Persistence and Change in Tribal India

About the Author

Dr. M.V. Rao, currently Director General, National Institute of Rural Development (NIRD), Rajendra Nagar, Hyderabad, belongs to the Indian Administrative Service. He served as District Magistrate of Malda, undivided Midnapore and Paschim Medinipur districts of West Bengal, India. He also served as Senior Consultant to UNICEF.

Dr. Rao has been working with the community for many years on innovative, practical and action oriented ideas for participatory development of the people at the grassroots. His earlier publications include *Community Health in Community Hands* (2003), and *Development for the People: Innovations in Administration* (2002).

Persistence and Change in Tribal India

Saga of Tribal People of West Midnapore

M.V. RAO
Director General
National Institute of Rural Development,
Hyderabad

Foreword by
Dr. B.D. Sharma

CONCEPT PUBLISHING COMPANY PVT. LTD.,
NEW DELHI-110059

ISBN-13: 978-81-8069-895-8

First Published 2014

Published and Printed by

Concept Publishing Company Pvt. Ltd.
A/15-16, Commercial Block, Mohan Garden
New Delhi-110059 (India)
T: 25351460, 25351794, *F*: 091-11-25357109
E: publishing@conceptpub.com W: www.conceptpub.com
Editorial Office: H-13, Bali Nagar, New Delhi-110 015, India.

Cataloging in Publication Data--*Courtesy:* D.K. Agencies (P) Ltd. <docinfo@dkagencies.com>

Rao, M. V., 1962-

Persistence and change in tribal India : saga of tribal people of West Midnapore/ M.V.Rao ; foreword by B.D. Sharma.

p. cm.

Revision of the author's thesis (Ph. D.)—Sambalpur University.

Includes bibliographical references (p.) and index.

ISBN 9788180698958

1. Santal (South Asian people)—India—Paschim Medinipur (District)—Social life and customs. 2. Lodha (Indic people)—India—Paschim Medinipur (District)Social life and customs. 3. Santal (South Asian people)—India—Paschim Medinipur (District)—Economic conditions. 4. Lodha (Indic people)—India—Paschim Medinipur (District)—Economic conditions. 5. Santal (South Asian people) Government policy—India—Paschim Medinipur (District) 6. Lodha (Indic people) Government policy—India—Paschim Medinipur (District) 7. Rural development India—Paschim Medinipur (District) I. Title.

DDC 305.80095414 23

Foreword

I am happy to be associated with this study about the continuity and change in tribal life. It has been undertaken at a time when the tribal people are facing the worst crisis in their history concerning their very survival. The study has a special flavour. The scholar as an administrator has had the privilege of looking at the events from both ends, from State-end as an administrator and from people's end as a researcher.

The focus of this study is on Lodhas at one end of the spectrum and on Santals at the other. While Santals are traditional farmers, Lodhas are virtually landless. What makes the life of these people worse or virtual hell is that this community was designated during the British rule as a 'Criminal Tribe'. It was renamed after Independence as 'De-Notified Tribe' (DNT). The Lodhas are lucky to have been further included in the category of 'Scheduled Tribes', a privilege not extended to most of the DNTs. As we move on in time, the most vulnerable groups amongst the Scheduled Tribes were classified in 1970s as 'Primitive Tribal Groups' (PTG). It was envisaged that the natural rights of these groups will be specially honoured as members of tribal communities. They will also be provided the protection of the Constitutional shield through designating the tribal areas as 'Scheduled Areas'. Specific problems of each community designated as PTG or even a part thereof shall be identified and special group-centered plan for its development shall be prepared. The entire financial outlay for PTG development has been underwritten by the Central Government as a part of Special Central Assistance.

What the researcher finds again and again in his study about Lodhas is *"one strong necessity, desire and ambition . . . . their urge to own a piece of land*". And what was their ambition about land-holding, *'just one-tenth of an acre per family.'* Moreover, in the context of their traditional social system frame *"there was no necessity for 'ownership' of land as is understood in present times; nature has given plenty in forests and there was no dearth of food. Their entire life depended on the forest. It started there and ended there*".

The new era after Independence began with the grand dream of Jawahar's *Panchasheel*. Indira's unequivocal commitment for tribal cause followed in 1970s in the form of Tribal Sub-Plans including special dispensation for PTG's. Lastly, there was Rajiv's Grand Vision of 'Heaven on Earth of Self-Governance' in 1980s. It was especially adapted to the tribal situation in the form of 'the Provisions of Panchayats (Extension to Scheduled Areas) Act, 1996' (PESA), acknowledged as the most radical law of the twentieth century.

But what these children of nature, the Lodhas, who suffered the worst ignominy under the British rule as a criminal tribe, had in their share after Independence? The irony is that the Lodhas had the dubious distinction of being *'criminal tribe square'*. Their inherited epitaph was squared by a queer phenomenon that no one likes to discuss and acknowledge. *The entire tribal world managing its affairs in accordance with its customs and tradition stood criminalized on November 26, 1949 with the adoption of Indian Constitution that has no place for their tradition.* Thus the original stigma of Lodhas continues in the eyes of the system especially the police that makes them most vulnerable to sorts of ignominy. The irony is that the same sense of denigration is showered on Lodhas by other communities in the neighbourhood. As observed by the author *"One felt shocked, embarrassed and sad as an elderly person remarked, 'the scent of a Lodha's stool goes far and wide' "*.

The story of Santals in West Midnapur is in the general mould of tribal development. Here is an area of extensive resources inhabited by simple people in distress. However, the social system continues to be strong notwithstanding 'urbanization and movement of people to far away places'. The situation on the usury front is dismal. The worst situation is in respect of developmental programmes which suffer from the day one due to paucity of funds and are destined to fail. Here is a situation where the tribal is a victim of the malfunctioning of the system. Madhya Pradesh (including Chhattisgarh) has a unique provision that in case a tribal does not get the intended benefit of a scheme for which he may have been advanced the loan, for no wilful fault on his part, he shall have no liability for its repayment. This precedent is worth emulation.

The researcher has rightly shared the concern of the people about medium of instruction, a non-issue in the current tribal development discourse. That education in the elementary classes, at least in first two years, has to be in the mother tongue, was conceded by the government way back in 1950s. In the absence of this facility Santali children have to start their schooling with severe disadvantage in Bengali. Students of Science and Mathematics are the worst sufferers. Nevertheless even with this initial disadvantage there is significant vertical mobility. Reservation in self-governing institutions has provided a new experience of confidence and assertion as the tribal people themselves *'hold the steering of the ship'*. The hitherto influential groups have come to realise that *'seemingly voiceless and innocent representatives cannot be taken for granted'*.

I congratulate Dr. Rao for the indepth study of two tribal communities located at two ends of the spectrum in the same vein with confidence.

Dr. B.D. SHARMA

Preface

Living conditions and lifestyles of people belonging to different tribes have been undergoing change over a period due to many factors. They are also forced to change the way they live because of outside pressures. Modern ways of development brought outsiders into their habitations. They have no choice but to adopt and adjust to the new realities. Influence of other communities and the way the development and welfare schemes of government are administered also impact the thinking processes of tribal communities. New aspirations are being nurtured among them about modern education and material comforts. Tribal youths are looking for employment opportunities like their counterparts in other communities. In the process, their culture and traditions are also undergoing change. At the same time, we can also observe that there is inherent yearning to retain and preserve their identity. The prime objective of this study has been to capture what is changing and what persists in the lives and traditions of tribal communities. The book documents the tribal life in transition, their response to the external influences and how they are adopting to the change. The present book is a further revised and developed version of my Ph.D. thesis submitted and accepted by Sambalpur University.

I was encouraged by Late Professor Prabodh K. Bhowmick, former Professor of Anthropology, University of Calcutta to take up this study as he thought I was closely associated with tribal development and had continuous interaction with the community. As I had the opportunity and privilege of working as the District Magistrate of Midnapore and later West Midnapore, I was in a position to positively influence and initiate proper implementation of tribal development programmes based on people's needs and aspirations. As I was also fortunate to have a relatively longer tenure of nearly five years in the district before and after division of erstwhile Midnapore, I got opportunity to understand the field situations and mould my thinking and strategies towards tribal development. On several occasions, it turned out to be, to some extent, action research, as field realities and experiences were incorporated into the planning process of development initiatives. The book is a documentation of my living and working with the natural citizens of this part of the country. There have been wide ranging experiences in the process. I was shocked when I saw the living conditions and apathy of the machinery and system. On the other hand, there have been many instances to underline how the efforts can be effective when the decision and choice making has been done by the community themselves. There is need to transform totally the way our tribal administration machinery functions, as in majority of the cases, no attention is being paid to the views and thoughts of the community. It is a long journey ahead before tribal communities rediscover their spontaneity and ingenuity.

I express my deep sense of gratitude to my research mentor Prof. Deepak Kumar Behera, Department of Anthropology, Sambalpur University for his inspiring guidance and continuous support throughout the research, which enabled me to bring this study to its present form. I am highly indebted to him for the valuable time he has spared for my research study. I am also thankful to Professor R. Siva Prasad, Department of Anthropology, University of Hyderabad, for going through the manuscripts and offering his incisive suggestions. I also thank Dr. Kasi Eswarappa, Department of Anthropology, University of Hyderabad, for his assistance in going through the mauscripts.

I must acknowledge with gratitude the help that I received from Shri Naba Kumar Das, previously Pradhan, Khelar Gram Panchayat and other members of the Panchayat for their continued support during my research work. I am also grateful to many government officers and Panchayat representatives of West Midnapore district for their understanding and wholehearted cooperation during my study across the district.

My thanks are due to Dr. B.D. Sharma, renowned authority on tribal issues and relentless crusader for their rights, for the encouraging foreword to the book. I am grateful to M/s. Concept Publishing Company Pvt. Ltd. for accepting to publish the work.

My wife Annapurna Padma Sri and two sons, Srikant and Sreenath, always encouraged and supported me during this long period of work as well as study.

Finally and most importantly, I am grateful to people across the length and breadth of this fascinating district as they form the basis for my learning.

16th April, 2011 **M. V. RAO**
Hyderabad

Contents

List of Case Studies

List of Tables

List of Maps

List of Photographs

1
Introduction

The present work is a result of both extensive and intensive study of tribal people of West Midnapore in West Bengal, primarily during the period when I was working as District Magistrate (DM) of undivided Midnapore district and later West Midnapore. The period gave the researcher a lifetime opportunity to live with people, know their culture, traditions, problems, livelihoods, aspirations, frustrations and more importantly, vision of life. The entire period of association with people was education all through, which could not have been, perhaps, learnt in any formal institution. The whole exercise proved to be some kind of action research, with the experience and learning from people becoming action points for our interventions in the capacity of administrator with the help of elected representatives. Many lofty ideals, by and large, are inscribed in formal plans and programmes; only problem is the wide gulf between the intent and reality found in practice. Thoughts and inner feelings of people as well as ideas and plans germinating in their backyard were nurtured and nourished painstakingly, and at times fighting the system. Many a time, these were translated into new rays of hope for the needy. In the process, what was achieved was invaluable trust and confidence of thousands of people, living away from the mainstream.

***At this point, one is reminded of these observations of Gerald D. Berreman*:**

> . . . empathy—the ability to put one's self in the place of others, to experience the world as they experience it. Empathy is insurance against narrow complacency, ethnocentrism and

> sterile scientism. Only through empathetic ability can the scientist hope to understand the phenomenal world of the people he studies, to comprehend their motives, their hopes, joys, and fears, and their reactions to himself . . . He must be liked and trusted as an individual to win the trust and confidence of those with whom he works (Berreman, 1968: 162).

When there is true harmony in one's interest and work, it becomes a pleasure, worth living for ages. The present work is an honest account of working with tribal people, which later blended into an academic research. In the process, of course, there is always the possibility of being carried away into myriad ideas and losing track of the research objectives as set out initially; but the end result, despite the deviations and digressions, has been purposeful. One learnt in the process that life did not always follow the pre-written screenplay. It had been somewhat unexplored or uncharted path. Remaining open in approach and mind gave the researcher opportunities to know and participate with people in their efforts of making their lives better.

As James Laidlaw aptly observes

> In entering into informal collaboration with people in 'researching' social and cultural arrangements, either their own and those of others around them, the anthropologist is merely joining in with though also in the process no doubt heightening and giving his or her own twist to an activity that is always at least an implicit part of everyday social life. And the anthropologist's ability to elicit engaged collaboration is at least an indication that his or her ethnographic questions have some coherence with indigenous interests and concerns; that the ethnographic knowledge he or she is seeking is recognizable as knowledge of how things are with them. In fact, it seems worth taking a lead from potential collaborators even if their interests diverge from one's original research plans (Laidlaw, 2004: 236).

OBJECTIVES

The present study has the following key objectives:

1. Analyse changes that are taking place in the culture and lifestyle of tribal people of Western Midnapore in general and Santals and Lodhas in particular.
2. Examine those tribal traditions, festivals and rituals which continue to persist in current times despite the impact of modernisation
3. Discuss in detail the lifestyle of the tribal people in the sample village in order to understand the social dynamics through the eyes of tribal people.
4. Know the importance of traditional authority and modern governance in the life of tribal people in contemporary context.
5. Find out the changing livelihood patterns and health system of the tribal people in the present situation.
6. Critically examine the impact of development programmes on the lives of tribal people and their response to such programmes.
7. Understand the needs and aspirations of tribal people from their own perspective.
8. Suggest some recommendations for improvement in the life of the tribal people, based upon the findings of our research.

The observations in the study have been made in respect of the tribal population of the entire district of West Midnapore while one village of Bonpatna in Khelar Gram Panchayat has been closely studied. Emphasis has been given for extensive study of two tribes, Santals and Lodhas in relation to other communities. The field situations have been compared across several villages inhabited by tribal population. As the title of the study suggests, the effort was to study the changes happening in the lives of tribal people of the Western Midnapore district with particular reference to one village. Despite the sweeping changes happening in the tribal life, there are certain aspects and characteristics, which are alive and persisting. The researcher has attempted to study the changes in social, cultural and economic life of Santals and Lodhas and simultaneously recording the elements and features which have withstood the test of time.

METHODOLOGY

Selection of Study Village and Data Collection

Rationale for the Selection of Study Village

Bonpatna village is located in Khelar Gram Panchayat of Kharagpur-I Block of West Midnapore district. Before selecting this village, a number of other villages of tribal dominated Blocks of West Midnapore were considered.

The main reasons for selecting Bonpatna were:

1. The village has both Santal and Lodha population.
2. The village is close to Kharagpur industrial town and National Highway on one hand and dense forest on the other. The urban influence of Kharagpur and mobility offered by the highway are points of significance as these are likely to affect the living of people of this village. Likewise, the adjoining forest and people's dependence on it for sustenance offer scope to understand the continuity in their lifestyles.
3. The urban area closeby offers modern day opportunities for livelihood and at the same time, people's culture, attitude and behaviour goes through transformation due to interaction with other social groups and their practices and beliefs.
4. The daily journey to adjoining forest by many of the Lodhas and Santals for livelihood is somewhat close to the traditional lifestyle of their ancestors who used to rely heavily on nature for their survival.
5. The village with unique location offer near ideal setting to study both persistence and change in tribal lives.

The village Bonpatna, located in Khelar Gram Panchayat of Kharagpur-I Block of West Midnapore district was thus chosen for the study. Respondents from the study village belonging to Santal and Lodha tribe were covered for collection of data on various aspects of the study. Information on different members of the households was collected through the heads of the households. The key informants furnished detailed information on some aspects, which could not be collected from other respondents. Four heads of the households from Santal and Lodha backgrounds could not be covered, as three were absent during the entire length of the study. One person had severe problem of hearing. Group discussions were conducted to collect reliable historical information and their views on different aspects. Data pertaining to educational aspects was collected from sixty-five school students and fourteen teachers of Khelar Adibasi Primary School and Khelar Higher Secondary School. Interactions and discussions were also held with people belonging to Santal and Lodha ethnic groups of adjoining villages to Bonpatna like Nachna, Khelar, Bolla and Raghunathpur. This helped to gather more information and in better understanding of their thought processes. In order to supplement the data, information on change and continuity was also collected from a number of other Blocks of the district, *viz.*, Lalgarh (Binpur-I), Belpahari (Binpur-II), Nayagram, Jhargram and Jamboni blocks of Jhargram sub-division, Midnapore, Garbeta-I and Salboni blocks of Midnapore sub-division and Kharagpur-I and Keshiary blocks of Kharagpur sub-division. Those are the ten tribal-dominated blocks of the total number of eighteen tribal Blocks of West Midnapore district and thus a wider coverage was given to make the study more reflective of the area and the people.

The following methods/tools and techniques were used for the collection of primary and secondary data for the study:

Rapport Establishment

Rapport establishment is the most important part of an anthropological fieldwork. Without proper rapport, the authenticity and reliability of the field data is questioned. Therefore, considerable time was spent in the sample village and other areas from where the researcher gathered the field data. Initially, the villagers were not clear about the purpose and reason for undertaking the study. As the researcher was also the District Magistrate, they were interested and forthcoming about their problems and livelihoods. This indeed was important and helped the researcher-administrator to understand the issues and initiate steps for their redressal. One also needed information and understanding about their social and cultural life and the changes happening in these aspects. At one point of time, the researcher thought that it would not be easy to collect all the information needed for the study. With the passage of time, the researcher could put together relevant data for the study. As part of the duty as well as out of sheer interest, the researcher visited different tribal habitations to understand the situation and living conditions and was drawn and got involved into the problems faced by tribal population, including poverty, ill health, indebtedness and other livelihood issues. Together with the people, opportunities were found and various government agencies were approached for redressal of different issues and problems.

Participant Observation

The researcher spent considerable time with both the communities and took part in various activities such as rituals and festivals and also participated in different activities of the tribal communities to gain deeper understanding through observation. Finally, establishment of good rapport provided the researcher with an opportunity to observe them from a close quarter to study the continuity and change in their way of life.

Interviewing Respondents

Semi-structured interviews were conducted to collect specific information from the respondents on various aspects, like livelihood, culture and traditions, education and health facilities. An interview guide was also used to gather qualitative data from key informants on different aspects of continuity and change in the lifestyle of the Lodha and Santal communities of the sample village. Students and teachers of Khelar Adibasi Primary School and Khelar Higher Secondary School were interviewed for generating quantitative and qualitative information relating to education.

Case Studies

Case studies were collected to supplement the analysis. Each case study was developed with a focus on a particular aspect of the analysis in order to strengthen the observations and findings. The case studies also helped the researcher to draw conclusions on different aspects of change and continuity of the tribal life.

Focus Group Discussions

Focus group discussions were organized to gather information and opinions of the communities on different aspects. For this, the researcher acted as a facilitator and initiated the discussion and recorded major points of the group discussion. This helped in collecting authentic and reliable data through a group filtration process.

Field Notes and Field Diary

Field notes and field diary were maintained as important tools of the study. These sources provided valuable information to develop ethnographic profile of the Lodhas and Santals. It also helped the researcher to have a better understanding of different socio-cultural practices from the viewpoint of the communities studied.

Data from Secondary Sources

Secondary sources included published literature, census data, maps, and published and unpublished reports. These sources were used frequently in order to generate relevant additional information for the study. Such data helped the researcher to present a comprehensive depiction of the area and the sample tribes. Data available in various government documents were consulted and compared while observing the field situations. Overview of already existing literature also provided a comparative frame to notice the differences and similarities. Some relevant photographs, maps and other supporting information have been included to make the thesis more comprehensive.

Any attempt to present the total portrait of tribal life in the changing context definitely demands comparative study of their social, economic and political life. Emphasis has been given to compare and contrast the 'live frames' as one constantly observed, in historical perspective. Attempts have been made to visualize the likely course of events in the future. It was the constant endeavour of the researcher to see events, situations, conditions and problems through the people's eyes. Existing literature on tribal life in changing context has been studied and citations have been provided wherever found relevant.

It may be appropriate here to recall the following observation of Alan Macfarlane on "compare and contrast" as methods of anthropological study:

> There are two separate operations, which need to take place in comparative work, the establishing of similarities and the establishing of differences. Rousseau recognized that different methods were required to establish each of these, and that one could not be done without the other . . . . Rousseau implies that the final aim is to reach the deeper similarities, the attributes, the 'psychic unity of man' as it was later to be called. More recently, some anthropologists suggested the reverse, namely, that we are more concerned with differences than similarities. Evans-Pritchard wrote that 'I would like to place emphasis on the importance for social anthropology, as a comparative discipline, of differences, because it could be held that in the past the tendency has often been to place the stress on similarities . . . . whereas it is the differences which would seem to invite sociological explanation (Macfarlane, 2004 : 101).

It is believed that the book will help the discerning readers to re-examine the tribal life, their manners and customs, which are in a process of continuous change. As a participant observer, the researcher had the opportunity to feel and observe the processes and their impact from a close quarter. The observation of Andre Beteille is relevant here:

> Authenticity of experience and the voice of the insider are now valued as much as detached observation and objective analysis (Beteille, 2000: 6).

Organisation of the Book

This book is organised into nine chapters. The first chapter introduces the reader to the context of the study. It also explains about the rationale of the study and different methods and tools applied to carry out the study. In the second chapter, an attempt is made to provide systematic and chronological representation of the available literature on the concept of tribe and indigenous people. To put the theme of study in perspective, contemporary and recent literature is also referred to, wherever necessary.

The third chapter gives a detailed ethnographic profile of the scheduled tribes of West Bengal, in general, and the study villages, in particular. The chapter also gives details of land utilization by the tribes in the study area. In the fourth chapter, an attempt is made to present an ethnographic illustration of the customs, traditions, beliefs and lifestyles of Santal and Lodha tribes. This chapter also discusses the dynamics of cultural practices and social life that are prevailing among the Santal and Lodha tribes.

The fifth chapter specifies traditional authority and social control arrangements of Santal and Lodha tribes. It also discusses the mechanisms of modern governance prevailing in the Santal and Lodha society. In the sixth chapter, an effort is made to provide changing livelihoods of Santal and Lodha tribes, their economy and livelihood cycle. The role of moneylenders, exploitation and reasons for their backwardness are also explained. The chapter also points out the MGNREGA and SHGs' interventions in the livelihoods of Santal and Lodha tribes.

Health is one of the important indicators of human development and keeping this in view, the seventh chapter analyses tribal health and its changing nature in relation to tradition and modernity. The chapter also deals with initiatives and innovations to overcome the health problems through voluntary health workers and the positive impact of campaigns of sanitation and hygiene on health of tribal people. The eighth chapter illustrates various interventions and resultant changes in tribal development. It also critically analyses implementation of different schemes for the development of tribal people. Further, the chapter also depicts interventions consequent to the researcher-administrator's continuous field visits and interaction with tribal people of the district. In the last chapter, an attempt is made to present major findings and recommendations in order to ameliorate the conditions of the tribal people. It also specifies the areas which need immediate attention of the planners, policy-makers and functionaries involved in implementation.

2
Review of Literature

India is a vast country inhabited by people belonging to different and distinct cultures. Due to different geo-physical backgrounds, we find people's way of life differing from area to area. People have to adjust with the environment and many situations, which bring continuous changes in their material, social and cultural life. These changes may be slow, happening over a long period of time. These changes are discernable to an expert person but may not be observed by many. The cultural, social and religious life differs from one group to another and these differences are visible in their customs, beliefs, mores and traditions. The vast Indian territory with various geo-physical backgrounds is home to as many as 500 tribal communities. An attempt is made to present the definitions on the concept of 'tribe' or 'indigenous people'[1] by different scholars.

T.C. Das (1953) defined 'tribe' in a scientific way. According to him:

> A tribe generally has a common name, common habitat, a common language and a common culture and a feeling of unity among its members as against members of other tribes. These common features give the tribe its individuality and thereby keep it distinct and different from the other tribes or advanced groups.

D.N. Majumdar (1967) tried to define 'tribe' as:

> A collection of families or group of families having common

> name, members of which occupy the same territory, speak the same language and observe certain taboos regarding marriage, profession or occupation and have developed well assessed system of reciprocity, and mutual obligation.

F.G. Baily[2] (cited in Singh, 2009:220) seriously worked on the concept of tribe in India. For him 'tribe' is as :

> In opposition to caste citing the markedly distinct assumptions of isolation, language, religion (animism), economic backwardness, and finally the claim for original inhabitation (*adivasiness*) of tribes in India (Bailey, 1961).

Bose (1971) found that:

> Tribes have more or less retained their separate social identity and on the whole, can be regarded as comparatively isolated and economically backward. As such for administrative purposes, they have been scheduled so that special measures may be taken to improve upon their economic standard and educational level.

B.K. Roy Burman (2000:4) defined 'indigenous peoples' as those:

> Peoples rooted in their immediate physical and social environment in a manner that they amplify and elaborate their culture primarily with reference to such environment, while at the same time incorporating elements of culture from other sources at the secondary level.

Many anthropologists (Das, 1953; Majumdar, 1967; Bose, 1971; Roy Burman, 2004; Srivastava, 2008) indicate the following are some of the essential characteristics of the tribal communities:

- Primitive[3] /traditional traits;
- Geographical isolation;
- Distinct culture;
- Shy of contact with community at large and social isolation; and
- Economic backwardness.

It has been reiterated that some groups of people of the Indian sub-continent had to traverse a long path through prehistoric periods with many bitter experiences of stresses and strains for their social stability. In course of such travels, travesty and shifting for security, clashes with other groups followed. As a result, the cultures of these groups transformed to a considerable extent. Further, this had led to adoption of traits of neighbouring groups. These changes occurred according to the demands of the situations or circumstantial exigencies. Present day culture of these communities bears such marks, which have been incorporated into the core of their cultural matrix. Thus, it can be said that tribes do not present permanent crystalline structures belonging to any stage of historical or social development. The tribal people in general have some common cultural pattern or ways of life and similarity of traits in material culture, largely depending on ecology and geo-physical background. Many distinguished anthropologists studied the tribal life closely in diverse social settings at different points of time. Their painstaking efforts and analysis enhanced our understanding of these people.

For instance, Radcliffe-Brown (1922) did his fieldwork in the Andamans from 1906 to 1908. He was the first anthropologist to make a clear distinction between the Great Andaman Group (including all Great Andaman tribes except Jarawa) and the Little Andaman Group, which includes the Onge of Little Andaman, the Jarawa of South Andaman and the Sentinelese on North Sentinel Island. The family is the only unit of social organization among the present day Great Andamanese. Earlier a group of families, consisting of 40-50 persons, used to form a social division, which Radcliffe-Brown called the 'local group', a structure breaking down from the beginning of the twentieth century.

Kroebar (1948) conceives tribes as "a small isolated and close knit society where both societal and cultural aspects are largely organized on the basis of kinship".

Peddington (1960) in his writing delineates the primary characteristic of tribal communities as 'illiteracy, societal organisation on the basis of small social groupings, low level of technological achievement based primarily on kinship and locality and lack of economic specialisation and overlapping social groups'.

Godelier (1977) sees tribal societies as being characterised by certain positive and negative features, the negatives being the absence of literacy, civilisation, industrialisation, specialisation, etc. The positive features are those absent in modern societies: social relations based on kinship bonds, all-pervasive religion, frequency of co-operation for common goals, etc.

In Xaxa's (1999) observation, the characteristic of a tribe as a society is related through its boundaries. At the same time, boundaries have been defined linguistically, culturally and politically by anthropologists. Boundaries set certain limit of interaction in the legal, political, economic and social relations of its members.

Likewise, Evans-Pritchard's, *The Nuer* (1940) is one of the best known sources of all ethnographic studies. He gives a sparkling and discerning picture of an interesting and unusual people. The work is about pastoral people, the Nuer, living along the upper Nile. They were strongly individualistic and had no laws or leaders. The social order was maintained by community values, tribal and lineage system.

Elwin (1942) in his work, *The Agaria*, discussed the Agaria, their myth, magic and craft. Later, Elwin (1950), in his work, *Bondo Highlander*, threw light on the tribal life of Orissa, one of the most interesting ethnographic regions of India. The Khonds are discussed with their attachment to infanticide and human sacrifice. There is brilliant description of the Juangs and Bhuiyas. He also discussed about Gadabas, Porojas and Saoras.

In *The Tribes and Castes of Bengal*, Risley (1891) presented ethnographic glossary of all subjects related to tribes and castes of Bengal in an alphabetical order. In this important work, he also discussed relationship of caste to marriage.

Mukherjee (1939) discussed issues like Santal genesis and migration, kinship organization, the cycle of Santal festivals, magic and witchcraft, folklore and hunting in Mayurbhanj areas of present Odisa State.

"The Santals[4]", by Troisi (1979) gives a detailed account of various issues related to Santals, like religion, marriage, kinship, magic, myths, folklore, material culture, education, tribal polity, social organization, language, physical characteristics, social movements and change.

Majumdar (1965) in his *Races and Cultures of India* made a critical study of races and race elements in the Indian population. The tribal people formed the central theme of this study.

Social scientists and other interested readers immensely benefitied from the knowledge of some of the fundamentals of social life in the country.

Xaxa (2008), in his phenomenal studies in the tribal regions of Jharkhand and Chhattisgarh, found that a 'tribe' has generally been defined as :

> A more or less homogeneous community having common government, a common dialect and common culture.

Ray (1972) points to this in his introductory essay in the volume *Tribal Situation in India.* He says, we know that there were *janas* or communities of people like the Savaras, the Kullutas, the Lollas, the Bhillas, the Khasas, the Kinnaras and countless others whom today we know as 'tribes' and who bear almost the same names. Yet the term by which they were known to the multitudes of people were not 'tribes' but *janas* meaning 'communities of people' (cited in Xaxa, 1999:1524).

Majumdar (1955) dealt with the changes happening in Santal culture. Campbell (1915) studied beliefs and superstitions of Santals in detail.

In *Cultural Contours of Tribal Bihar*, Vidyarthi (1964) covered a wide range of issues like tribal education and economic programmes for welfare and development. He also dealt with issues like genetic study of the Oraons, culture types in tribal region of Bihar and the sacred complex in Maler Hill.

The Aboriginal Tribes of India, by Fuchs (1973) is a short but comprehensive account of all the aboriginal tribes of the Indian sub-continent. For the purpose of presentation, the aboriginal tribes are divided into five separate groups: The tribes of northern India; nomadic tribes in the plains of northern India; the tribes in the central area; the tribes in eastern India and the tribes in south India.

Ghurye (1960), in his study, *The Scheduled Tribes*, gave a historical account with a survey of the developments of these tribes after India attained independence. He critically examined both the constitutional provisions and the report of the Scheduled Areas and Scheduled Tribes Commission.

The life of most of the tribal population in India has been that of struggle for existence and survival. They had to weather the storms of physical alienation and cultural domination by their neighbours. Haimendorf (1982) graphically described the traumatising lives of tribes like the Gonds and Chenchus and the metamorphosis of beliefs and culture as a result of outside onslaught. The agony has been that the changes in tribal lives are not happening on their own seeking but thrust upon them.

As civilization and social processes are dynamic, changes are but natural in customs, beliefs and inter-relations among various social groups in a social setting. Beteille (1996:224) made an intensive study of a South Indian village, Sripuram, in Tanjore district. He showed the changing relationship between caste, class and power. Beteille showed how the locus of power shifted from the traditional caste structures to institutions like panchayats and political parties. He observed, "The growth of new political organs and institutions and the entire process of political modernization are likely to render still more complex the relations between caste and power" (*ibid.*).

"Collected Essays" of Srinivas (2002) occupies the position of a classic in sociology and social anthropology literature. His essays covered wide-ranging themes over a period of time. He had a deep knowledge and understanding of the caste system in India. He was a pioneer in village studies in India. His study of 'imaginary' Rampura village in the princely state of Mysore (present Karnataka State) has set the trend for many sociologists and anthropologists to follow. He bridged theory, method, fieldwork and social reality in his writings.

Srivastava's (1997) ethnographic monograph on religious renunciation among the Raikas, agro-pastoralists in western Rajasthan, thoughtfully combines the fine details of religious practices related to renunciation with descriptions of the Raikas everyday livelihoods.

Large scale development projects like, irrigation dams, steel plants, mega industrial ventures, power plants and highways have invariably displaced many poor people including those from tribal communities. These had enormous impact on social, cultural and economic life of these affected people. Vidyarthi (1968: 13-26) felt that establishment of great steel plants in the very core of the tribal's homeland led to the displacement of their population.

Ill-conceived and non-participatory development programmes for rural and tribal development has been one of the biggest problems faced so far. Srivastava (1990) felt development made tribal people clowns of human society, throwing their social life in a conundrum. State agencies may show them as beneficiaries of development, but seen from their perspective, they have lost their pre-development social life without gaining much in the process.

In respect of tribal and non-tribal interaction, Sachchidananda (1992: 12) makes an interesting observation when he says:

> It must be urged upon them that their problems are common with the other weaker sections of the Indian society with whom they can join forces to find common solutions. They must be assured against the submergence of their group identity.

Das and Banerjee (1962) discussed impact of industrialisation on the life of the tribal population of West Bengal. The book studied the impact on the economic system, social life and psychology of the tribal people. Das and Banerjee (1964) also analyzed, in a separate study, the impact of tea industry on the life of the tribal people of northern region of West Bengal.

As the contours of social sciences widened, the studies started reflecting understanding of contemporary social, political and economic processes across the globe. These writings also present sprinkling of other social sciences like sociology, political science and economics.

Hackering (1967) viewed that many large tribes and entire nations are represented in the ethnographic literature only by reports of "customs" or "norms" based upon single studies of "sample" communities. Later, Lindner (1982) observed that for the anthropologist, government control reduces a tribe to an exhibit of a particular ecological adaptation, one that can no longer enforce its ideology on the encapsulating society.

Bailey's (1969) classic political-anthropology work, *Stratagems and Spoils*, provides insights into principles of political competition that operate alike in "exotic" and "developed" societies. The book is a new addition to the conceptual methods for analyzing the rules of game that govern political tussles in different environments and cultures.

Bailey's (2001) another work, *Treasons, Stratagems and Spoils* is a sequel to his *Stratagems and Spoils*. Treason points to an increased attention to morality, to ideas of duty and conscience, as a foil to rational calculations of advantage. This book helps in understanding struggles for power, politics and political leaders in different cultures as it provides propositions and raises issues on political events. The methods can be applied to comprehend power struggles in different settings.

The idea of "liminal" and "liminality" was introduced to the field of anthropology in 1909 by Arnold Van Gennep in his seminal work, *Les Rites de Passage*. He described rites of passage like certain rituals and marriage as having three part structure of separation, liminal period and reassimilation. These concepts gained further recognition through the works of Victor Turner. His well noted works which extensively dealt with these themes include "Betwixt and Between: The Liminal Period in *Rites de Passage*," from *The Forest of Symbols: Aspects of Ndembu Ritual* (1967), "Liminality and Communitas," from *The Ritual Process: Structure and Anti-Structure* (1969), and "Passages, Margins, and Poverty: Religious Symbols of Communitas," from *Dramas, Fields, and Metaphors* (1974).

Thus, like any social science, anthropology has been undergoing changes in content, methods and reach. The enormous time spent and invaluable efforts made by many anthropologists over the years enriched our understanding and appreciation of dynamic social processes in relation to politics, economy, lifestyle and culture.

Despite all these explanations, there has been controversy and ambiguity regarding definition and classification of tribes for many years. A careful analysis clearly reveals that many of the traditional features of tribe are no longer valid in our fast-changing society. There have been many inconclusive anthropological debates on the concept of tribal society (*e.g.*, Pfeffer and Behera, 2005). The term 'Scheduled Tribes' first appeared in the Constitution of India. The Constitution of India does not define Scheduled Tribes as such. Article 366 (25) refers to Scheduled Tribes as "such tribes or tribal communities or parts of or groups within such tribes or tribal communities as are deemed under Article 342 to be Scheduled Tribes for the purposes of this Constitution". According to Article 342 of the Constitution, the Scheduled Tribes are the tribes or tribal communities or part of or groups within these tribes and tribal communities, which have been declared as such by the President through a public notification. Article 342 prescribes procedure to be followed in the matter of specification of scheduled tribes.

In West Bengal, there were only seven Scheduled Tribes in 1951 but the number has now gone up to thirty eight. Even before the Scheduled Caste and Scheduled Tribe Reorganisation Act (1976) came into force, "Bhumij" was a tribe in Midnapore (West Bengal) but its counterpart "Bhumijis" of Purulia (transferred territory from Bihar) were treated as members of Scheduled Caste.

Throughout the study, variations have been recorded from place to place and community to community. Nature, extent and causes of change, its impact on the life of the people and the persistence of tradition have been recorded to give a clear picture of the situation. It is true to some extent that due to developments and changes in social and political spectrum of the region, traditional life style and ideas are in a process of transformation. Modern educational facilities and new type of employment brought various changes. These changes have been recorded while processing data. Various methods for collection of data such as case history and personal observations have been applied and recorded. Along with these, a systematic reference of earlier records has been made for correlation. Facts have been recorded with interpretation. References have been provided at the end. It is hoped that an overall collection in the form of a monographic account will be a new contribution to the subject.

NOTES

1. For Xaxa (1999), the idea of 'indigenous people' is an issue of considerable contention today. In fact, social workers, administrators, politicians and even scholars widely used the term to refer to a particular category of people. The term indigenous has been used in anthropology to describe groups called tribes for quite some time. See also Southall (1970), Behura (2002), Pati & Dash (2002), Roy Burman (2002), Dove

(2006) and Uberoi *et al.* (2007), for detailed discussion and analysis on the concept of 'indigenous people'.

2. See for further reference, Fried (1968), Beteille (1986), Bates (1995), Skaria (1997), Zimmerman (1999) and Srivastava (2008) for more definitions on the concept of 'Tribe'.
3. In the Draft National Tribal Policy (2008), Ministry of Tribal Affairs, Government of India, it has been suggested that the term 'primitive' is derogatory and instead the term 'particularly vulnerable tribal groups' may be used.
4. Menz and Hansda's (2010) book picturises the writings on Santal community vividly. Also see Orans (1965), Kochar (1966), Prasad and Sengupta (1973), Raychaudhuri (1973), Ray (1975), George (1979), Troisi (1979), Prasad (1985), Singh (1985), Mahapatra (1986), Duyker (1987), Carrin (2002), Bhowmick (2004), Culshaw (2004), Behera and Pfeffer (2008), Bhowmick and Jana (2008), and Carrin (2008) for other related references on Santal community.

3
The Universe

Area and the People

West Midnapore or Paschim Medinipur district is situated in the south-western direction of West Bengal State of India. Bankura and Purulia districts in the north, Mayurbhanj and Balasore districts of Orissa in the south, Hooghly and Purba Medinipur district in the east and Singhbhum district of Jharkhand and Purulia district of West Bengal in the west bound the district. The district is located between 21°47′N to 23°00′N latitude and 86°40' E to 87°52' E longitude. Map 3.1 gives location of West Midnapore district in West Bengal. It also shows location of West Bengal in India. The Map also reflects boundaries of all the Blocks in the district. The district consists of four Sub-Divisions, 27 Police Stations, 29 Blocks and 8 Municipalities. The district has 290 Gram Panchayats and 8,735 mouzas or revenue villages.

West Medinipur district has been carved out from the erstwhile Midnapore district[1] and came into existence from 1st January, 2002. It has 9295.28 sq. km. of geographical area and population of 52,18,399 as per Census 2001. The district is predominantly rural with over 87 per cent of population living in villages. There are 6,41,315 cultivators, 6,63,626 small and marginal farmers, 7,46,209 agricultural labourers, 1,62,797 artisans and 5,84,197 other workers. Percentage of people belonging to Scheduled Castes is 18.06 and that of Scheduled Tribes is 14.87. Population density of the district is 561.40 persons per square kilometre. Around 36.64 per cent of families have been identified as families living below poverty line (BPL) in the year 2008. About 60 per cent of people of the district are literate according to Census 2001. Literacy coverage among men is 70 per cent and whereas it is 50 per cent among women.

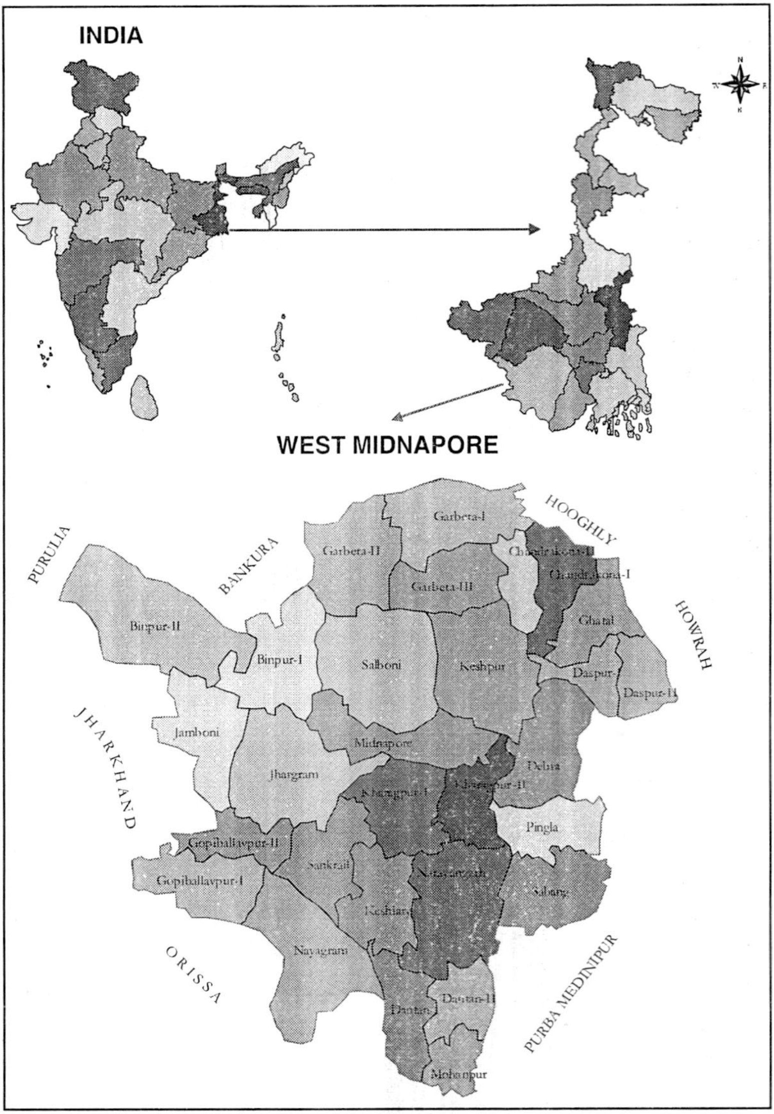

Map 3.1: India : West Bengal and West Midnapore

The climate is tropical and the land surface of the district is characterised by hard rock uplands, lateritic covered area, and flat alluvial and deltaic plains. Extremely rugged topography is seen in the western part of the district and rolling topography is experienced consisting of hard red soil covered area. These rolling plains gradually merge into flat alluvial and deltaic plains to the east and south-east of the district. The soil is fairly fertile. The normal rainfall of the district is 1656 mm. Hot summer, cold winter, abundant rainfall and humidity characterize the climate.

Kangsabati, Silabati, Subarnarekha, Keleghai and their tributaries are the main rivers of the district. Irrigation is provided to both *kharif* and *rabi*[2] crops. Kangsabati canal system is the main irrigation scheme. Ground water supports supplementary irrigation. About 48 per cent of gross cropped area is irrigated. Paddy occupies the first place in production; other important crops are potato, wheat, jute, oilseeds, betel vine, groundnut, sugarcane, cashewnut and mat stick. Vegetables are grown in some areas. The district has some areas where cultivation of mulberry and horticulture crops such as mango, banana, guava, lemon, musambi, papaya, cashew and jackfruit are undertaken. There are large water areas in the district, which are exploited for inland fisheries and also used as source of irrigation.

Western Midnapore has a lot of barren land with undulating topography and hard red soil. In many areas of Jhargram, parts of Midnapore and Kharagpur sub-divisions, huge area of land remained both unutilized and underutilized. These areas also have significant tribal population.

Over the years, farmers made desperate attempts to cultivate rice in all kinds of lands in the area. The conditions did not suit rice cultivation but farmers continued with it, as they did not have suitable alternatives. Viable technologies and alternatives were not available with the farmers to grow alternative crops. In a district where over half of the farming is rainfed without any assured irrigation facilities, dependence on water intensive rice crop alone together with the vagaries of monsoon made life difficult for the farmers. There is considerable area of cultivable wasteland available in these places.

The main industrial area of the district is around Kharagpur.[3] Small-scale industrial clusters are coming up in Jhargram, Chandrakona Road, Garhbeta and Midnapore. These units are based on agriculture, forest produce, animal husbandry, chemicals and engineering. Handloom is a traditional industry, which engages a considerable number of artisans.

National Highway No. 6 and 60 run through the district. A

network of State Highways connects the various places of the district. This district has reasonably developed railway network of South Eastern Railway.

Census Directorate categorized altogether thirty-eight tribal communities in West Bengal of which the following tribes are found in West Midnapore district: Lodha, Mahali, Munda, Santal and Bhumij. The list of declared Scheduled Tribes in West Bengal is displayed in Table 3.1.

Table 3.1: List of Scheduled Tribes in West Bengal

Asur	*Kora*
Baiga	Korwa
Badia, Bediya	Lepcha
Bhumij	Lodha, Kheria, Kharia
Bhutia, Sherpa, Toto, Dukpa, Kagatay	Lohara, Lohra
Tibetan, Yolmo.	Magh
Birhor	Mahali
Birjia	Mahli
Chakma	Mal Pahariya
Chero	Mech
Chik Baraik	Mru
Garo	Munda
Gond	Nagesia
Gorait	Oraon
Hajang	Parhaiya
Ho	Rabha
Karmali	Santal
Kharwar	Sauria Paharia
Khond	Savar
Kisan	

The total population of West Bengal as per 2001 Census has been 8,01,76,197. Of this, 44,06,794 persons belong to Scheduled Tribes (STs) constituting 5.5 per cent of the total population of the State. The State has registered 15.7 per cent decadal growth of ST population in 1991-2001.

The Santal represent more than half of the total ST population of the State (51.8 per cent). Oraon (14 per cent), Munda (7.8 per cent), Bhumij (7.6 per cent) and Kora (3.2 per cent) are the other major STs having sizeable population. Along with Santal, they constitute nearly

85 per cent of the State's total ST population. The Lodha, Mahali, Bhutia, Bedia, and Savar are the remaining STs having population of one per cent or more. Population and proportion of ten major scheduled tribes is given in Table 3.2.

Table 3.2: Population and Proportion of Ten Major Scheduled Tribes in West Bengal, 2001 Census

Sl. No.	*Name of the Scheduled Tribe*	*Total population*	*Proportion to the total ST population*
1.	All Scheduled Tribes	4,406,794	100%
2.	Santal	2,280,540	51.8
3.	Oraon	617,138	14.0
4.	Munda	341,542	7.8
5.	Bhumij	336,436	7.6
6.	Kora	142,789	3.2
7.	Lodha	84,966	1.9
8.	Mahali	76,102	1.7
9.	Bhutia	60,091	1.4
10.	Bedia	55,979	1.3
11.	Savar	43,599	1.0

The Lodhas[4] are treated as Particularly Vulnerable Tribal Group (PVTG) for administrative purposes. Their way of life is almost pre-agricultural economy. In some places, they have taken to agriculture recently. The Mahalis are traditional basket makers while the Santals and Mundas are predominantly agriculturists.

West Midnapore harboured these groups in different areas and in course of time, they have accommodated themselves in different changing situations. In this study, an attempt has been made to examine the persistence and change noticed in their socio-economic life, their customs, beliefs, traditions and festivals. Table 3.3 shows the total population and tribal percentage of West Midnapore district as per Census 2001. Incidence of poverty in different blocks of the district can be seen in Table 3.4. Table 3.4 shows percentage of population living Below Poverty Line (BPL). A correlation can be easily made with proportion of tribal population and high incidence of poverty. For easy reference, the proportion of tribal and BPL population in different Blocks of the district has been shown in Map 3.2 and Map 3.3, respectively.

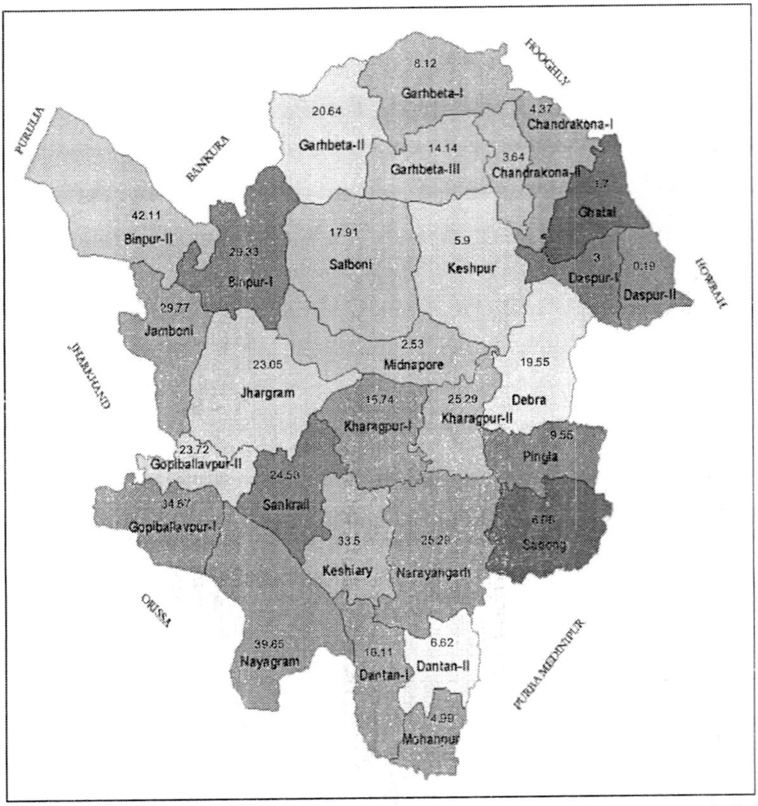

Map 3.2 : West Midnapore District: Block-wise Percentage of Tribal Population

Belpahari (Binpur II) Block of the district has over 43 per cent of population who belong to scheduled tribes. There are sixteen tribes identified in the district. There are 19 Blocks and 2,043 mouzas (revenue villages) identified under Integrated Tribal Development Programme (ITDP). These areas are identified because of incidence of tribal population and backwardness. In some of these Blocks, percentage of tribal population to total population ranges from 20 per cent to 43 per cent. Map 3.4 gives indication of forest incidence in West Midnapore district. It has been observed that there is natural correlation between forest coverage and location of tribal habitations. It is interesting to note two distinct parts in the district, the western

Map 3.3 : West Midnapore District: Block-wise Percentage of BPL Population

half and the eastern half. The western half is where maximum number of tribal population live and it is also the region with good forest coverage. The areas with dense forest cover have been the traditional habitat for tribal living over generations.

Santals are the largest among tribal population in the district. The Backward Classes Welfare Office at Midnapore estimates population of Lodhas in the district to be around 46,000. Their habitations are spread over 123 mouzas across 22 blocks though their concentration is more in Blocks of Narayangarh, Keshiary, Jhargram, Kharagpur-I and Nayagram. The district is also home to other tribes like Munda, Mahali, Kora and Bhumij.

Table 3.3 : West Midnapore: Total Population and ST Percentage—Census 2001

Sl. No.	Name of Block / Municipality	Population			ST Population			% of ST Population
		Male	Female	Total	Male	Female	Total	
1.	Midnapore Sadar	81043	76902	157945	14911	14737	29648	18.77
2.	Garhbeta I	102815	97587	200402	8133	8136	16269	8.12
3.	Garhbeta II	66940	64163	131103	13480	13575	27055	20.64
4.	Garhbeta III	74900	70954	145854	10449	10178	20627	14.14
5.	Keshpur	147720	140769	288489	8526	8486	17012	5.90
6.	Salboni	84253	80995	165248	15028	14576	29604	17.91
7.	Midnapore Muni.	76503	73266	149769	1887	1906	3793	2.53
8.	Pingla	88433	82633	171066	8476	7869	16345	9.55
9.	Debra	129224	125996	255220	25157	24745	49902	19.55
10.	Keshiary	67427	64634	132061	22675	21562	44237	33.50
11.	Dantan I	77203	74173	151376	12320	12068	24388	16.11
12.	Dantan II	68823	65537	134360	4476	4417	8893	6.62
13.	Mohanpur	49147	47176	96323	2451	2356	4807	4.99
14.	Kharagpur I	121717	115511	237228	19114	18232	37346	15.74
15.	Kharagpur II	82350	79478	161828	20563	20357	40920	25.29
16.	Sabang	122867	115819	238686	7504	7012	14516	6.08
17.	Narayangarh	136169	130506	266675	29216	28311	57527	21.57
18.	Kharagpur Muni.	97721	91040	188761	3382	3386	6768	3.59
19.	Jhargram	78363	74968	153331	18003	17338	35341	23.05
20.	Lalgarh (Binpur I)	71097	68051	139148	20398	20410	40808	29.33
21.	Belpahari (Binpur II)	73624	72353	145977	30697	30772	61469	42.11
22.	Jamboni	51880	49838	101718	15347	14938	30285	29.77
23.	Nayagram	62629	61308	123937	24932	24455	49387	39.85
24.	Sankrail	52066	50568	102634	12751	12480	25231	24.58
25.	Gopiballavpur I	48828	46006	94834	16740	16137	32877	34.67
26.	Gopiballavpur II	47914	45392	93306	11230	10903	22133	23.72
27.	Jhargram Muni.	27136	26009	53145	2589	2468	5057	9.52
28.	Ghatal	96678	94060	190738	1639	1612	3251	1.70
29.	Chandrakona I	60299	57786	118085	2649	2514	5163	4.37
30.	Chandrakona II	54686	52145	106831	1997	1893	3890	3.64
31.	Daspur I	87167	88607	175774	2621	2653	5274	3.00
32.	Daspur II	100853	105234	206087	191	205	396	0.19
33.	Ghatal Muni.	26852	24730	51582	69	54	123	0.24
34.	Kharar Muni.	5894	5686	11580	102	100	202	1.74
35.	Khirpai Muni.	7439	7109	14548	491	474	965	6.63
36.	Ramjibanpur Muni.	8924	8440	17364	166	133	299	1.72
37.	Chandrakona Muni.	10464	9934	20398	181	188	369	1.81
District Total		**2648048**	**2545363**	**5193411**	**390541**	**381636**	**772177**	**14.87**

It may be mentioned that all festivals are not common to tribal communities referred to before. These vary with different tribal groups and their traditions. In some cases, local caste Hindus in neighbouring areas also participate in the celebrations of tribal festivals. We also find influence of other historical factors in the observance of the tribal festivals. Worshipping and rituals reflect many aspects of tribal socio-economic activities. There have been many changes in tribal life due to the influence of various modernizing forces. More socio-political

Table 3.4: West Midnapore: Total Population and BPL Percentage (2008)

Sl. No.	*Name of the Block*	*Total Population*	*% of BPL Population*
1.	Midnapore Municipality	149769	31.30
2.	Midnapore	157945	29.11
3.	Keshpur	288489	30.13
4.	Salboni	165248	30.68
5.	Garhbeta I	200402	30.45
6.	Garhbeta II	131103	32.44
7.	Garhbeta III	145854	29.72
8.	Kharagpur I	237228	19.83
9.	Kharagpur II	161828	34.03
10.	Pingla	171066	34.13
11.	Sabong	238686	29.58
12.	Debra	255220	33.27
13.	Dantan I	151376	34.05
14.	Dantan II	134360	36.47
15.	Mohanpur	96323	47.49
16.	Keshyari	132061	51.85
17.	Narayangarh	266675	32.17
18.	Kharagpur Municipality	188761	58.93
19.	Ghatal	190738	34.53
20.	Chandrakona I	118085	30.91
21.	Chandrakona II	106831	30.07
22.	Daspur I	175774	29.45
23.	Daspur II	206087	35.42
24.	Ghatal Municipality	51582	24.43
25.	Kharar Municipality	11580	26.92
26.	Ramjibanpur Municipality	17364	33.25
27.	Khirpai Municipality	14548	30.85
28.	Chandrakona Municipality	20398	24.06
29.	Jhargram	206476	48.47
30.	Lalgarh (Binpur I)	139148	53.68
31.	Belpahari (Binpur II)	145977	49.14
32.	Jamboni	101718	52.85
33.	Sankrail	102634	47.36
34.	Gopiballavpur I	94834	47.71
35.	Gopiballavpur II	93306	52.98
36.	Nayagram	123937	51.78
Total		**5193411**	**36.64**

events are being depicted in their songs, while retaining the core aspects of their culture. They have also imbibed many modern values and practices in recent times. As a result, we can observe changes taking place in their festivals and life style. An attempt has been made to study closely how customs, rituals, festivals and life styles are witnessing changes over a period.

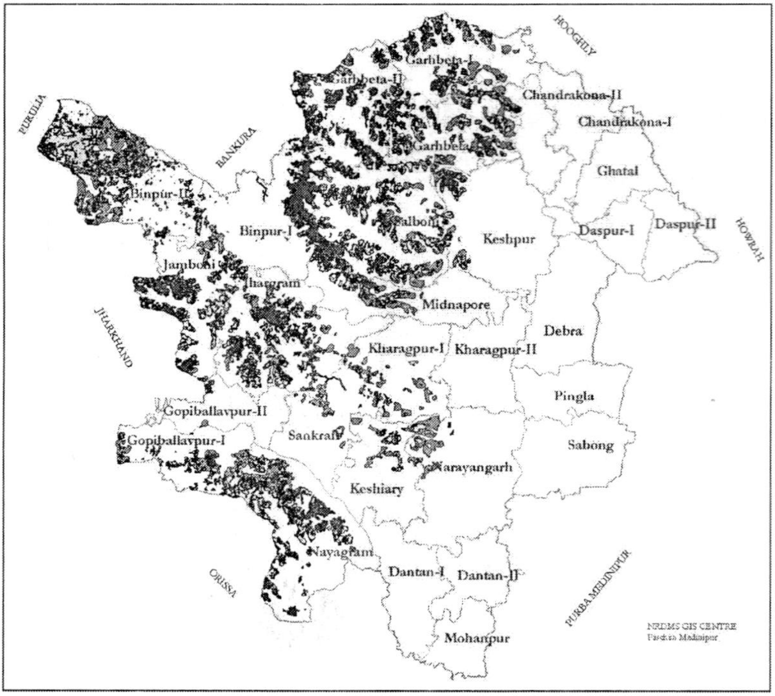

Map 3.4: West Midnapore District: Forest Coverage and Tribal Habitations Coexist

Khelar Gram Panchayat and Bonpatna Village

Khelar is one of the seven Gram Panchayats of Kharagpur-I Block. The area is close to two urban centres. One is the more prominent Kharagpur and the other is a commercial centre, Belda. Map 3.5 shows Kharagpur-I Block area including Gram Panchayats like Khelar and Kharagpur town. Khelar has fourteen *gram samsads* or Wards and twenty villages. The population of the Gram Panchayat is 16,035 as per 2001 Census. Out of them, 6,414 (40%) belong to scheduled castes and 5,612 (35%), to scheduled tribes. As it can be observed, the proportion of people belonging to SC and ST is significantly high and way above the district average. These details normally signal a comparatively poor and socially backward situation. There are forty-nine mouzas or revenue villages in Khelar Gram Panchayat, out of

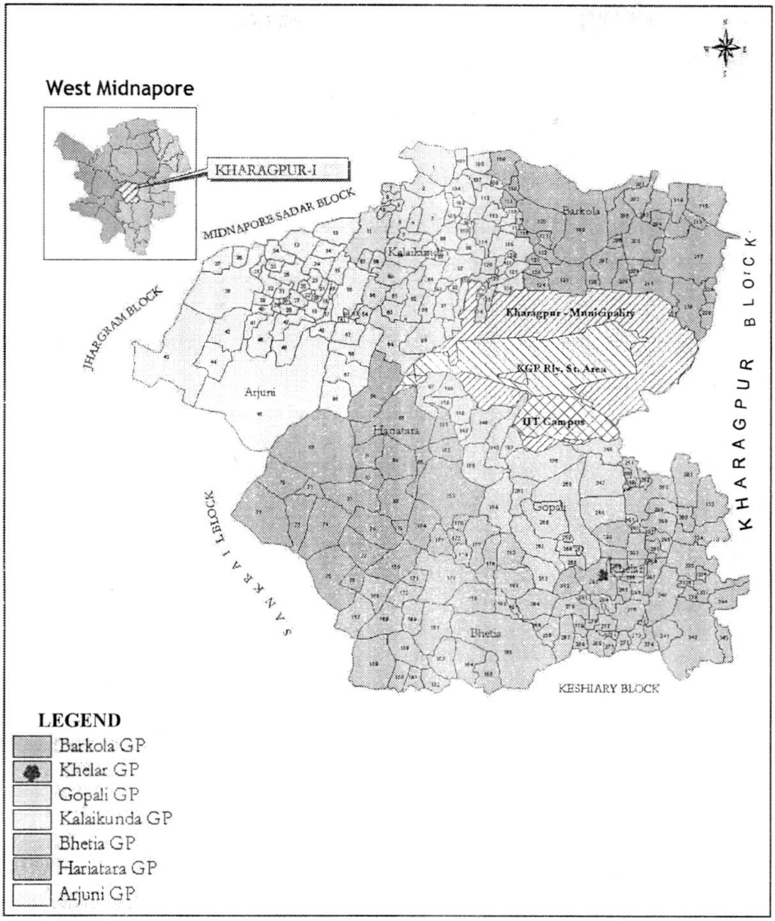

Map 3.5: Kharagpur-I Block showing Khelar and other Gram Panchayats, Municipality, IIT and Railway Settlement

which thirty-nine are inhabited. The remaining ten mouzas consist of agriculture and forestland. Table 3.5 gives detailed land utilization pattern in Khelar Gram Panchayat. There are fifteen primary schools and one higher secondary school in Khelar Gram Panchayat. In addition, there are fifteen community-managed schools also in the area.[5]

Table 3.5: Land Utilization Pattern in Khelar Gram Panchayat

(Area in Acres)

Total area	*8779.16*
Agriculture land	7512.17
Non-agriculture land	393.14
Bastu land (Residential area)	197.7
Water area	82.61
River	36.52
Forest	557.0

The villages have influence of nearby towns. There is forest cover also in some areas, which extends up to adjoining Narayangarh Block. Tribes such as Santals and Lodhas inhabit the area. There is also small population of Kora tribe in some areas. As already indicated, there is a significant proportion of population belonging to the scheduled castes. Agriculture is the main livelihood for the majority of people living here (Photograph 3.1 shows people working in countryside after harvesting of paddy.) There are cultivators, landless wage earners in agriculture fields and many who need to supplement their income from small piece of own land, by working in lands of others. Income from agriculture is supplemented by other activities like collection of firewood and leaves from the forest (Photograph 3.2 portrays tribal women collecting firewood from nearby forest.). This image is perhaps symbolic of life of tribal girls and women in rural West Midnapore. Most of the areas grow single crop of paddy, whose success depends on the monsoon. Hence, the economic condition and livelihoods of the people are susceptible to the vagaries of nature. Some work as labourers in brickfields, quarries and construction works. Some earn livelihood by pulling three-wheelers, popularly known as *rikshaws* and *thelas*. Photograph 3.3 shows a villager, Montu Soren belonging to Santal tribe, transporting hay on his three-wheeler. Photograph 3.4 visualises changing occupations among tribal people of the study area. Here, Badal Murmu, also a Santal, has taken to enterprise with a tailoring and readymade dress shop in village Bonpatna. His shop has an appropriate nameplate, "Murmu Tailors". Similar to any other rural place, the proportion of people having permanent jobs in the Government or private sector is insignificant. They form the new elite or most respected lot in villages.

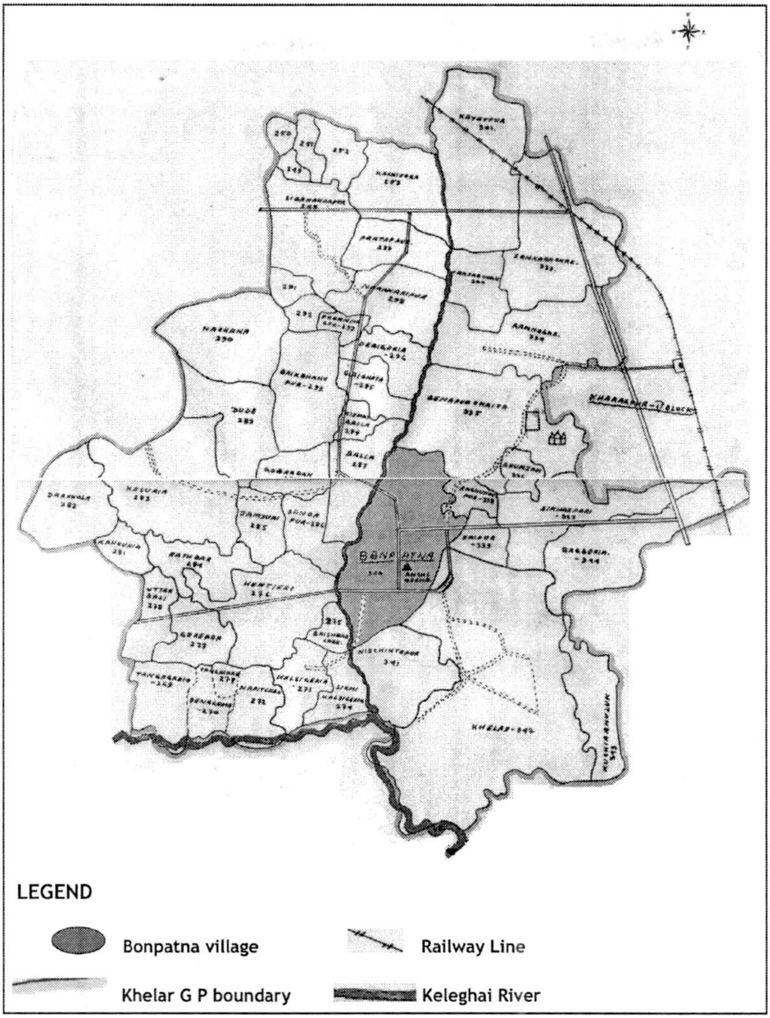

Map 3.6: Khelar Gram Panchayat and Bonpatna Village

Bonpatna is one of the villages of Khelar Gram Panchayat and it is shown in Map 3.6. Various utilities in the area are shown in Map 3.7. The population of Bonpatna is 2,244. There are 1,118 men and 1,126 women in the mouza. Out of them, 983 belong to scheduled tribes and 641 to scheduled castes. Remaining 502 belong to other castes.

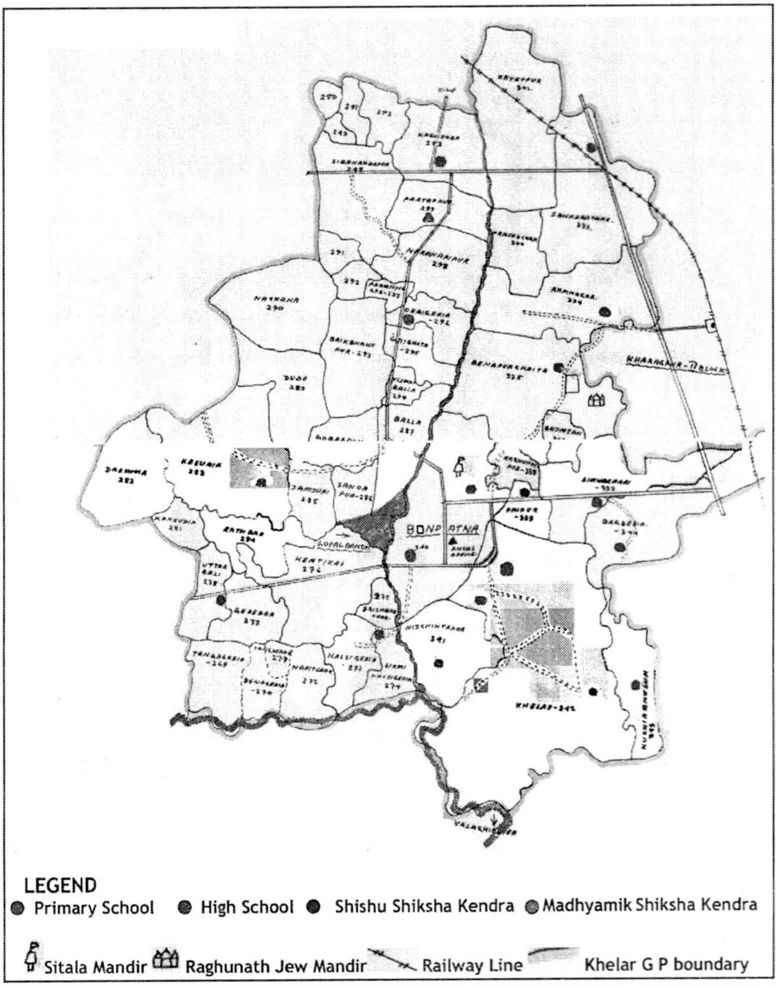

Map 3.7: Khelar Gram Panchayat and Bonpatna Village : Location of Various Public Utilities

Table 3.6 gives detailed break-up of population of Bonpatna mouza.[6] Table 3.7 depicts age group-wise details of Santal and Lodha respondents of Bonpatna village. The village has different hamlets or *paras*, as locally called. Uttar Bonpatna and Dakshin Bonpatna[7] are two well-marked hamlets where people from Lodha community live. Agriculture is the main source of livelihood for most of the people of Bonpatna village. There is *Sitala* temple, where the Goddess *Sitala* is worshipped, in both the hamlets. Whenever the researcher visited one hamlet, women of the other hamlet always complained saying that he did not go to their village.

Table 3.6: Category-wise Population Details of Bonpatna Mouza

Category	*Number of families*	*Male*	*Female*	*Total*
General	73	254	248	502
SC	142	310	331	641
ST	188	498	485	983
OBC	16	56	62	118
Total	**419**	**1118**	**1126**	**2244**

SC: Scheduled Caste. ST: Scheduled Tribe. OBC: Other Backward Classes.

Table 3.7: Ethnic Group-wise Age Group Details of Respondents of Bonpatna Mouza

[N = 172]

Ethnic Group	*20-30*	*30-40*	*40-50*	*50-60*	*60 and above*
Santal*	13 (17.6%)	21 (28.4%)	15 (20.3%)	14 (18.9%)	11 (14.8%)
Lodha**	15 (15.3%)	28 (28.6%)	26 (26.5%)	17 (17.4%)	12 (12.2%)
Total	**28 (16.3%)**	**49 (28.5%)**	**41 (23.8%)**	**35 (20.3%)**	**19 (11.1%)**

*Santal: 74. **Lodha: 98.

In Dakshin Bonpatna, there are thirty-two families of Santals. Among them, only one family owns a plot of land. Shyam Mandi owns three acres of land, which is comparatively a large holding for any family in the area. Others work as labourers either in fields or construction work. Some of them also go to other districts during agriculture season. Santals' houses are built of mud, roofed with straw or tin sheets. The houses are kept very neat and clean and the outside walls are painted with beautiful designs.

In *Danga para*, fourteen families of *hari* community reside. They belong to scheduled caste. Elderly women of this community work as *dayi* or midwife who help during pregnancy and childbirth. In olden days, men from this community used to be *palki* (palanquin) bearers.[8]

They also work as labourers nowadays. There are also four families belonging to *mahar* community. They also belong to scheduled caste and mostly work as labourers.

In *Madhya para*, six families of *Brahman* community stay. They used to be *jamindars* or landlords once upon a time. Now they are mainly into jobs. There are also sixty families of *jalia koibartha* caste. They belong to scheduled caste. They work as labourers and also do fishing in *Gopal bandh* and other waterbodies in the area.

In *Pal para*, eight families belonging to *Teli* community inhabit. They own agriculture land. There are also people belonging to *Bagdi* caste. They also earn their livelihood mostly as agriculture labourers. They also belong to scheduled caste.

It is observed that each *para* or inhabitation is separate from the other and can be distinguished. There is no mixing of *paras* generally. In *Uttar para* of course, houses of *jalia koibartha, bagdi* and general castes can be seen together and mixed. In entire Bonpatna village, all houses are *katcha* or thatched except the five *pucca* or permanent houses of *satpathis* in *Brahman para*. Map 3.8 indicates location of different habitations and important landmarks in Bonpatna village.

Most of the houses in the village are very small mud houses. Some houses have tin roof. Typically, a house of a Lodha family is not built at normal height; it is dark inside the house even during day. There are two to three small windows in the walls. Photograph 3.5 shows a Lodha couple painstakingly rebuilding their mud house and Photograph 3.6 is the picture of a Lodha man sitting in front of his simple mud house in Dakshin Bonpatna Lodha habitation.

There is no electricity in the village. People get about one and half litres of kerosene from ration shop and buy about two and a half litres from market. The price is rupees twenty per litre in the open market, which is twice that of ration shop.

Khelar Adibasi Primary School and Khelar Higher Secondary School are located in Bonpatna village. The Gram Panchayat office and the primary health centre are next-door and also are located in Bonpatna village. There is a temple, which is four hundred and ten years old in this village. This is known as *Raghunath Jew mandir*, built by *Satpathis,* the then landlords of the area. With all these, the village is always bubbling with activity.

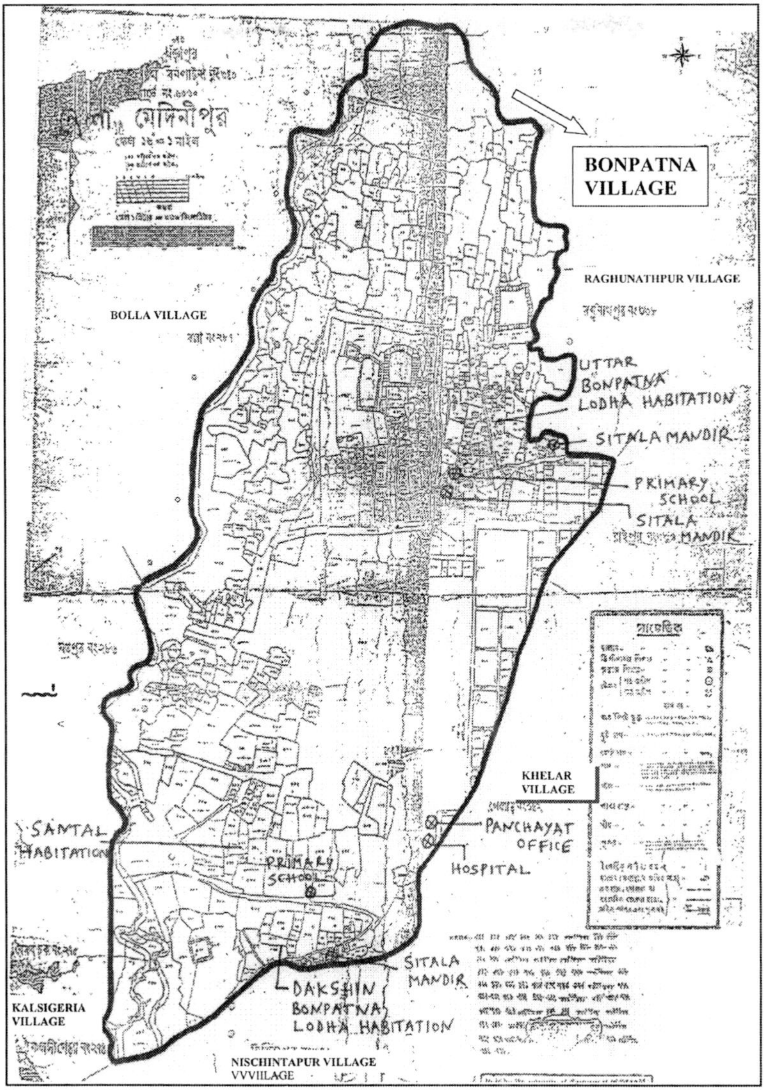

Map 3.8: Bonpatna Village: Habitations and Landmarks

NOTES

1. With nearly ten million people, Midnapore district used to be the largest district in India.

2. *Kharif* is summer crop and *rabi* is winter crop.
3. Kharagpur is a cosmopolitan town of the district, historically known for the workshops and establishments of the Railways, even from the British times. The town is also better known for the Indian Institute of Technology (IIT). The town has sizeable sections of population speaking languages of Telugu, Oriya and Hindi.
4. There are number of anthropological and sociological studies on Lodhas and see for instance Jana (2010), Chakravarty *et al.* (2005), Paty (2005), Mondal (1999), and Bhowmick (2004; 1981 and 1963).
5. These are known as SSK (*Shishu Shiksha Kendra*) at the primary level and MSK (*Madhyamik Shiksha Kendra*) at the upper primary level. The local school committee drawn from the village manages the school. The committee selects teachers from the educated women of the village. The salary is significantly less compared to the 'normal teachers' of Government run schools. One interesting study was published by *Pratichi Trust*, with which the Nobel laureate Amartya Sen is associated, signifying that education standards of SSK were comparatively better than those were found in normal primary schools run by the Government.
6. This is as per house-to-house survey done by Khelar Gram Panchayat in June 2008.
7. Uttar means the north and Dakshin means the south.
8. *Palki* was used in olden days for carrying bride and bridegroom during marriage processions. It is tastefully decorated for the occasion. Also women of upper castes and landlords used to move in *palki* carried manually by *palki* bearers.

4
Customs, Traditions, Beliefs and Lifestyle

The Santals : Historical Introduction

In eastern India, the Santals are the largest tribe. The traditions of the Santals symbolize them as a group wandering from one place to another and they finally settled in Chhota Nagpur and the adjoining districts. On the basis of their traditions, several theories have been put forward to explain their origin. The Santali language is part of the Austro-Asiatic family, distantly related to Vietnamese and Khmer. A few of the Indian anthropologists also believe that humans first came to India about 65,000-55,000 years ago. The earliest of them were Proto-Australoids followed by the Proto-Dravidians. The Proto-Australoids can be identified with some facial characteristics such as low forehead, thick lips, wide jaw and wavy hair. Historians believe that they were the ancestors of the tribal community residing in the eastern part of India (excluding hilly portions). Hence, the Santals, Kols, and Mundas may be the descendants of them.

In the middle of the eigheenth century, Chhota Nagpur was the main habitat of the Santals. By the end of the century, due to the demands of population, the forests started getting cleared. The Permanent Settlement of 1793 during the British rule over India forced the landlords to pay more attention to land reclamation and improvement. The Santals were increasingly used for this purpose. In 1832, the Government set apart a large area in the Santal Parganas for the settlement of the Santals. This area was known as Damin-i-Koh. As a result, from the middle of the last century, Damin-i-Koh turned out to be the major concentration of the Santals.

The Santal Rebellion : Background

Before the advent of the British in India, the Santals resided peacefully in the hilly districts of Cuttack, Dhalbhum, Manbhum, Barabhum, Chhotanagpur, Palamau, Hazaribagh, Midnapore, Bankura and Birbhum. They started their agrarian way of life by clearing the forest and also engaged themselves in hunting for subsistence. But as the agents of the new colonial rule claimed their rights on the lands of the Santals, they peacefully went to reside in the hills of Rajamahal. After a brief interlude of peace, the British operatives with their native counterparts jointly started claiming their rights in this new land as well. The simple and honest Santals were cheated and turned into slaves by the zamindars (landlords) and the moneylenders who first appeared to them as businessmen. They allured the Santals first by giving goods to them as loan. These loans, however hard a Santal tried to repay, never ended. Through corrupt measures of the moneylenders, it multiplied to an amount for which a generation of the Santal family had to work as slaves. Furthermore, the Santali women who worked under labour contractors were disgraced and abused. This loss of freedom, which they enjoyed once, turned them into rebels and finally they took oath to launch an attack on this axis of evil.

The Santal Rebellion[1]

On 30 June, 1855, two Santal rebel leaders, Sidhu and Kanhu Murmu, mobilized thousands of Santals and declared a rebellion against the British rule. The Santals initially gained some success but soon the British found out a new way to tackle these rebels. As the legend goes that the Santals, so skilled in archery, could throw arrows extremely accurate and with great power. The British soon understood that there was no point fighting them in the forest. They decided to force the Santals come out of the forest. So in a conclusive battle, which followed, the British equipped with modern firearms and war elephants stationed at the foot of the hill. As the Santali fighters neared the foot of the hill, the British army attacked them with full power. Thereafter, attacking every village of the Santals, they made sure that any trace of revolutionary spirit was annihilated. Although the revolution was brutally suppressed, it marked a great change in the British colonial rule and policy. The day is still celebrated among the Santal community with great respect and spirit for the thousands of the Santal martyrs who sacrificed their lives along with their two celebrated leaders to win freedom from the rule of the landlords and the British.

Ol Chiki: The Santali Script

The Santali script is a relatively recent innovation. Santalis did not have a written language until the twentieth century and used Latin/ Roman, Devnagari and Bangla writing systems. As none of the existing scripts were sufficient enough to correctly express the Santali language phonetically, a need for a separate script was felt by some visionary Santals, which resulted in the invention of new script called *Ol Chiki* by Pandit Raghunath Murmu in 1925. For his noble deed and contribution of the script *Ol Chiki* for the Santal society, he is revered among Santals. He wrote over 150 books covering a wide spectrum of subjects such as grammar, novels, drama, poetry, and short stories in Santali using *Ol Chiki* as part of his extensive programme for uplifting the Santal community. *Darege Dhan*, *Sidhu-Kanhu*, *Bidu Chandan* and *Kherwal Bir* are among the most acclaimed of his works.

The Santal Community of Bonpatna

There are two hamlets of Bonpatna and Kantabani in Bonpatna village with Santal habitation. The Santal people of Bonpatna believe that the word Santal is a combination of two words; *san* means organised, *tal* means united and Santal means united community or tribe. There are twelve surnames (lineage/clans) or titles of this community found in the research area. These are Kisku, Murmu, Hembram, Hansda, Tudu, Mandi, Besra, Baskey, Soren, Koyra, Badli and Pauria. The Santals of Kantabani and Banpatna have the surnames of Kisku, Murmu, Tudu, Baskey, Soren, Mandi, Hansda and Hembram. The Santal community is devoid of any caste system and there is no distinction made on the basis of birth. There is no social differentiation among them though no marital relationship occurs between Mandi and Kisku, Tudu and Besra.

Table 4.1 shows the family details of respondents of Bonpatna village.

Table 4.1: Ethnic Group-wise Family Details of Respondents

[N=172]

Ethnic Group	*Nuclear Family*	*Extended Family*
Santal*	21 (28.4%)	53 (71.6%)
Lodha**	32 (32.7%)	66 (67.3%)

*Santal: 74. **Lodha: 98.

The Santals have distinct customs and rituals[2], which they observe during various phases of a human being's life. Starting from the birth of a child, the rituals are performed during different phases of life cycle of a person, including marriage and death. These rituals are well defined and performed by the priests of the village. These also serve to unite the community socially on a regular basis. Santali culture is depicted in the paintings and art works on the walls of their houses. Local mythology includes the stories of the Santal ancestors Pilchu Haram and Pilchu Bhudi.

Purification after Childbirth

After the child is born, the village mid-wife, commonly known as *daima*, cuts the umbilical chord. Afterwards, on a determined day, the *majhi* or the Village Chief/_Headman summons all the adult male members of the Santal households. In the presence of all, the *Dharma* God is worshipped by offering oil and vermilion and it is believed that initial purification is done.

Later, during the first rice feeding ceremony of the newborn, ultimate purity is attained. This ceremony can take place when the child is six to eighteen months of age. The *majhi* is informed of the date fixed for the auspicious ceremony. *Khichdi,* a rice preparation, is cooked with *atap* (raw) rice and fried and crushed neem leaves. All the invitees are served with a spoon full of the *khichdi*. In addition to this, the father of the newborn serves the community with five pots of *haria,* home-made rice beer. The *namkaran* or naming ceremony of the new born also takes place on the same day. It is believed that the child is purified from the birth related impurities.

Santal Marriage[3]

How are Marriages Arranged ?

In case of a negotiated marriage, the groom's side goes to check the prospective bride. The *majhi* accompanies them. After reaching the native village of the prospective bride, the groom's party initially goes to meet the *majhi* of the village. The *majhi* and his associates properly receive them and the *majhi's* men inform the bride's family about their arrival. Then the groom's party visits the house of the prospective bride. There, the mother or the aunts of the prospective bride receive them with an earthen pot full of water. They also touch the feet of the elderly member of the groom's party. The young ones of the party show respect to the women by touching their feet. Then the prospective bride comes to touch the feet of the elderly members of the party. During the process, the party gets opportunity to see and assess the girl. After she has completed the task, she returns inside. If the party chooses her, one of the members sprinkles drops of water thrice from the earthen pot containing water. The sprinkling of water is the sign of choosing the girl. If the bridegroom side does not like the girl, no water is sprinkled. If the party chooses the girl, then the prospective groom is sent to the girl's house. His friends accompany the prospective groom. Again the *majhi* first receives the party. Then the bride's family receives the groom and his friends. If the groom likes the bride, water is sprinkled from the earthen pot. After this custom, the bride's family is invited to visit the groom's house. The groom receives the bride's family by touching their feet. He also provides the party with an earthen pot full of water. If the bride's party sprinkles water from the pot thrice then it is a sign that the bride's party has accepted the groom. After this initial phase, the matchmaker contacts both the families and fixes up the wedding date. The transactions, if any, are also settled at this moment. In their society, there is no dowry demand from the groom's side. It is the groom who has to pay the bride price in the form of, *viz*., a calf, a bull, and a she-goat. If one is unable to meet the demand immediately then, later on, a pig has to be paid as fine along with the above-mentioned animals. The bride's family gives three saris, measuring 21, 15 and 11 arm lengths.

The Marriage Proper

Marriage takes place at the bride's place. When the groom goes to marry, he takes along with him, a marriage party. Initially, the marriage party visits the *majhi's* house. From there, the elder sisters of the bride take the groom to the wedding place on their laps. If it is not possible, the groom is taken by holding his hands. The groom takes bath and wears new clothes. He is seated on the groom's throne. After this, the sisters of the groom take him to the wedding site. The groom's brothers bring the bride to the wedding site in a bamboo basket. In the next step, the brother-in-law of the groom (groom's sister's husband) carries him on his shoulder. At this moment, the sisters-in-law of both the bride and the groom carry pots, containing water and mango leaves, on their heads. They sprinkle water from the pots with the mango leaves on both the bride and the groom. Then the groom puts *sindoor* (vermilion) on the bride. The *sindoor giving* ceremony is accompanied by a dancing ceremony under the direction of the *majhi*. The bride and the groom are taken inside and given food. As a custom, the groom shows vanity and refuses to take food. He is then told by the bride's party to shed off his vanity and he is promised his share of gifts. After receiving assurance, the groom takes his food. The menu for the marriage feast generally consists of rice, lentil soup, vegetables, pork and chicken. *Haria* is also offered. Usually, members of other communities are not invited. However, those who can afford do invite people from other castes, and separate arrangements are to be made for them.

On the next day, after taking meal, the bride and the groom leave the bride's house for the groom's house. After six to nine days, her family members bring the bride to her parental house. She stays in her parental home for equal number of days that she has spent at the groom's home. Later, she leaves her parents' house to stay with her in-laws.

Apart from arranged or negotiated marriages, one can also observe that there are occasions when a Santal boy falls in love with a girl of his community and takes her away to marry. However, such marriage needs to be socialized under the supervision of the *majhis* of both the parties. The boy's side may have to pay penalty also for the boy's adventure.

Separation of a Married Couple

If the couple fails to have an understanding, the husband sends the wife to her parental home. If the wife does not want to cohabit with her husband, she leaves the husband's house and returns to her parental home on her own. If the wife appears willing, but the husband is found unwilling to cohabit, then the *majhis* along with dignitaries of both the sides try to settle the matter. If they fail, the separation takes place between the couple by a written agreement. In this case, the husband's side pays the wife cultivable land measuring one *bigha*, ten *maunds* of rice, plough and a bullock, a bull, a calf and a she-goat. If the husband's side fails to pay the wife on time, then the wife's party takes away, by force, the cattle of the husband's family as well as that of the *majhi* of the husband's village. After the payment is made, such cattle taken away by force are returned to their owners. In cases when the wife is unwilling to continue marital relationship, the wife's side has to pay the husband's side, the amount spent by them on the occasion of marriage.

The Last Rites of the Deceased and Purification Process

The dead body is usually burnt. The head of the body is placed in the southern direction and the son performs the *mukhagni*. It is to be noted that the dead body of lepers and tuberculosis patients are not burnt, but buried in a grave due to fear of spread of disease.[4] However, the *mukhagni* rite is performed. After the body is burnt, the skull is put in a bowl and taken to the deceased's house. After covering it with turmeric, it is placed in a bottle. The bottle is buried under a tree in front of five community men. A chick is taken to the holy place belonging to the *Dharma Debta* and is sacrificed by remembering the God. The detached head of the chick remains lying there. The body of the chick is taken to the deceased's house and after cleaning, is cooked without using oil, spices and salt. The dish is placed in an old plate along with cooked rice. The rice and the curry are divided into two parts. Three bowls made of *Karma* leaves or *Sal* leaves are taken. Water, curry and rice are kept separately in the three bowls. All the three bowls are put in a straw basket and is made to hang in the loft. The son of the deceased person performs the *achaman* (purification) ceremony twice and consumes the remaining half of the curry and the rice. The half that is hung on the loft is shown to the community men on the next day. It is believed that, if the soul of the deceased person has consumed the offering, then the rice will contain traces of the curry. After performing this rite, the family of the deceased gain back the right to have oil and non-vegetarian food. After this, a ceremony called *ghat-shraddha*[5] is performed. But there is no fixed date for it. The family performs it as per its discretion. The eldest male member of the household of the deceased informs the *mukhia* (village chief/headman) that he wants to perform the *ghat-shraddha*. He fixes a date and all the friends and relatives are invited.

It is interesting to note that during the process, it is chanted to the soul of the deceased, "From this date onwards you will not scare us off. For freeing your spirit, we are offering blood of chicken to the *Dharma* god, the villagers and the relatives." During the occasion the tribe's men play the role of barber, washerman and *Brahmin* (priest). The one who plays the role takes a fee from the head of the family. The married women do not gain their right to wear *sindoor* till completion of this funeral ceremony. The feast starts from the next morning (around 8 am). However, the cooking starts from the previous night. The menu consists of rice, pork/chicken, *dal* and vegetables. Sometimes, invitations are also sent to members of the other communities. But normally, separate arrangements are made for them.

Afterwards, a day is fixed and after obtaining permission from the *mukhia*, the bones that remain buried under the tree are unearthed and are submerged in the river waters of the *Damodar* or the *Subarnarekha*. These days, many also use the nearby river waters of the *Keleghai* for the purpose.

The Supernatural World of Santals

The Santals believe in balance and equilibrium between the world of men and the world of spirits. Their belief is that there are some supernatural beings that control their destiny. The supernatural world comprises *bongas* of various orders, spirits of the dead ancestors. It is believed by some scholars that *bonga* means the same as *Bhaga* (*Bhagavan* or God). They believe these *bongas* retain interest in the matters of their next generations. The *bongas* wander about and interfere in the affairs of human beings. Photograph 4.1 shows the clay statues of horses and elephants believed to be carriers of *bongas*. There are *bongas* at the periphery of the village and also within the village limits. There are different *bongas*—forest *bongas*, mountain *bongas*, spring *bongas*, tree *bongas*, home *bongas* and underground *bongas*. There are benevolent *bongas* who are kind and caring. They wish wellbeing of the village people. They give them valour, strength, prosperity, peace and harmony. Some of the benevolent deities of the Santals are *Maran Buru*, *Jaher Era*, *Moreko-Turuiko* and *Sima bonga*. They are propitiated for good agricultural products or trouble free harvesting. They are worshipped at family level and community level at different times of the year.

There are also malicious and harmful *bongas* who are found in everywhere in the universe. They cause sufferings, misfortunes, and mishaps. The Santals also believe that troubles and sufferings may come, if the supernatural beings are displeased with them. Deities like *Karam* and *Bagut* are regarded as malevolent in nature and thus they are propitiated solely out of fear.

Maran Buru gives life to people for a definite time. The Sun God causes day and night. He brings rain and bestows sunlight. He helps people to get good crops. He also punishes them too with starvation and deficiency if they break the rules of conduct and go against social taboos.

All these *bongas* are frequently propitiated on several occasions or else they would cause destruction. People believe that they are hungry, thirsty, angry and discontented. Hence, sacrifices are offered to them so that they do not ruin the health and happiness of the people. They also believe in *rakhas* (monsters) and *bhut* (evil spirits).

According to *binties* of Santals, which are oral compilations passed on to successive generations, the sun is considered a male God and the moon is his wife. Stars are believed to be their children. The sun is called *sin cando* and the moon, *ninda cando*. Santals distinguish constellations in the sky with local names. For example, the Milky Way is known as *hat dahar*, the path to the market. The Great Bear is nothing but *burhi parkom*, the old woman's bed. D. N. Mujumdar (1955) gave graphic description of these interesting beliefs.

Some of the major *pujas* or prayers and rituals performed by Santals of Banpatna and Kantabani are presented here :

- *Magha sime (Magha puja)*: During this *puja* the next *majhi* of the village is decided. It is also decided which are the new households that will be included in the village *pujas.*
- *Baha bonga*: This *puja* takes place during April and May (Bengali months of *Chaitra* and *Baisakh*). This *puja* is done with pomp and gaiety. Due to the heavy expenditure involved in it, in some villages, it is performed once in five years.
- *Ayaree puja*: This *puja* takes place in the Bengali month of *Asad*. After this *puja*, the farmers start with their tasks.
- There are many other *pujas* that they perform either individually or collectively, such as, *Karam bonga* and *Aram bonga,* performed to, what they believe, destroy the evil spirits.

Santals of Bonpatna and adjoining villages celebrate '*Salui puja*' on the day of '*Dol purnima*' in the month of *Phalgun* coinciding with Holi. During this *puja, 'Ma More'* is worshipped. *Ma More* is combination of five goddesses. Shyam Kisku mentioned that in the year 2010, five persons were possessed by the deity. Within a span of half an hour, these five persons were possessed by the deity. They were in the age group of 25 to 40. As a result, these people started shivering and shaking. In this stage, the deity speaks to people. The priest offered sacrifice of a he-goat to the goddess. This period lasted for about two hours. The priest asked the deity through them, whether the *puja* arrangements were proper and the deity was satisfied. The priest also enquired whether there were any mistakes in the rituals. He also enquired about future. People were keen to know whether they would be free from diseases. Shyam mentions that when a person is in such a stage, he even drinks blood coming out of the animal sacrificed. At times, a cock also is sacrificed to please the deity. Among Lodhas, this phenomenon occurs among men as well as women. In contrast, only Santal men are possessed by the deity. Shyam has not seen in his life, any Santal woman being possessed. At the end of this period of trance, water was spread on the faces of people and they slowly became normal.

Belief in Witch : Persisting with Superstitions

Many Santals still believe in the adverse effects of *dayin*, *dayini* or witch. A man is called a *dayin* and a woman, a *dayini*, on the suspicion of possessing control over evil forces. It is believed that a *dayin* or *dayini* has the power to unleash evil forces on people resulting in ill health and problems. In some cases, when the patient dies, it is attributed to the evil effects of *dayin* or *dayini*. Even today, there are many cases where the villagers kill a person who is marked as a *dayin* or *dayini*. The *ojha* or *janguru* identifies the *dayin* or *dayini*. They are socially ostracized and penalized.

In April 2003, Montu Singh of Bonpatna village was killed on the suspicion of being a *dayin*. He was forty-five years old. His wife was threatened not to speak out; otherwise she would also be killed. She had to keep silent. The police came and went without much progress in the investigation. Their son used to work in a farmer's house in a village in Punjab. About seven people went to Punjab in search of work. Montu's son returned to the village after the incident and never went back to Punjab.

In Nachna village, about five kilometres from Bonpatna, Lakshman Mandi was killed on suspicion of being *dayin*. It is relevant to mention that throughout India, mostly in tribal societies, such cases of marking people as *dayinis* or witches and killing them are happening repeatedly. Local people feel that on the excuse of *dayini*, motivated persons eliminate personal and political adversaries.[6]

Educated Santal persons of Bonpatna made one interesting and important observation. One of the reasons why some people from their community converted to Christianity[7] were the superstitions like witchcraft and persistent persecution of people associated with such branding. The more liberal Christian religion, comparatively, appeared to them as an option to overcome the social stigmas. The other familiar reason was, of course, gratitude for and being influenced by the help received from Christian philanthropic organizations.

Cultural Celebrations: The Rhythm of Life

Culture is a way of life of people in the society, the pattern of behaviour and the expression of feeling and thought in different situations. These patterns are understood by other members of the same society. They can understand, appreciate and recognize these behaviours and experiences together. This helps in development of quality of life of the people in that particular society.

Culture is also understood as bond among human beings themselves, human beings and societies, and human beings and nature. Culture is classified into spiritual, societal and material aspects. It can be accumulated and passed on from one generation to the next one, from one society to another society. Culture is so precious that it needs conservation, rehabilitation, development, transmission, promotion and exchange as it helps human beings to live in peace, happiness and freedom, which are the foundation of human civilization.

In UNESCO's definition, culture includes 'the whole complex of distinctive spiritual, material, intellectual and emotional features that characterize a society or social group. It includes not only arts and letters, but also modes of life, the fundamental rights of the human being, value systems, traditions and beliefs' (UNESCO: 1982:41).

Analysing these various thoughts about culture in relation to Santals of Bonpatna, their view of happiness is that of well-being and freedom from disease and sickness. Disease and sickness are unnatural. Human beings have a natural right to health and life. They must live healthily up to old age. They would love to enjoy themselves without any time restriction.

The festivals are occasions to dance for men and women and each festival has distinct dance form and songs associated with it. The Santal men and women perform dances individually as well as collectively. Some of these are:

- *Dong enech* (Dong dance): This dance is performed only on the day of wedding ceremony. Here the men and women dance separately but they follow the same steps. Men also play instruments.
- *Mongri*: This is a dance to celebrate and there is no restriction regarding its performance. This is an exclusive dance performed to tide over the hardships of life. Men and women dance separately, but they follow the same steps.
- *Baha bonga*: This dance is performed during *pujas*. Here also both men and women participate, but they dance separately.

- *Dongel enech*: This dance is performed exclusively by men. This is performed in association of *shikar* (shooting) and is performed any time during the shooting season during *Chaitra* and *Jaistha.* (April and May)
- *Dansai enech*: This dance is performed only by men, during the occasion of Durga *puja*. No instrument is played in this dance and the participants dance as per the rhythm. A bow is tied with a string to the skin of a gourd. The string is pulled as per the rhythm and it makes a sweet sound. The dancers also use a pair of bells.
- *Sardsa* dance: During the occasion of Durga *puja,* women only perform this dance. Women carry two steel plates with spoons attached to them. The dancers beat the plates with the help of the spoons.
- *Karam* dance: This dance is performed only during the occasion of Karam *puja*. Men and women perform the dance, but separately.

Mukherjee (1962), Campbell (1915) and Risley (1851) chronicled the rituals and festivals of Santals in great detail. The researcher attempted to study the changing patterns in their celebrations and observations, rocked by the tides of time.

What has changed?

Modern Day Marriages are Short

Nowadays, the time span of marriage ceremony has come down and is generally completed in two days. On the first day, the groom's party arrives at the bride's place. The following day, marriage is performed and the bridegroom returns to his village with the bride. There are, however, many places in the district, where the marriage ceremony lasts for at least three days. The shortening of the ceremony is a modern phenomenon, as people feel that they do not have that much time and resources to spare. As Bonpatna village is close to Kharagpur urban centre and the national highway, the process of modernization has taken its toll on the leisurely marriage ceremony of yesteryears, as the Santals now prefer at the most a two-day marriage.

Educated Santal parents take Doctor's advice regarding children, family welfare and methods to be followed. They do not prefer more than two to three children. Earlier, families used to have six to seven children. In some cases, the number of children used to be up to 10 to 12. According to Lal Mohan Kisku, elders in his community do not like the youngsters to restrict the family size. Interestingly, Lal Mohan says, boys who are not much educated or not doing a job, tend to marry at the age of 18 to 19 years even in present times. In such cases, the bride's age is around 14 to 15 years.

Incidents of Marriages Outside Community

1. Rabi Kisku of Bonpatna village married Chandmani, daughter of Jamini Singh, who belongs to the Kora tribe of Rupnarayanpur. At present, both the communities have accepted their marriage and they are living happily with two sons and two daughters.
2. Kuntu Kisku, daughter of Late Deena Kisku, a Santal woman, got married to Rabi Singh of Kora tribe. Their marriage has received acceptance and they are leading a happy married life. The couple has two sons.
3. Widow re-marriages do take place among Santals; Rabin Kisku married a woman from his community who had lost her husband before.
4. Mantu Singh belongs to Kora tribe and he married a girl from 'general caste', a term locally used for castes other than scheduled castes and tribes.

Social Ostracization

In case of violation of social customs and norms, there is system of punishment in Santal society. The most common violation referred to is marriage outside the community. To compensate the violation of son marrying outside the community, the father has to perform *shraddha* ceremony as if the son is dead; then only the family is readmitted to their society and restrictions are withdrawn. The strongest social action is expulsion from the society, known as *bitlaha*. However, these restrictions are getting less and less binding on the members of the community because of the effects of modern education and interactions with other communities and their social behaviour.

Will Traditions Continue ?

When asked, Raghunath Tudu of Bonpatna said they followed and observed social customs of Santal community. When persisted with the question as to how it was possible for him, living far away in a different social setting because of job, to manage to do so. He mentioned he would always try to come home for important occasions like marriage and festivals. He admitted that it was not possible for him to come home on all occasions and he felt sad about it. The researcher asked Diwakar Kisku, Raghunath Tudu and Lakaram Kisku to visualize a situation about forty to fifty years from now. With the spread of urbanization and movement of people to far away places due to education and employment, would their customs and culture survive? They were emphatic that these would survive despite the sweeping changes happening in society. They felt so because they would pass on the essence of their culture and traditions to their children. They would also maintain their links with their 'village.' One may tend to observe here that it is not known whether the 'village' itself in present form would remain at all at that time.

Raghunath was particularly mentioning about *Baha* festival they celebrate on the full moon day coinciding with *Dol* or *Holi* festival, celebrated widely in the country by the *Hindu* community. They pray to the goddess *Sitala* on this occasion. Sacrifice of goats and poultry birds is compulsory on this occasion, he said. Men and women sing and dance separately throughout the night on the occasion. There is merry making throughout the period. He said the elders would teach their children the importance of festivals and rituals like *Baha*, even if they were staying away from their village and the community. Interestingly, when educated and employed Santal people stay away from village in places like Kolkata, the issue regarding observance of rituals comes up, particularly when a child is born. In such cases, the *mukhiya* and representatives of the girl go to the place even if it is Kolkata. *Puja* is performed for '*Maramguru*' there itself.

According to Lal Mohan Kisku, every Santal parent wants children to be educated and well settled in life. They do not prefer that their children stay in villages and do cultivation. Lal Mohan says *haria* or country liquor is prepared in almost every house. People consume '*haria*', which is made from rice. Regarding consumption of '*haria*', he says, men and women consume in moderate quantities on occasions of festivals. It is a part of tradition and does not cause any intoxication when taken in small quantities. He also says when people do not understand the limit of drinking it creates problems. He also feels that observance of rituals and festivals has decreased over a period. When he looks back to his childhood, he remembers greater involvement of people and their interest on rituals and festivals. He is apprehensive that these will further come down as years pass by and we may not be able to see anything in distant future. He feels sad about the changing situation. At the same time, he does not agree that educated boys and girls are not inclined towards festivals and rituals.

Education

Education status among the Santals and recent developments are discussed here in this chapter as the customs, traditions and beliefs have been undergoing significant changes due to modern education and interaction with other communities and social groups. Table 4.2 shows the education levels of respondents belonging to Santal and Lodha communities of Bonpatna and Kantabani villages. As it can be seen from the table, three Santal persons completed graduation and one Lodha respondent completed Class 10.

Table 4.2: Ethnic Group-wise Educational Details of Respondents of Bonpatna Mouza

[N = 172]

Ethnic Group	*Illiterate*	*Literate without formal education*	*Standard 5 completed*	*Class 10 completed*	*Graduate*
Santal*	21 (28.4%)	23 (31.0%)	19 (25.7%)	8 (10.8%)	3 (4.1%)
Lodha**	54 (55.1%)	27 (27.6%)	16 (16.3%)	1 (1.0%)	0 (0.0%)
Total	**75 (43.6%)**	**50 (29.1%)**	**35 (20.4%)**	**9 (5.2%)**	**3 (1.7%)**

*Santal: 74. **Lodha: 98.

The formal education system as it is today puts the Santali children at a disadvantage. The following discussion with Diwakar Kisku, an educated, elderly and respected person of their community, throws up pertinent issues regarding tribal education.

DM	:	How do your children compare with others when they start going to schools?
Diwakar Kisku	:	The Santali children start with severe disadvantage when they enter school for the first time. Their mother tongue is Santali whereas they study in Bengali in school. An average student loses two to three years of time because of this. He will be a laggard in school. His confidence level is low and suffers from inferiority complex. A Santali boy finishes his schooling late when compared to his counterparts from other castes and communities.
DM	:	Why cannot they study in their own language itself?
Diwakar Kisku	:	We do not have schools here offering Santali as medium of instruction. I heard they have schools in Bihar, which teach in Santali language.
DM	:	*Ol Chiki* is the script for the Santali languge, I learnt.
Diwakar Kisku	:	Yes, that's right.
DM	:	Do people know here to write in *Ol Chiki* script?
Diwakar Kisku	:	Many of us in our village can write in the script. We organized a school in Benapur, three kilometres from here, to teach the script.
DM	:	Did you teach children also?
Diwakar Kisku	:	No, mainly people in the age group of 25-30 learnt in that school.
DM	:	If the Japanese can learn in Japanese language and the French in French language, why cannot our children study in their mother tongue?

Diwakar Kisku : I hope that day will come. It will be of enormous advantage to our children.

Role of Christian Missionaries

As in other parts of West Bengal and India, one can find many schools and facilities run by Christian Missionaries in West Midnapore also. Children from poor families get an opportunity to study in these institutions. Usually, these institutions are found in remote areas and inhabited by tribal population. As the facilities are provided free, it becomes a boon for poor families to afford for their children. Children can stay in hostels; they get free clothes, books and food. One may hazard a statement here that without these organizations, thousands of children, particularly from tribal families, might not have seen the light of education. Diwakar Kisku, thinking of situation nearly forty years back, feels it was because of such organizations that many could pursue education in his community. This is in spite of the oft-repeated grouse and complaints of religious conversion against these organizations. One can find 'Christian way of life and values' in the children in many schools visited; the prayers and the beliefs shown by children are reasons for this observation. These are alien to traditional tribal beliefs and customs. These are imparted. However, these organizations take pains to 'promote' the tribal culture by joining their festivals and at times helping them financially. Near Keshiary[8], the researcher met an octogenarian father from a European country, in a large school and hostel facility. He came here and settled down many decades back. He was instrumental in organizing many educational institutions in the region.

At Raipur, one of the villages of Khelar Gram Panchayat and very close to Bonpatna, a Christian missionary established a hostel for orphan children. In February 2005, seventy-eight children were staying there. As usual, the boys and girls are provided free boarding, food, clothes and books. The children study in nearby schools. The organization faced tough time in the first year, as some villagers were suspicious about the intentions of the work. Schools refused to admit the children. There was propaganda that religious conversion is the motto behind this work. The Pradhan, Naba Kumar Das, helped them in convincing the school authorities to admit the needy children.

Children are drawn from even far-flung places. Mostly poor, needy children, some of them orphans also, from scheduled castes and tribes got a chance to improve their lives in this *ashram*, named "Oasis". At present, the organization is running well with villagers getting over their doubts and fears.

Interestingly, there are some schools run by the Hindu religious organizations in the district on the same lines. Only difference: the prayers are different ! One observes, of late, such organizations are coming out publicly against what they perceive as the "hidden agenda of religious conversions" by the Christian missionaries behind running schools and hospitals. One meets several persons belonging to Santal community professing Christianity. Religion is supposed to be an individual's choice. The boundary line between advocating a religion and indirect coercion and enticement for conversions is thin and many a time, causes social tension in many parts of the country.[9]

Customs and Traditions[10] of Santals as observed in other parts of West Bengal

An attempt is made here to describe the customs, traditions, festivals and beliefs of Santals as observed in other parts of West Bengal, mostly in the North Bengal districts of North Dinajpur, South Dinajpur and Malda[11] . The Santal proper are divided into twelve clans—Murmu, Kisku, Hemrom, Hasda, Soren, Mardi, Tudu, Besra, Baske, Chore, Bedea and Paurea. The legend goes that the first-two human beings to be created were Pilchu Haram and Pilchi Budhi. They were blessed with seven sons and seven daughters. The sons were given the first seven names of the groups mentioned above. The seven daughters were married off. In this way, seven groups arose and later five others were added. It is interesting and important to note that each is exogamous. For example, A Murmu cannot marry the daughter of a Murmu.

In a village setting, the Santal community normally builds their houses together in a group. This is known as the Santalpara, and is generally, at some distance from the Bangalpara, where people belonging to other communities reside. The Santals construct their houses well, with solid walls of clay. They keep their houses meticulously clean. The Santals are fond of growing flower plants like *java* or hibiscus shrubs in front of their houses. The women wear the red java flowers in their hair on festive occasions. However, in modern times, a young Santal woman would prefer a colourful rubber band to tie her hair while going out to *haat* or bazaar.

The social system is under the direction of village headmen, called Majhis. Their houses are identifiable by a mound of earth outside it, in the centre of which is fixed a wooden post, known as the *manjithan*. On ceremonial occasions, the post is painted with vermilion in places, and sacrifices are offered to the spirits of departed chieftains. Majhi's office is normally hereditary, but if the successor of a Majhi is found unfit, or incurs the displeasure of his co-villagers, he is replaced by another. The ordinary duties of the Majhis include exercising control over his community people and their punishment by fines or other means for breaches of social customs. When there are disputes between villages, the Majhis of three or five villages sit together as a tribunal. When a family leaves the village in a year of scarcity to make a living elsewhere, their immovable property remains in the custody of the Majhi.

The social unity among the Santal community is remarkable. Inter-marriage with any non-Santal is forbidden. Moreover, the disregard of a Majhi's commands, or the commission of a serious social offence, brings the entire Santal community to oppose the offender. On a market day, the branch of a tree is held up and this attracts the entire Santal community present at the market. The incident is then briefly narrated and all are directed to be present on a given day. On the day fixed, the whole community appears and judgment is passed on the offender. It is described by elderly people that, in olden days, the offender's house used to get ransacked and a branch is planted in it as a sign that he has been excommunicated. Until he has paid the penalty, and the ban has been lifted, the whole village will not have any dealings with him.

It is recounted as stories that the British officers used to try and understand the so-called tribal secrets, without much success. The *sahebs* (or Lords, as the British officers were known) were interested to know the name of the plant from which poison for arrowhead is extracted and the Santals always feigned ignorance.

Santal customs are distinct and interesting. The first ceremony observed is the *Nasta*, which takes place on the third or fifth day after birth. The men are shaved and bathed at noon and when they have assembled, the father names the child in their presence. The first is named after his grandfather and the daughter after her grandmother. After the child has been named, the midwife goes round the assembly, sprinkling a solution of flour and water on the chests of all present and repeating on the child. Rice, which has been boiled with *neem* leaves, is then served to the guests after being offered to the Hafram or deceased ancestors.

The next ceremony is the *Sekhi*, which is the name for the branding marks on the wrists of all Santal men. The branding is done with a piece of burning rag, when the child is five or six years old. The girls are not branded, but are tattooed on the breast and on one of the arms. After marriage, the other arm is tattooed, but if a woman loses a child before the second arm has been tattooed, it remains as it is. The idea is that in such cases the child would not be able to recognize the mother in the after life.

There are several systems of marriage. The negotiation may be carried through a *Ghatak* or matchmaker; but this is an imitation of Bengali society and not a tribal custom. It is, however, less costly as the bride price is smaller. Generally, marriages are arranged by mutual selection, or the young man carries off the girl, and takes her to live with him. In such cases, the bride's father approaches the *Majhi* of the bridegroom's village and demands a bride price. If this is paid, and the girl is willing to stay with the young man, the marriage is concluded: otherwise a penalty is realized from him and the girl returns to her father's house without any stigma.

The *Majhis* adjudicate in cases of divorce. If they decide that there should be a divorce, the tearing across of a leaf indicates the termination of the marriage. The co-respondent is required to pay double the wife's bride price to the husband as compensation.

The Santals generally cremate their dead though it is gathered that in earlier times the dead also were, at times, buried. There was no hard and fast rule in the matter, but they preferred cremation when fuel was available. Great respect is shown to the dead and almost the whole village attends the cremation or burial.

Of the Santal festivals the most important is the *Bandna*. This is a kind of harvest festival, which takes place after the winter paddy has been reaped. There is no fixed date for it. However, the village headmen decide the day on which the festivities are to commence. On the first day, sacrifices are made to *Jahar* at the place of worship outside the village. A few fowls and an egg are offered in sacrifice. The cattle are washed and made to walk over the place of worship. If one of them tramples on the sacrificial egg, it is considered an auspicious omen for the owner. Then for three days, there will be continuous round of festivity in which everyone joins irrespective of age. The elders enjoy drinking while young men and girls get engrossed in amusement. The whole period is one of unrestrained recreation, and all restrictions are thrown off. On the last day, a feast is arranged in which the whole village participates.

The *Sakrat* festival is generally held about a fortnight after the *Bandna*. Its special feature is dancing with *lathis* (sticks). On the second day, a contest in archery is held. A plantain tree is set up at a distance, and the first competitor who hits it, is carried shoulder high by the Jog Majhi or joint headman and receives the homage of the spectators.

The *Fagua* is a counterpart of the *Doljatra* festival. On the appointed day, the villagers go to the place of worship and offer sacrifices. On the way back to the village, they sprinkle water on each other, but it is considered highly objectionable to use coloured water.

The *Chata* and *Karam pujas* are also celebrated by the Santals. In the former, an umbrella is tied to the end of a pole, which has been embedded on the ground. In the latter, a branch is cut from the jungle and planted in a pathway. The younger people dance round it from evening until dawn. The branch is then uprooted and immersed in a neighbouring tank with great ceremony.

The *Charak* festival takes place in April on a moonlit night and is attended by the younger people. It is understood that normally, Santals will not stay out of house after dusk for fear of ghosts, but on this occasion, they stay past midnight singing and dancing.

By nature, the Santals are simple and straightforward, though contact with other social groups tends to make them different. In spite of their simplicity, however, the Santals can be very reserved in certain matters affecting their tribal customs. They are independent by nature and resentments are put under any restriction. It is often said that no Santal could ever lose his independence; he would prefer starvation than begging. They are cheerful and easygoing by nature. Their life is full of festivities, and they enjoy drinking and music. In their villages, one hears the music of bamboo pipes, especially towards the sunset. The women are more hard working than men. In addition to the household work, they do most of the transplanting of paddy seedlings, a backbreaking job, and much of the harvesting.[12]

The Lodhas : Historical References

The Lodhas take pride in claiming themselves as 'Savaras'. They believe Vishwavasu, the mythical chief of Savaras spent time with Lord Jagannath of Puri. The Census of India 1901 has reference to Lodhas where it is described that the traditional occupation of the tribe is collection of jungle produce, such as, cocoons, lac, resin, honey, wax, etc.

It is also mentioned that polygamy is allowed among Lodhas. The bridegroom puts an iron bangle across the bride's wrist and smears her forehead with vermilion and the ceremony is completed. They cremate their dead and their mourning period is 19 days; on the eleventh day, they shave themselves, wash their clothes and present rice and small sums of money to a *Brahmin*.

The District Gazetteer Midnapur (1931) contains remarks that the crime and dacoities committed in Midnapur were largely committed by the Lodhas, an aboriginal tribe mainly found in Narayangarh and the neighbouring areas.

The Census of 1951 has references to the Lodhas as a tribe of hunters. Several Police officers of the British period mentioned 'about the criminal propensities of the Lodha tribe' during their times.

Lodhas : The Stigma and Suffering of being De-notified Tribes

In 1871, the British passed the Criminal Tribes Act. As a result of this Act, many tribes and social groups were notified around the country as "criminal". It gave the police wide powers to deal with members of such tribes, including restricting their movements and requiring them to report at Police Stations regularly. In 1916, the Lodhas were declared a criminal tribe under Government Notification No. 7022-23 dated 20th May, 1916 (Bhowmick, 1963).

After India achieved independence, this Act was repealed in 1952 and the tribes were "de-notified". From that time, the expression, de-notified tribes (DNTs) has become popular, or notorious one may say. Even after many decades, Lodhas are mostly referred to as criminal tribe. They suffer immense disadvantage in their day-to-day life because of this historical incident. Administrators also loosely and irresponsibly use the term, furthering further credence to such wrong prejudices. As a result, their human and constitutional rights are in constant threat of being violated. For the police, any theft or dacoity will point to their involvement. It was common that they were treated as habitual offenders and found in police lock up or jails. This treatment resulted in the community feeling alienated and frustrated for many decades after independence.

> As the Lodhas wear the stigma of criminality, many people do not trust them wholly. And there were a good number of inter-tribe hostilities. Naturally, a new mentality has to be grown to tackle this problem......But such attempts to bring them to the fold of the bigger society still remain a far cry......The results of the projects have not, however been as satisfactory as one desires. ...They have pseudo-friends in the form of receiver of stolen property who want to exploit them and keep the pot of criminality boiling......Mass killing of the Lodhas took a different turn when their humble huts were set on fire......with nothing to fall back upon in life (Bhowmick, 1994:53-54).

Lodhas used to suffer discrimination in almost every walk of life. Their habitations cannot coexist with other social groups. Admission of their children in schools was a problem. One must add that the situation has slowly changed to some extent over a period. The State support in education for these groups and reservations in local bodies have slowly started showing results but it is still a long way to go.

The Lodha Community of Bonpatna

Pregnancy and Childbirth

Pregnant Lodha women normally avoid hard manual work in the advanced stages of pregnancy. There are other restrictions and taboos on pregnant women. It is believed that they should not eat fish caught by a basket trap or by a hook as it might adversely affect the child in mother's womb. A pregnant woman also avoids sewing old and torn clothes with a needle as the belief goes that the new born child's eyesight may get affected.

The Birth Pollution

The Lodha Community celebrates the birth pollution on the 9th day as *"Notta"* and on the 21st day as the *"Ekusha"*. They clean up the pollution with the help of their own barber and washerman.

Marriage

In the olden times, boys and girls were married off in their teens. The ideal age for suitable boys was 16-17 and that for girls was 13-14. These days, a man marries when he is 22-24 years of age. Girls are married when they are 16-17 years of age. The girl's parents do not wish to delay the marriage, as it gets more and more difficult as the girl becomes older. These days, in most of the cases, negotiation precedes marriage.

Even now, in Jyotirampur village under Makrampur Gram Panchayat of Narayangarh Block, Lodha boys marry at the age of 18 and 19 whereas Lodha girls at the age of 15 and 16. Marriages outside Lodha community happen. However, these are not many. Asit Naik mentions the case of a *bagdi* girl getting married to a Lodha boy in his village. The ratio of such marriages outside their community is about one in ten. Normally, Lodha parents do not disagree to such marriage proposals. There are also occasions when a boy and girl fall in love and get married. This is a trend happening in the last 10 years or so and such instances are rising.

Dowry

Nearly thirty to forty years ago, the groom had to pay bride price and it used to be around rupees sixty to hundred and some gifts were also given in kind. But there is a real shift in this pattern. These days, as in other communities, dowry is given to the bridegroom at the time of marriage. Dowry often amounts to rupees two to three thousand. A bicycle is also demanded at times. Those who can afford, also give bedding and utensils. It is found in Bonpatna village that dowry includes cash, a bicycle, a watch and household items. In cases where they can afford, the bride's parents offer cash in the range of Rs. 10,000 to Rs. 15,000. These cases pertain to those who have sizeable landholdings or those employed. However, such cases are negligible. There are some occasions when marriages also take place without any payment of dowry. Nevertheless, a pattern is clearly emerging and dowry is becoming a part of accepted norm.

Separation

Usually, if the couple fails to reach an understanding, the husband sends his wife to her father's place. If the wife loses interest to cohabit with the husband, she on her own deserts her husband and returns to her father's place. In both the cases, attempts are made to come to a settlement with the help of the village "Mukhia" (Headman) and the other dignitaries of the village. If there is no settlement, the separation, commonly known as "*Char Kat*", is done with the help of a written document known as "*Lekhi*".

Among the Lodha community, there is no system of any maintenance. After the separation, both men and women can remarry. However, not all separated remarry. In the village of Bonpatna, Jharna Paramanick (28), daughter of late Bhutka, deserted her husband after he got married for the second time. She has not gone back to her husband since then.

CASE STUDY 4.1

Life of a Struggling Lodha Woman: Jharna Paramanick

Jharna Paramanick (28) does not have any child. At present, she is living with her brothers. She earns her livelihood as an agricultural labourer. During the lean period, she collects fuel wood from the forest and sells it in the market to earn her living. However, during the festive season, especially during the *puja* (prayers and rituals done, annually) of Goddess *Sitala* or when she suffers from any ailment, she does not go to the forest; otherwise, she goes to the forest regularly. On an average, by spending six to seven hours, she collects fuel wood weighing about 30 kilograms and earns roughly an amount of rupees ten by selling it.

Jharna lost her father and her mother is alive. Her mother and her neighbours are sympathetic towards her. She said that she was living at her paternal home because her husband never came to take her along. She would have definitely gone with her husband had he come to take her. In this way, she has spent her days for the last ten years by waiting for her husband. She added that she had information that her husband had remarried. After receiving the news, she became very depressed initially. After four to five years of the incident, she became habitual to the pain. She managed to forget about the past and is trying to live a self-sufficient life by working hard. Though her economic condition is not very good, she neither wants to go with her husband nor does she want to remarry. She wants to stay back at her parental home and wants to live an independent life. No Government assistance has touched her so far; she is a single woman, belongs to identified vulnerable tribe and direly in need of assistance.

In general, in case of a divorce, the villagers first try to resolve the matter by consulting both the parties. They also try to reach an agreement about the maintenance. If the problem is not locally solved, then the woman's side in some cases approaches the Court of Law seeking maintenance. However, in the Lodha community, if there is a divorce, maintenance becomes an insignificant issue. The woman's side hardly ever plays any role to arrange for the maintenance.

The Death Pollution

On the ninth day, they do the ritual known as *"Kshourakarma"*, that is they shave their head, moustache and beard. On the eleventh day, they perform the funeral rites. Their community men perform the rites. However, if the death becomes polluted with faults like *"Ekpad", "Dwipad", "Tripad"* or *"Chatushpad",* then the *brahmin* is summoned to purify the death.

The Last Rites of the Dead Body

The community buries the dead body by the riverside. During the monsoon, the body is made to float in the river. In the modern times, those who can afford to arrange for wood, burn the body. In those cases, after the head of the body is placed towards the north direction, the ritual of *mukhagni*, that is burning the mouth of the dead with a jute stick by uttering hymns, are performed.

The Rituals and Prayers of Lodhas

Sitala is the main deity of Lodhas. It is widely believed from ancient times that she controls serious diseases and epidemics like small pox and cholera. Lodhas also believe Sitala has six sisters who control many other diseases. In Bonpatna, the Lodhas celebrate Sitala *puja* in the month of Baisakh (April-May), on a Saturday or Tuesday. Along with Sitala, Yugini is also worshipped. In May 2004, the researcher was invited by the Lodhas of Uttar Bonpatna and Dakshin Bonpatna to be with them during Sitala puja.[13] It provided first hand account and knowledge of the celebrations and the importance given to that ritual by the Lodhas.

A platform is made normally with jute on which an earthen pot is placed in the sanctum sanctorum. The earthen pot should not have any black mark on it as black colour is considered *asubh* or inauspicious. Water for the *puja* (prayer and ritual) is collected in the pot from designated pond.[14] A green coconut or *dab* is placed on the pot. *Sindoor* or red colour substance (vermilion) is applied on the pot and coconut. Red *sari* is decorated on the neck portion of the pot. After these arrangements, *puja* is held.

Once the *puja* proper was over, dance festival started. The entire village assembled under the large tree and in the open space before the temple. The dance was accompanied by beating of *changals* or drums. The *changal* is a locally made drum using animal skin. Traditionally, only men used to dance on these occasions and ladies were present and witnessed the carnival. Photograph 4.2 and Photograph 4.3 show a dance scene at Sitala *mandir* in Uttar Bonpatna Lodha habitation. However, some women also can be seen here matching steps with men on this event. This points to the changes happening over a period in observance of rituals and celebrations.

The researcher gathered that almost every year, the deity 'possesses' one or even more persons of the village. This phenomenon is locally called *dhupar*. As a result, the person behaves hysterically, moving his head violently and making shrieks and loud sounds. This time also, one girl of the village started behaving in the same manner. The priest offered her incense smoke from a cup. She became normal after nearly three hours. The belief is that the deity will foretell the future that beckons them through her. Sometimes, the person also points out any mistake or inadequacy in performance of the rituals. She may also identify any person in the village who is evil for the society. Some villagers told the researcher that this identification of a person as evil creates tricky and problematic situations at times. It may so happen that a respectable person of the village, a *bhadralok*, is identified.[15]

During *Sitala puja* on the first day of *Jaishta* in 2010, the *goddess* possessed Bankim Pramanik (55), the priest. Bankim is a resident of Bonpatna. Lodhas believe that the *goddess* possesses a person so that he or she becomes a medium through which the deity talks to humans. When the possession or trance begins, the Bankim fainted and started shaking as if in an epileptic fit. When this happened, elderly people of the village enquired whether *Ma Sitala* was pleased with the *puja* done by the villagers which they did with great care and effort. They also asked whether *Ma Jugni* would go to her home in the forest as she is taken to her abode in the forest on completion of the rituals. In physical terms, the remainings after *puja* are taken and left in the village forest. *Ma Sitala* was happy about the arrangements about which she spoke through Bankim Pramanik. They also enquired whether their children would be safe and free from disease.

On completion of *puja*, remainings or left overs after the ritual are taken to a place inside the forest and this place has to be far from the village. It is believed that all evil and bad effects from the village are also taken away along with these things after *puja*.

One may recall here observations of Victor Turner in his essay "Social Dramas and Ritual Metaphors" in *Dramas, Fields, and Metaphors: Symbolic Action in Human Society*:

> In moving from experience of social life to conceptualization and intellectual history, I follow the path of anthropologists almost everywhere. Although we take theories into the field with us, these become relevant only if and when they illuminate social reality. Moreover, we tend to find very frequently that it is not a theorist's whole system which so illuminates, but his scattered ideas, his flashes of insight taken out of systemic context and applied to scattered data. Such ideas have a virtue of their own and may generate new hypotheses. They even show how scattered facts may be systematically connected! Randomly distributed through

> some monstrous logical system, they resemble nourishing raisins in a cellular mass of inedible dough. The intuitions, not the tissue of logic connecting them, are what tend to survive in the field experience (Turner, 1974).

During *Makar Sankranti*, held in the middle of January, *pujas* of *Chandi*, *Borham* and *Hanuman* (*Bir puja*) are performed. *Chandi* is the goddess of forest. She protects people from wild animals.

CASE STUDY 4.2

Lodha Village of Jyotirampur offers a contrasting scenario

One can see a contrasting picture in the Lodha village of Jyotirampur in Makrampur Gram Panchayat in Narayangarh Block. Out of 200 Lodha families in Jyotirampur, 15 families converted to Christianity. These families do not practice traditional rituals. Initially, there were some problems and reservation among Lodha people about religious conversion. However, at present there is no such problem. The families who converted to Christianity do not perform traditional *puja* of Lodhas like *Sitala puja*. Huge expenditure used to be incurred on traditional *puja*. Asit Naik says there used to be large amount of subscriptions for conduct of *puja*. This used to range to about Rs. 500 per family. Most of the Lodhas were poor and found it difficult to pay. Anybody who could not pay or refused to pay was put under pressure from the organizers saying that they would be ex-communicated from the society. He says they are happy now. There is no pressure on them. At the same time, he says they have built a Church in the village Jyotirampur. It is a mud structure with corrugated sheet as roof. The church house got damaged during cyclone in 2009 and the villagers got together and built it again. They do prayers on Sundays and on other special occasions. Christian followers among Lodhas get together twice a year and also for any important event. There is affinity and linkage among Christian followers of Lodha villages like Doharpur, Jyotirampur, Balarampur, Makrampur and other nearby areas. Marriages happen generally among the followers of Christianity and such marriages take place in the Church as per Christian traditions. Asit also says this is a step forward for them towards modernity, as people need to re-look at old beliefs and systems. One *Mukhiya* of Lodha village in Jyotirampur himself converted to Christianity. There are some more who would like to take up Christianity. Asit Malik says people who have converted to Christianity do not observe any traditional rituals. At a time of childbirth or when a person dies, rituals which were followed traditionally are no more followed. According to Christian traditions only, the dead body is buried.

Culture

Chang is the customary folk dance of Lodhas, which is now on the verge of extinction. In this dance, participation of women is not allowed. *Chang* is the only entertainment in annual worship, marriage celebration and also funeral functions. In the past, the Lodhas used to be nomadic hunting tribe moving from one forest to another. Due to this reason perhaps, their musical instrument *changu* is light and easy. On the other hand, the Santals have been agriculture-based tribe and used to settle at a specific place and so their musical instruments like *dhamsas* and *madals* are heavy.

The present day Lodha youth are not generally interested about their traditional folk art of *chang*. Most of the folk artists are old and the new generation is not interested to learn their traditional folk dance. They are more inclined to electronic media like television and video. They also feel *chang* is old fashioned and is not for the current generation, which is comparatively more educated. Photograph 4.4 captures the interesting sight of a child trying his hand on the drum as his father looks on.

Babulal Bhakta is from village Bhaliachati under Nayagram Police Station. He is aged about seventy years. He used to rear cows from childhood. When he was fifteen years old, his father died. His father was a singer of *chang* songs but Babulal was not interested in *chang*. After his father's death, one day, he saw a dream that an old lady, red in colour, sat by the side of his head. Perhaps, she was goddess Sitala, he thought C*hangu*, the musical instrument was there in his house, which his father used to play. Once, in full darkness, called *amabasya*, he took *changu* in hand and started *chang* in the shrine of *Sitala*. He organized some of the local Lodha youth as his *chang* team. On several occasions, they have been invited to play *chang* dance in nearby Lodha villages. He feels their traditional folk art *chang* is declining due to poverty and negligence. It is very difficult to maintain family on forest products alone. Musical instruments got broken and they are not able to revive *chang*.

In the festive season, be it Durga Puja, Kali Puja, Makar Sankranti, or during *puja* of Sitala, the Lodhas celebrate by performing the *chang* dance. They use the local instruments like *madol* and *bailo*. About five to ten men, dance to the rhythm of song and music. Women do not participate in the dancing.

Ram-Sita, Radha-Krishna and Jagannath[16] of Puri are the topics of religious songs. The language of these folk songs is a mixture of Bengali and Oriya languages. There is no written form of *chang* songs and it is in the form of oral literature.

Incidents and references from famous Hindu epics are commonly found in *chang* songs. Some examples of *chang* with religious theme are mentioned here:

> *"Ailo rey Ravana raja*
> *Jugivesh niyey*
> *Duarey iduarey Ravan bhikkya magilo*
> *Hatey dhorey Sitay rathey chapailo*
> *Thamo thamo boli Jata daurey asilo*
> *Hat bhangilo Jatar Paa bhangilo*
> *Parey rayilo Jata parbata saman"*

Free Translation

Ravana came in the disguise of a saint and took away Sita forcibly in his chariot. Jatayu came running and shouted at the offender to stop; he opposed and resisted Ravana, but could not succeed. He fell on the earth and remained like a mountain.[17]

> *"Ram dhoren taru dal*
> *Lakshman dharen Sirey*
> *Chalitey nan pareu Sita*
> *Banero bhitarey"*

Free Translation

Ram and Lakshman carry on holding on to tree branches and creepers but Sita is unable to walk in the forest.

Chang songs also mirror the moods and thoughts of Lodhas in different circumstances.

"Dibir dibir bajna bajey
Kiser bajna bajey
Bara Raja taro Sepai
Sikarey Sajey
Dukho harani rey-kala harani rey
Dur bon Palayey jabo cholo na rey.
Karo Kanda Khai nai
Karo lata khai nai
Khai boner lata
Tabu asiche uyara
Katbey hamader matha
Dukho harani rey....
Sikari Sikar Karey
Ghach taley thakey
Choudice gherache jal jabo kon dikey
Dukho Harani rey kala harani rey
Dur bon palayey jabo chalo na rey"

Free Translation

Drums are being beaten as the king is coming with his army to our forest for hunting. They will cut our throats. Let us flee to the distant forest. We have no fixed shelter. We do not eat anybody's wealth except tuberous roots collected from forest. In spite of that, they would torment us.

Interpretation

This song shows the fear and insecurity of Lodhas due to onslaught of outsiders into their abode. They have been victims of outside attacks. This also explains the mindset and preference of a Lodha to remain exclusive and away from other social groups and settings.

The philosophy of life and a Lodha's attitude to life is depicted in these *chang* songs:

"Ohgo jimut kaley upay korey lakhaya takar sona
Moron kaley songey jabey sudhu kalsikhana"

Free Translation

A person can earn gold, lakhs of rupees in life but he will not take any of these with him when he dies.

"A hator panch paiko hauyachi dak-hat
Hata sori goney bhet paunai kirey mon
Janu nahiki
Michi pari bhula mon bhula kanhiki
Sunnarey bhasuche bhela
Janu nahiki"

Free Translation

We have come here on this earth for a short time and we will be back when our task is over. Life is temporary.

Chang songs also amply display the romantic bent of Lodha people, particularly young men and women. Some examples are:

"Tobha narango pholo
Pakchi daley dalo
Pakuchi hey madhu malati
Mu rashaboti
Mu nari abala juboti"

Free Translation

It is spring; nature is beautiful with different flowers and leaves. I am a young and youthful lady, longing to meet my sweetheart.

"Akela dihir majhey
Jagey railam micha Kajey
Balana rasher katha duti suni
Ai na Pakhir Kalkalani
Kalmilata taru ami
Tumi na rakhiley katha khani"

Free Translation

I am alone in house; please tell me some sweet and enchanting words. You are like a bird and I am like a tree.

'Bai-kundali' is the other name of *chang* in some areas of the district. *'Bai'* means mad and *'Kundali'* means circular in local language. The Lodhas, in fact, go mad while doing this folk dance and it is performed in a semi-circle throughout the night. It is a folk belief of Lodhas that when *changu* is rung, the Hindu God Lord Shiva's seat gets shivered. The musical instrument *changu* is prepared from wood and is tempered with sunshine and fire. The frame of this musical instrument is covered with either goat skin or that of a snake. Lodhas worship various gods and goddesses throughout the year and would arrange for *chang* on these occasions.

Education

The Lodha community has remained underdeveloped in education. In the village of Bonpatna, there are a total of 130 families of Lodha community, 54 families reside at *Uttarpara* and 76 families reside at *Dakshinpara*. Table 4.3 gives age group-wise break-up of Lodha population of Bonpatna village. In the entire Lodha community of the village, only one boy, Abhay Bhakta, son of Santosh Bhakta, passed the Madhyamik Pariksha. At present, he is studying at Higher Secondary level at Gokulpur High School of Kharagpur Block.

Table 4.3: Age Group-wise Distribution of People belonging to Lodha Tribe of Bonpatna Village

Name of the Hamlet	*Age-group-wise population distribution*						*Total*
	0 to 14 Age		*15 + Age*		*60 + Age*		
	Men	*Women*	*Men*	*Women*	*Men*	*Women*	
Bonpatna Uttarpara	50	49	66	64	08	07	244
Bonpatna Dakshinpara	52	51	87	85	07	10	292
Total	**102**	**100**	**153**	**149**	**15**	**17**	**536**

Out of 536 people belonging to Lodha tribe of this village, 15 men and 17 women are above sixty years of age.

In both the *paras*, there are Primary schools, one in each area. In the Uttarpara primary school, there are 16 boys and 17 girls of Lodha community. There are 11 boys and 11 girls of Lodha community who study at the Dakshinpara primary school. Though they have enrolled, yet the percentage of their presence is very poor. Table 4.4

and Table 4.5 give details of primary education status of Lodha and other children in Bonpatna village.

Table 4.4 : Primary Education Status of Bonpatna Village

Academic Session : 2006-2007
Name of the School : Dakshin Bonpatna Adibasi Primary School
Village : Bonpatna
Circle : Kharagpur Paschim, Khelar Gram Panchayat
District : Paschim Medinipur
Names of Teachers : Mr. Keshab Chandra Roy, Head Teacher; Mrs. Kalyani Dutta, Assistant Teacher
Number of Students : 93

Class	*Lodha*		*Santal*		*Kora*		*SC*		*OBC*		*Others*		*Total*	
	B	*G*	*B*	*G*	*B*	*G*	*B*	*G*	*B*	*G*	*B*	*G*	*B*	*G*
I	2	4	5	—	—	4	—	1	—	—	—	—	7	9
II	1	—	8	16	1	—	—	—	2	—	—	—	12	16
III	3	2	3	3	5	4	—	—	—	1	—	—	11	10
IV	5	5	6	7	2	2	—	1	—	—	—	—	13	15
Total	**11**	**11**	**22**	**26**	**8**	**10**	**—**	**2**	**2**	**1**	**—**	**—**	**43**	**50**

B: Boys. G : Girls.

Name of the School : Bonpatna G.S.F.P. Vidyalaya
Village : Bonpatna
Circle : Kharagpur Paschim, Khelar Gram Panchayat, Kharagpur-I Panchayat Samiti
District : Paschim Medinipur
Name of Teachers : Mr. Haripada Maity, Head Teacher; Mrs. Rita Satpathi, Assistant Teacher; Mrs. Sandhya Chowdhury (Rout), Assistant Teacher; Mr. Badal Chandra Sheet, Assistant Teacher; Mr. Bhabesh Bhanja, Assistant Teacher.
Number of students : 185

Class	*Lodha*		*Santal*		*Kora*		*SC*		*Minorities*		*OBC*		*General*		*Total*	
	B	*G*	*B*	*G*	*B*	*G*	*B*	*G*	*B*	*G*	*B*	*G*	*B*	*G*	*B*	*G*
I	9	10	—	—	—	—	15	20	1	1	2	—	5	5	32	36
II	4	3	1	1	—	—	9	14	3	5	2	—	1	3	20	26
III	3	2	2	1	1	—	6	4	4	4	1	—	2	5	19	16
IV	—	2	2	—	—	—	5	8	2	2	5	1	5	4	19	17
Total	**16**	**17**	**5**	**2**	**1**	**—**	**35**	**46**	**10**	**12**	**10**	**1**	**13**	**17**	**90**	**95**

SC: Scheduled Castes, OBC: Other Backward Classes, B: Boys, G: Girls

Table 4.5: Educational Information of Children belonging to Lodha Tribe of Bonpatna village

Name of the School	*Boys*	*Girls*	*Total*
Uttar Bonpatna G.S.F.P. School	16	17	33
Dakshin Bonpatna Adibasi Primary School	11	11	22
Khelar High School	06	04	10
Total	**33**	**32**	**65**

In Khelar Gram Panchayat, there are fifteen primary schools. The district administration provided rupees one and half lakh to the Dakshin Bonpatna Adibasi Primary School for construction of additional classrooms. This requirement was brought out by the Panchayat Pradhan and the local people. This was after many years that the school received any government grant. The school is the mainstay for all Santal, Lodha and other village children of the area. The people were happy that the need was felt and redressed.

In many Lodha villages, the researcher observed that children of school going age look after their younger ones when their mothers go out for work. This is more so in case of girls. For this reason, children often miss their schools. Many children do not get anything to eat before going to school or after returning from school. So these children refuse to go to school. Again, in many cases, the parents go out for work and their children do not go to school and spend the day playing by the roadside.

Over this issue, the discussion with villagers of Bonpatna went like this:

DM : Is every child above five years in school?

Nilu Pramanik : Yes, children are going to school. They go to Khelar Adibasi Primary School.

DM : Do they stop after primary level? Do children pursue study in the High School?

Ganesh Pramanik : I can say about my family, my children are studying.

Bhushan Dandapat : It is difficult for all to pursue education at higher level.

DM : Why? Is it because of financial condition?

Bhushan Dandapat	:	It is because parents just cannot afford the expenses involved.
DM	:	But, the Government provides all support.
Ganesh Pramanik	:	Not all children can get into the hostel. One of my sons is in Khemasuli[18] tribal hostel. But I could not get chance for my daughter in a hostel.
DM	:	What is the reason? Is it because of lack of adequate seats?
Bhushan Dandapat	:	Where are so many seats in hostels? Everyone cannot get admission. And we don't have the money to bear the expenditure for their studies.
Nilu Pramanik	:	We need a hostel in Bonpatna; you please arrange one.[19]

It is relevant to recount here one experience of visiting a hostel for Lodha boys in Nayagram Block. Bharat Sevashram Sangha ran the hostel with financial assistance from Ministry of Tribal Welfare of Government of India and it was found that officials had to certify proper utilization of funds received for the previous year from the Government without which no new allotment would be made for the following year. There were doubts and suspicions regarding the running of this facility. The researcher alongwith a team of officers including the local BDO, Sub-Divisional Officer, officers of Backward Classes Welfare Department, visited the place without prior notice.[20]

The picture was very discouraging to the researcher and other inspecting officials. Some of the shocking points which we found were:

- the number of students supposed to be benefiting and actually existing were no match;
- the land purchased for the income generation of Lodha families was exorbitantly higher than the prevailing price in the area; and
- expenditure shown for food, utilities and books was more fictitious than real.

The local people, who gathered by this time, had lots of stories to tell about misappropriation of government funds by the set-up. They had a lot of complaints against the *swamiji* (saint!), in charge of the centre. Honestly, one was dejected to find the picture as the organization had reputation of working for welfare of the needy. The factual position was reported to the higher authorities. Tremors were felt in the organisation's hierarchy. Senior *swamijis* landed in the District Magistrate's office at Midnapore and tried to explain and retrieve the situation. As a corrective step, the *swamiji*, in charge of the centre was removed; serious efforts were started by the organization to redeem the position. The incident highlights again, the problems in implementation of plans and programmes. Here, the objective has been that Non Government Organizations (NGOs) will be encouraged and financially assisted to run schools and hostels for tribal students in remote areas, as it is presumed that they would do a better job of it when compared to the bureaucratic and tested government machinery. In this case, the experience had been no different or rather same as before.

Understanding the Dynamics of Change in Cultural and Social Life of Tribals

Culture is an accumulated store of symbols, ideas and material products, which are transmitted from one generation to the other. Cultural forms regulate social activities. Cultural processes of change show the various ways through which any culture responds to numerous changes over a period of time. The sources of change can be classified into two broader categories—endogenous and exogenous. While endogenous sources of change get initiated from within the society, exogenous sources flow from outside a particular society[21] . Changes in the cultural structure have emanated from both endogenous and exogenous sources.

The process of secularisation has considerably reduced and weakened the ideas of pollution and purity among Santals and Lodhas. People no longer try to know the social background of fellow passengers in a bus or a train. They hardly bother about it while visiting restaurants and hotels. The rules of pollution are not observed at the place of work, particularly in the urban settings. The styles of life are influenced more by the requirements of jobs and occupations than by caste and religion. The orthodox elements of caste, tribe and religion are gradually losing significance in the face of growing secularisation of life and culture. Due to increased secularisation and mobility, social system is unable to sustain those values which were so far considered essential. At the same time, it is important to remember that while religious values attached to the castes and tribes are disappearing, its role in secular domains like politics is increasing. These days, people are being mobilised on caste and tribe lines for political purposes. It is a fascinating sociological question.

There are two other areas, which have been affected by the process of secularisation. These are family system and village community. While the gradual structural transformation in family produces change in interpersonal relationships, other elements of family life are equally affected. Ceremonies and rituals performed in family, such as marriage rituals, funeral rites and worship of family deities are assuming a different character. They are either curtailed or shortened to suit the convenience of the concerned family. Some of these ceremonies are used as occasions to display and advertise affluence. The ostentation associated with wedding receptions has got nothing to do with religious practices. Similarly, several community festivals have acquired new meaning and observances. A festival is celebrated more as a cultural event than a religious one. People from different religious groups join and enjoy its festivity. *Durga Puja* and *Kali Puja* have assumed new character and their religious rituals have receded into the background. Hundreds of *pandals* are tastefully decorated displaying various contemporary social and political issues. The tribal community is also influenced by changes taking place in economic, political and cultural fields. The internal differentiation created by economic forces has altered the harmonious community feelings among the community. Levels of aspirations have increased because of various developmental measures undertaken by the government. The attitude of surrender before fate and divine will, commonly found among the poor and deprived, has been replaced by the attitude of defiance. These changes are the products of the process of secularisation.

Preserving Tribal Culture[22] and Identities: Some Observations

In the area of study, as may be in other areas too, indigenous people, Santals and Lodhas, clearly distinguish themselves from the other segments of society by way of historical and structural features as well as their self-identification. Their cultural distinctiveness is often based on language, social organization, religion and spiritual values, modes of production, as well as laws and institutions. Government policies over the years, to some extent, resulted in denting the indigenous identities in the name of civilization, progress, development and modernization. Over a period, indigenous peoples were expected or compelled to assimilate into the majority or dominant mainstream. In some areas, they were simply neglected and their existence forgotten.

In recent decades, awareness increased among the Santals and Lodhas and they recognize their rights. Emerging standards provide them with some extent of protection and security from oppression and exploitation. However, they are still far away from the point of full realization of their cultural, social and economic rights.

State policies were traditionally designed to assimilate or incorporate tribal people into the dominant national mainstream. These policies were also successful on many occasions. However, resistance of tribal people to such processes has also taken place. They now demand full respect for their cultures and identities with scope for self-determination. Increasingly, the State and society are adopting pluralistic policies and accommodation with a view to respect the cultural identities of tribal people.

Many features are associated with this cultural distinctiveness, the main one being the relationship of Santals and Lodhas to the natural environment, which results from ancestral links between traditional native cultures and the earth ("Mother Earth" as it is normally expressed in local terms). These links have frequently been broken, sometimes irretrievably, as a result of state policies and economic development. Nevertheless, they continue to shape the universe of tribal population. The preservation, reconstitution and rejuvenation of these links make up one of the continuing themes of indigenous cultural debate.

For tribal communities like Santals, the use and maintenance of their own language is not just a medium of communication. It is also a crucial element in providing meaning to their natural and social environment. This constitutes another crucial and distinctive factor of tribal cultures. The identification of cultural identity with language is such that linguistic criteria are often used to identify and classify indigenous peoples.

Santali language is very ancient and while it has undergone changes—just as any other language—it is transmitted from generation to generation and thereby, helps preserve the continuity of the Santal cultural community. This is also, why religious missionaries and governments have for a long time attempted to change these ways and in a way impose on the tribal people their own or dominant cultures through their languages and doctrines. The school system has of course played a crucial role in this process in most of the cases.

Language rights are today considered an essential element of the cultural rights that all persons enjoy under international human rights standards. Therefore, language rights are nowadays proclaimed as human rights, which entail respect, protection and promotion by others and, especially, by public authorities. Numerous States have now adopted legislation concerning the protection of regional, minority or indigenous languages.

These developments have many implications for cultural diversity. Santali language may have been used only in the domestic ambit or the local marketplace on a limited scale; we may one day find its way into the local public administration, the courts, the community radio stations and other public spaces.

The use of the mother tongue in education and public communications is an important issue for the Santals. Bilingual and intercultural schooling has become the object of educational policy for indigenous communities in many parts of the world. Specialists in education agree that early schooling in both the native mother tongue and the official language of the State is of great benefit to indigenous children, who may become proficient in the language of the wider society without losing their own language. This implies that oral indigenous languages will become written ones and require the training of school teachers and interpreters, and the preparation of materials like textbooks.

Similar issues remain with other expressions of culture like folklore. Folklore is fundamental experience of human life. Folklore is the wisdom of being and becoming. It is a dynamic force. The researcher was reminded of an experience at a government run tourist hotel, a few kilometres from Santiniketan in Birbhum district[23] . The researcher alongwith other members in a group were given 'flavour' of Santali culture through a traditional dance programme, on a winter evening. No doubt, the programme was beautiful but the question arises: Why salvage tribal culture and folklore? Is it only to satisfy modern man's ego? Must it stay as a museum specimen, for tourist attraction? Many among the intellectual circles tend to take a view that tribal culture is not only a showcase for satisfying the modern man's vanity. It should not be treated as an 'object' of curiosity. Traditional societies need not be romanticised but it must be given what is due. One may add here, it may be better to replace the term 'safeguarding' by 'rejuvenation'. 'Rejuvenation' includes restoring the earlier form by generating confidence in the self-organizing system rather than dependence on outside agencies. It is necessary to understand people in totality, to appreciate that man, nature and social structure are mutually dependent and interrelated.

The idea of cultural pluralism does not imply the artificial preservation of indigenous (or tribal) cultures in some sort of museum, but only the right of every human community to live by the standards and visions of its own culture. It is clear that cultural rights pertain to every individual, yet these rights can only be fully enjoyed by all persons in community with other members of the group.

It has been observed that tribal culture is closely linked to the concept of land rights and the occupation and possession of territorial homelands. A question frequently asked of tribal communities is whether their cultural identities can survive in dispersed settlements and urban centres where indigenous migrants live interspersed with non-indigenous populations. The answer to this question depends on particular circumstances and is contingent on the specific definition of indigenous identity in each case. The right of any individual or group of individuals to preserve, practice and develop their own culture is related to self-identification. Indigenous identities have indeed been diluted in the process of urbanization. In spite of this, in certain circumstances, the urban environment is favourable to the emergence of new kinds of indigenous cultural identities.

A major issue facing indigenous peoples is the protection of their cultural heritage, including traditional knowledge, skills and techniques of all kinds.

In 2000, the UN organized an international seminar on the protection of the cultural heritage of 'indigenous peoples', which adopted a set of principles and guidelines, among others, which are as follows :

1. The effective protection of the heritage of the indigenous peoples of the world benefits all humanity. Its diversity is essential to the adaptability, sustainability and creativity of the human species as a whole.
2. To be effective, the protection of indigenous peoples' heritage should be based broadly on the principle of self-determination, which includes the right of indigenous peoples to maintain and develop their own cultures and knowledge systems, and forms of social organization.
3. Indigenous peoples should be the source, the guardians and the interpreters of their heritage, whether created in the past, or developed by them in the future.
4. Recognizing, respecting and valuing their customs, rules and practices for the transmission of their heritage to future generations is essential to indigenous peoples, their identity and dignity.
5. Indigenous peoples' ownership and custody of their heritage should be collective, permanent and inalienable, or as prescribed by the customs, rules and practices of each people. (Stavenhagen, 2004: 27)

The wealth of knowledge that communities like Santals and Lodhas possess concerning the environment, the plants and animals of their traditional habitat and the multiple uses that such knowledge can be put to is one of the principal assets of indigenous cultures. Historically, such knowledge was widely used and shared, particularly in connection with traditional herbal medicine, nutrition, colours used for weaving textiles and making handicrafts, hunting, fishing and gardening.

Tribal people demand respect for their traditional knowledge and the freedom to use the products of their environment according to custom. Moreover, some tribal communities have been able to trade in such products and thereby increase their incomes. More recently, multinational corporations have discovered the commercial potential inherent in much of this traditional wealth, and the race is on to patent, privatize and appropriate what has been part of the cultural heritage of indigenous peoples from time immemorial. Once again, the tribal people are being dispossessed of their legitimate collective property, only this time within the framework of multilateral commercial and financial agreements. Only through concerted action will they be able to save whatever little is left of their cultural heritage.

NOTES

1. There are numerous writings on Santal rebellion and other social movements, see for instance Macdougall (1977), Rottger-Hogen (1982), Derne (1985), Misra (1986), Bandyopadhyay (2001), Jogdanand and Michael (2003), Judge (2005), Kumar (2005), Mishra (2006), Patel (2006), Shah (2006), Roy (2007), Crossley (2009), Roy (2009), Padhi *et al.*, (2010), and Pati (2010) for detailed analysis and explanation.
2. Mahapatra (1986) systematically explained the rituals and activities and actions associated with Santal rituals in his book. Similarly see Parkin (1990), Kochar (1966) for more analysis.
3. Anthropological explanations on marriage patterns and related practices among tribal communities received greater attention and importance, for instance see, Ghosh (2011), Kumar (2006), Pfeffer (1983), and Yorke (1979).
4. Such patients are not normally allowed to stay inside the village and kept outside the village. Villagers provide them food and other requirements at that place itself.
5. It can be described as part of funeral ceremonies performed on the banks of a river.
6. People's belief in the system of witch and witchcraft is equally prevalent, if not more, in various parts of the country. Incidents of killing and humiliating such persons, identified as witches, keep getting reported in the media. It is surprising that the vast network of administration and elected representatives at field level cannot get information before hand, as the killing of a person does not happen suddenly. Ignorance, superstition or some ulterior motive drives these incidents.
7. Proselytisation of tribal communities has got prominence in the contemporary Indian society. For detailed literature and analysis, see

Pati (2010), Bara (2010), Thong (2010), Subba *et al.*, (2009), Kumar (2008), Saumya (2008), Claerhout and Roover (2005), Nadakarni (2003), Chaube (1999) Tharamangalam (1989) and Wiebe (1970).

8. Keshiary is about thirty kilometres to the south of Midnapore and Kharagpur. The Block has sizeable Santal and Lodha population. Another point that strikes about Keshiary is high prevalence of leprosy in the area. Christian organizations also run hospitals in the vicinity for treatment and rehabilitation of patients. By correlation, many Santal and Lodha persons suffer from this disease due to lack of awareness and social stigma attached to leprosy. Repeated efforts and campaigning by the Government are showing results, but slowly.
9. The researcher recounts one experience in Malda district of West Bengal in the year 1999 when he worked as District Magistrate, which was debated for long time. Some Hindu religious organizations arranged "purification programmes" and reconversion campaigns for Santal persons who earlier converted to Christianity. The issue generated huge controversy and the administration had to ultimately intervene and stop the show, as tribal people, after rituals, were to walk on fire to attain purification!
10. For rituals and forms of relatedness of tribes and others , see Hardenberg (2009), Strumpell (2008), Agarwal (2004), and Säävälä (2001).
11. The researcher worked as District Magistrate of Malda in West Bengal during 1998-99. He visited these areas and spent considerable time to study the patterns for correlation of same tribe separated by significant geographic distance.
12. Cooking is tedious and drudgery for most Indian women and Santal women can be no exception. They spend enormous amount of time on firewood collection, a job left for women and girl children to perform as the menfolk, the researcher observed, spend time in homes, some of them consuming *heria* (country liquor).
13. The warmth and affection of the people was such that the researcher had to be with them during this *puja*. When the researcher said in a lighter vein that he was with them anyway at that time also (the time of discussion), and would be coming time and again, they did not agree. '*Apnake o somoye nischoy asthe hobe*', meaning, 'you have to definitely come at that time'. The incident underlined the importance of the annual ritual in their lives. It provided the researcher a good opportunity not only to observe the ritual but also their customs, songs, dances and intimate social bonding.
14. It is locally called *pratishtitho pukur*. A waterbody or pond is called *pukur*, all over Bengal. This pond is not used for other daily uses. Water from tube wells or wells is not used as the water from these sources is not considered fit for prayers.

15. During childhood, the researcher saw such incidents in a different social setting in the South Indian State of Andhra Pradesh. There, some persons were possessed by *Hanuman* (the God in monkey form and an ardent devotee of *Ram*).
16. As per Hindu mythology, Ram and Krishna are incarnation of Lord Vishnu. Jagannath is another name for Krishna. Sita is wife of Ram and Radha is consort of Krishna.
17. The story is from *Ramayana*, the epic of Hindus. Jatayu is a courageous bird, which fought Ravana, the King of Lanka and died in the end.
18. Khemasuli is about thirty kilometres from Bonpatna. When the researcher enquired about the boy, he was bought to the front, as he was watching the discussion from a distance. The researcher took him closer and held his hand. The boy suddenly started crying leaving the researcher shocked. The villagers said the boy had lost his mother. As he was staying away from home also, the boy became emotional. The researcher recounted to the villagers his experiences of visiting the hostel at Khemasuli. The management of the hostel made elaborate arrangements of snacks though the researcher had gone to that place to see the Lodha village nearby. It was embarrassing for him to see their insistence on having food. The researcher politely refused their requests and instead asked them to give the food prepared to the children. The researcher got curious and asked what all the children eat daily. The picture given by the hostel-in-charge was rosy; but when the researcher persisted, the children gave a distressing picture about the food given to them.
19. Her voice is so personal, insisting and innocent as if one is talking to a member of family.
20. It is a pity that the supervising officers at various levels resort to blind recommendations, even not visiting the field. Reasons are lack of devotion to duty, dishonesty or both.
21. For related discussion and information see Lee (2010), Rapport and Overing (2007); Rao (2004); Ramaswamy and Bhangya (2002), Mahapatra (1992), Malhotra (1992), Mann (1992), and Redfield (1960).
22. Studies on tribal culture received attention of anthropologists and sociologists since beginning of these two disciplines. For related discussion and arguments see, Singh (2010), Inayatullah (1999), Misra (1986), Mohanty & Bailey (1984), and Southall (1970).
23. Santiniketan is famous for Rabindranath Tagore, the renowned Nobel laureate poet and scholar. He developed this place as a centre of learning and excellence

5
Traditional Authority and Modern Governance

There is significant difference between simple and modern societies regarding law and its enforcement. There were no written laws and the knowledge is passed on to generations orally. This is in contrast to the modern day laws, which are written and codified.

Some Characteristics of Law in Simple Societies

1. There is prevalence of customary law.
2. Law is backed by physical force.
3. There is legitimate use of physical coercion.
4. Prevention of the breach of social norms is the goal.
5. The objective is to maintain social control and establish social order.
6. Punishment for the breach through economic deprivation, confiscation of property; Ostracism (excommunication): gossip; ridicule; fine in shape of cash and/or kind; avoidance and denial of favours; direct physical compulsion;
7. Law is built on precedents and social norms form the core of law.
8. Law has official authority. It is regular and consistent.
9. Law is characteristically found in unwritten form.
10. The legal system is more or less self-developed.
11. There is absence of legislative enactment.
12. During administration of justice or judicial hearings, there is prevalence of supernatural legal methods, such as divination, oath and ordeal.
13. The need for law is minimum.

14. There are no legal practitioners or lawyers.
15. The wrongdoer violates social norms, which are believed to be not allowed.

Traditional Authority and Social Control Among the Santals

The social system among Santals is under the direction of village headman, called *Majhi.* His house is identifiable by a mound of earth outside it, in the centre of which is fixed a wooden post, known as the *manjithan.* On ceremonial occasions, the post is painted with turmeric in places, and sacrifices are offered to the spirits of departed chieftains. Each *Majhi* also keeps a hut, generally unfenced, for village meetings. His office is normally hereditary, but if the successor of a *Majhi* incurs the displeasure of his co-villagers, he is replaced by another.

The *Majhi* organization consists of other officials like *paranik, jog majhi, naeke* and *godet* (Risley, 1892). The *paranik* is the assistant headman, *jog majhi* arranges feasts, *naeke* is the village priest and *godet* is the bellboy of the *Majhi.* This *Majhi* organization is responsible for performance of village business and activities like social, cultural and spiritual ceremonies. It is observed that these different officers represent different clans of the Santal village. However, the *Majhi* clan represents the founder of the village. The *Majhi's* presence is required in all rituals, social gatherings and ceremonies. The *Majhi* could impose punishment by fines or other means for breaches of social customs. When there are disputes between villages, the *Majhis* of three or five villages sit together as a tribunal. Whenever a family had to leave the village in the year of scarcity to make a living elsewhere, their immovable property used to remain in the custody of the *Majhi.*

CASE STUDY 5.1

Experiences of a Mukhiya of a Santal Village

Shyam Kisku (59) is *Mukhiya* of Khelar Santal village. He is presently a Member of Kharagpur -I Panchayat Samiti.[1] That he was chosen as a candidate and subsequently selected as a Member of Panchayat Samiti is significant for the reason that his position as traditional authority in Santal society earned him a formal position in modern power structure.

According to him, 95 per cent of disputes in his village are sorted out through traditional conciliation process. It is rare that they go to police and courts for any complaint or dispute. On the other hand, among *Lodha* community, it is gathered that not even 50 per cent of disputes are resolved at the traditional panchayat level. Lodhas go to police comparatively more often than Santals for settlement of their disputes. This can be attributed to stronger social bonding among *Santal* society when compared to *Lodha* community.

Kisku mentions, on a given day, when the Panchayat is called by him, meeting starts generally in the evening. The meeting can last for one and half to three hours. Family disputes are the major issues, which come before him for conciliation. Kisku mentions he doesn't normally get any dispute related to land between two Santal members of his village. In these meetings, representatives of both sides are called and the *Mukhiya* hears both the sides. If a mistake or wrong is committed by a person, efforts are made to make him understand the same. Normally, no monetary fine is imposed. Even if fine is imposed, it is in the range of Rs. 50 to Rs. 100. This amount is normally spent on meeting the expenditure for the meeting. In earlier days, he mentions, a feast was used to be organized by the offending side. This practice has come down over a period.

Some cases come to him where a Santal girl marries a boy from outside the community. In such cases, after meeting, the girl's father is asked to arrange a feast for the villagers. Once it is done, the marriage is accepted and no more conditions or stigma is attached to the marriage.

In the month of January 2010, a family dispute came to him for conciliation. Mohan Tudu (31) used to beat his wife Sankari Tudu regularly. Mohan and Sankari have a son and a daughter. The girl's parents complained to the *Mukhiya* about the ill treatment. One of the reasons for his ill treating his wife was said to be mistrust about his wife. A meeting was held in which Mohan Tudu confessed his mistake. He was fined Rs. 5,000 by the *Mukhiya* and this amount was used for feast for the people of the village. Kisku mentions that there is no further complaint of harassment by Mohan Tudu. There has been change in his behaviour. The main reason for these disputes, according to Kisku, is the effect of intoxication.

Kisku also referred to another case of Pardana Baske who also used to beat his wife Sombari Baske. In the village meeting, Pardana accepted his mistake with folded hands and promised that he would not ill treat his wife again. However, the *Mukhiya* says Pardana is undone. He does not have any control over himself when he is intoxicated. Even now, he beats his wife.

Traditional Authority Arrangements in the Lodha Society

The Lodha Panchayat

The Lodhas have a well-defined political organisation among them. Historically, the village political set-up had enormous powers and control to settle disputes among the people.

Each Lodha village has a panchayat or a council consisting of all adult male members of the village. Normally, women and children are not members of the council. There are some exceptions in some villages where women also are members. The Lodha Panchayat has office bearers who run the affairs. They are the prominent members of the village and enjoy special social status.

The important office-bearers of the Lodha Panchayat are:

1. *Mukhia*, who is the headman of the village.
2. *Dakua*, who is the village messenger.
3. *Paramanik*, who is the village cook for social functions and ceremonies.

These posts are normally hereditary. If the incumbent does not have a son, the villagers select a new person. An office bearer can also be removed from the post because of improper conduct.

Conventionally, the Lodha Panchayat used to perform the following functions:

- Settlement of disputes among villagers;
- Administration of justice;
- Maintaining peace;
- Promotion of the welfare of the village;
- Fostering traditions and customs of the community which are un-codified;
- Religious and social ceremonies; and
- Marriage negotiations and feasts.

The Lodha Panchayat has meetings when complaints are received from the villagers. They have the power to impose fines on the offenders and, if required, can ostracise a member for a serious offence. Among disputes, discord between wife and husband is the major reason. These disputes are referred to the Lodha Panchayat. For dispute resolution, meeting of the Lodha villagers is called which is known as *Raj Sabha* or the king's court. Elders of the village refer *Mukhiya* as *Maharaj* in the meeting.

The normal complaints received by the Lodha Panchayat are of this nature:

- Adultery;
- Witchcraft and black magic;
- Breach of traditional taboos; and
- Ignoring and not maintaining wife and children.

Efforts are made to conciliate between the two sides of the dispute. In many cases, there is no agreement. Nowadays, there are growing instances of villagers seeking the assistance of the police to settle disputes. Thus, the role of the Lodha Panchayat as the sole arbiter of disputes is on the wane.

Influence on Traditional Power Structures

When the researcher asked Diwakar Kisku of Bonpatna, he mentioned that the traditional authority of their community, even in present times, disposed 95 per cent of disputes among the community, as in olden days. People feel it advantageous to have conciliation at the village level as enormous delay occurs when cases go to police and in subsequent court proceedings. The process is both time consuming as well as costly.

It is a fact of life for the Santals and the Lodhas that the traditional village power structures and organizations are coming under influence of changes happening in their society and lifestyle.

These influences are many and complementary:

- Modern day Panchayat set up based on democratic elections deriving authority and power from the Constitution and laws.
- Rule of law and elaborate judicial system of our country after India became independent.
- Spreading of modern education among the tribal population.

- Mobility among them due to employment and work.
- Influence of other social groups.
- Mass-media and improved communication networks.

It may not be out of place here to recall the observations of Andre Beteille, made in the context of a different social setting in Southern India, on the changing relationships and influences between traditional power structures and the modern day economic order:

> In sum, the processes of economic change and political modernisation have led the productive system and the organisation of power to acquire an increasing degree of autonomy. In the concrete, the overlap between the hierarchies of caste, class, and power has been progressively reduced. . . . . The economy of the village is drawn increasingly into the orbit of this new economic order. Similarly, the new political order is at least formally independent of caste and it too has an important effect on the social life of the village (Beteille, 1996: 225).

Constitutional Guarantees for the Persons Belonging to the Scheduled Tribes

We may look at the safeguards and guarantees provided in the Constitution of India to the members of the scheduled tribes, which speaks volumes about the vision, and commitment of its framers. The free India that emerged from centuries of foreign rule yearned to be a just and egalitarian State, providing equal opportunities and protection of human rights to all its citizens. There was strong necessity to expressly point out these entitlements in respect of those social groups, which suffered neglect and subjugation for generations.

For the protection, socio-economic and political development of Scheduled Tribes, the Constitution of India guarantees:[2]

(i) Social

- Equality before Law (Article 14);
- The State to make special provisions for the advancement of any socially and educationally backward classes of citizens

or for the Scheduled Castes and the Scheduled Tribes [Article 15 (4)];

- Equality of opportunity for all citizens in matters relating to employment or appointment to any office under the State (Article 16);
- The State to make provisions in matters of promotion to any class or classes of posts in the services in favour of the Scheduled Castes and the Scheduled Tribes [Article 16 (4A)];
- A National Commission for Scheduled Castes and Scheduled Tribes to investigate, monitor and evaluate all matters relating to the Constitutional safeguards provided for the Scheduled Castes and the Scheduled Tribes (Article 338);
- Appointment of a Commission to report on the administration of the Scheduled Areas and the welfare of the Scheduled Tribes in the States (Article339);
- Appointment of a Commission to investigate the conditions of socially and educationally backward classes and the difficulties under which they labour and to make recommendations to remove such difficulties and to improve their conditions (Article 340); and
- To specify the Tribes or Tribal communities to be Scheduled Tribes (Article 342).

(ii) Economic

- The State to promote with special care the educational and economic interests of the weaker sections of the people, and in particular, of the Scheduled Castes and the Scheduled Tribes and protect them from social injustice and all forms of exploitation (Article 46);
- Grant-in-aid from the Consolidated Fund of India each year for promoting the welfare of the Scheduled Tribes and administration of Scheduled Areas [Article 275 (1)]; and
- The claims of the members of the Scheduled Tribes in the appointments to services and posts in connection with the affairs of the Union or of a State to be taken into consideration consistent with the maintenance of efficiency of administration [Article 335].

(iii) Political

- Through the Fifth Schedule, the administration and control of Scheduled Areas and the Scheduled Tribes in any State, other than the States of Assam, Meghalaya, Tripura and Mizoram by ensuring submission of Annual Report by the Governors to the President of India regarding the administration of the Scheduled Areas and setting up of a Tribal Advisory Council to advise on such matters pertaining to the welfare and advancement of the Scheduled Tribes [Article 244 (1)];
- Special provisions through the Sixth Schedule for the administration of Tribal Areas in the States of Assam, Meghalaya, Tripura and Mizoram by designating certain tribal areas as Autonomous Districts and Autonomous Regions and also by constituting District Councils, Autonomous Councils and Regional Councils [Article 244 (21)];
- Reservation of seats for the Scheduled Castes and the Scheduled Tribes in the House of the People [Article 330];
- Reservation of seats for the Scheduled Castes and the Scheduled Tribes in the Legislative Assemblies of the States [Article 332];
- Reservation of seats for the Scheduled Castes and the Scheduled Tribes in every Panchayat [Article 243D]; and
- Extension of the 73rd and 74th Amendments of the Constitution to the Scheduled Areas through the Panchayats [Extension to the Scheduled Areas] Act 1996 for effective participation of the tribals in the process of planning and decision-making[3].

The Experience So Far

The experience of nearly fifty-five years, after the Constitution has been adopted, has been mixed. Perhaps, no one can deny that the democratic process provided positive opportunities for the various social sections hitherto neglected to voice their identity and discover their capabilities. We find representation of these social groups in the Parliament, State Legislative Assemblies, Panchayat bodies and top ranks of the bureaucracy

CASE STUDY 5.2

Climbing the Social and Political Ladder

Raghunath Tudu is a constable with the Border Security Force (BSF). He has been working for the last fifteen years and presently posted in Kashmir. He is married and has a daughter. His family lives in Kantaboni village of Khelar Gram Panchayat Lakaram Kisku is a diesel engine mechanic with the Indian Railways. He is working in Kharagpur. Diwakar Kisku is employed as an *amin* (surveyor) in the Land Revenue office at Belda, about twenty kilometres from Khelar. In Khelar, according to Diwakar, ten persons belonging to Santal community are in different Government service. Some are working as teachers.

Gupta Mallick of Gopali village works as a Group 'D' employee in Land Reforms set up in Kharagpur. His son and daughter are graduates. In Bonpatna village, Santosh Bhakta passed class 10 examination. He works as a temporary labourer in telephone department. The work is seasonal in nature.

Lal Mohan Kisku retired after working for 33 years in Government service. He has two sons and a daughter. His elder son discontinued study while pursuing B.Com at Kharagpur College. Reason given by Lal Mohan is disinterest of his son to pursue education. He wants to do some job or work like driving, etc. His younger son is 10 years old and studying in Class III in a private convent school at Khelar village. His daughter is 22 years old and married five years ago. His son-in-law has a multipurpose shop at Ranibandh in Bankura district, dealing with telephone, copying, fax and computer works. His son-in-law's father retired as Assistant Secretary at Secretariat, Government of West Bengal. His daughter's marriage was arranged through a known person who used to travel to Bankura often. She passed higher secondary examination at the time of her marriage. After marriage, her in-laws encouraged her to study further. As a result, she is about to complete B.A. from a college at Khatra in Bankura district.

Dhiren Kisku became Up Pradhan after the Panchayat elections held in May 2004. He passed B.A. from Sabang College in 1997. He stayed for two years in a hostel run by the Government for tribal students. He used to get three hundred rupees per month as stipend, which was adjusted against his food bill. There used to be seventy-five boys in the hostel. Out of them, thirty-five students were studying in graduation courses like B.A., B.Com. and B.Sc. Rest forty boys were studying at Higher Secondary level. There was also a hostel nearby for girls. He recounted that five to six girls belonging to tribal community were studying at that time.

His family has five *bighas* of cultivable land. The Government gave one *bigha*. They were cultivating the land for twenty years but it was recorded in their name only in the year 2000. Two *bighas* of land is on tenancy. His father purchased two *bighas* of land.

Dhiren is married to Lakshmi in 2001. They do not have any child yet. Dhiren is 29 years old and his wife is 19. She passed class 10. Both of them feel that one or two children are sufficient in present day times. He says the days of big families are history now in his community. The couple does not follow any family welfare method. People feel two to three children are enough. The woman normally undergoes family welfare operation after two to three children.

When the researcher visited Bonpatna village and the Khelar Gram Panchayat after a gap of two months in December 2004, the Pradhan mentioned that Dhiren got a job in a Central Cooperative Bank in Nadia district, located about hundred kilometres north of Kolkata.

Santosh Bhaktha is a Gram Panchayat member from Bonpatna ward. Presently, he has about 10 *bighas* of land. He has two sons. One is in class IX and the other is in class VI. He started his life as a rickshaw puller. He also used to cultivate land on lease. Through sheer hard work, he improved his economic condition. He bought agriculture land from his earnings. Compared to the landholding pattern among Lodha tribe, his land holding size can be considered significant. Because of his standing in his village and among the Lodha community, he was elected to Khelar Gram Panchayat in 2007 elections.

Bakul Naik (34) is Pradhan of Makrampur Gram Panchayat. She belongs to Lodha community. She studied up to Class VIII. She was a housewife before getting elected as Pradhan. The post was reserved for ST woman in the Panchayat elections held in the year 2007. Asit and Bakul have two daughters and a son. Son is studying in Class III and daughters are in Class VII and V. They study at Makrampur High School. As Pradhan, her social status has increased. Asit says his status also increased because of her elevation. She gets due recognition from her office staff. Car or other vehicle comes to their home from the office to pick her up whenever she has to go early for work or in case of any official tour.

Dr. Pulin Behari Baske is a doctor by profession. He was working in a Government hospital. He contested Panchayat elections for the post of Zilla Parishad member as a candidate of Communist Party of India (Marxist) and won from Dantan Block of the district. He was elected as Sabhadhipathi of Zilla Parishad as the post was reserved for a tribal candidate in 1998. When the post became a general one in 2003 due to rotation, he continued as Sabhadhipathi for another term of five years. The incident shows the stature of Dr. Baske who started his political career on a reserved seat as a tribal candidate but went on to gain experience and political position to be accepted at par with other candidates on merit. The incident is significant in the sense that tribal people through education and participation in the democratic process have moved up the social ladder.

They became almost equal with other social groups and castes. Later, Dr. Baske became a Member of Parliament from Jhargram parliamentary constituency. On personal front, Dr. Baske married a Brahmin girl and they have two children. It shows that educated people among the community are open to inter-ethnic marriages. However, in this case, a tribal man married an upper caste woman; the reverse may not be too frequent yet.

Such examples are many in West Midnapore and West Bengal, as members belonging to tribal community have become members of Gram Panchayats, Panchayat Samithis and Zilla Parishad. Among them, there are many women members also, as reservation provisions were made for women in Panchayat bodies. Sri Rupchand Murmu had been a Member of Parliament for many years from Jhargram Parliamentary constituency. Sri Shambhu Mandi was elected as Member of Legislative Assembly from Binpur constituency. He is a veterinary doctor by profession. He served as a Minister in the West Bengal Government previously. There are others who are MLAs winning from the reserved constituencies. This has been mainly possible because of the Indian Constitution and subsequent Acts of Parliament and State Legislatures providing reservation of seats for tribal community people in these posts. Though they represent the entire electorate after winning the elections, they provide their community sense of self-belief and achievement. Tribal people also get an opportunity to voice their problems.

As it happens, initially other members do not take many of these Panchayat members from tribal and other disadvantaged sections seriously. Though these members have statutory position, they tend to be silent spectators to the proceedings in meetings and decisions are sometimes thrust on them. But experience shows that it is only a question of time before these members get confidence and experience and start asserting. The 'outside' interference and influence slowly gets less as the influential group of people who wield control realizes that these seemingly voiceless and innocent representatives cannot be taken for granted.

Various political parties have been wooing these sections and groups to their fold for better representation in the elections. The very fact that these parties had to take cognizance of the importance of these social groups is an achievement in itself. Probably, the journey towards self-expression and realizing aspirations and hopes for the millions belonging to the so-called scheduled tribes, castes and other backward classes has begun in the right earnest. It may be necessary to point out here that the process may not be perfect and textbook style; but one only hopes that the issues of development or lack of it for these groups shall not remain limited to the electoral arithmetic.

NOTES

1. Shyam Kisku has three *bighas* of monocrop land. He cannot cultivate second crop for want of irrigation facilities. His son Bishal Kisku (30) helps him in cultivation. Bishal is married and has a son and a daughter. Bishal's wife Sabitri studied up to third standard and she is from the same village. Shyam Kisku regrets that his son, though educated up to higher secondary, could not find any employment. His son presently works as LIC agent. The small amount he earns is spent on coaching for his children. Shyam Kisku had also a daughter who died after marriage at in-law's place.
2. As is the case, many of the tribal people, for whose benefit the provisions are made, may not be aware of the existence of such constitutional safeguards and arrangements, as yet. This is true with several other issues and welfare programmes of the State. Awareness and consciousness of their rights and entitlements will propel them to seek and demand them, when denied. There is still a lot which needs to be done in this regard.
3. It is surprising to scholars and activists of tribal rights like Dr. B.D. Sharma that West Bengal tribal areas are left out of this very important constitutional empowerment process, bestowed to the tribal communities of India.

6
Changing Livelihoods

Tribal Economy: An Introduction

It is widely understood and agreed that tribal economies[1] were traditionally subsistence oriented; there was no concept or necessity for surplus and profit. There was also no notion of individual ownership of land or property. There used to be common ownership of land and collective use of available natural resources, mainly forest based. People used to make use of the easily available natural resources with simple technologies. The tendency was not to produce beyond the immediate necessity. Thereafter, available time was spent in leisure. One can say land and forest were the two natural and necessary resources available to tribal societies.

Over the years, other peasant classes and middlemen started taking interest in land grabbing and commercial exploitation of forest resources. The State had also stepped in with various land settlements and imposition of land revenue. The tribals were put into new dynamics of land ownership and creation of surpluses from agriculture. They were naturally not up to this task and started losing their freedom of use of forest and natural resources. They were either further pushed deep into the forests or they became victims of greedy land grabbers and moneylenders. The situation was further accentuated by not so sensitive administration in most of the cases.

Setting up of many industries and mining activities in traditionally tribal areas dislocated the tribal population from their natural habitat. The consequent urbanization also affected the living styles of tribal population. Many, after losing their traditional sources of livelihood, have become industrial workers and unskilled wage earners in various enterprises. The industrialization and urbanization process, though inevitable, left deep scars on the minds of older generation. It also led many in the younger generation into frustration due to unfulfilled desires and expectations.

Many of the tribal communities continue to be techno-economically backward for various reasons. Their economy is not similar and they are at different levels of the techno-economic parameter. Vulnerable tribal groups inhabit areas with poor communication facility and who are still at the pre-agricultural stage of economy (i.e., gathering, collection and hunting) and amongst whom the rate of literacy is very low. Notwithstanding variations in the techno-economic domain, tribal economies exhibit three basic features, namely:

1. Common ownership of land and joint control over forest and other natural resources;
2. Non-acquisitive but community oriented economic value system; and
3. Lack of an ulterior motive and lack of interest in the generation of surpluses for capital formation.

Tribal economies are "undifferentiated" or "mixed" in nature which encompass several types of economic activities, such as, collection and gathering of various edible items, hunting and catching of game, fishing, herding, shifting cultivation, settled agriculture, handicraft, wage-labour, etc. On the basis of the general features of their (a) habitat, (b) production technology, and (c) belief system, tribal economies may be classified into six types on an analytical plane. The six types are:

1. Food-gatherers and hunters;
2. Shifting cultivators;
3. Simple artisans;
4. Livestock raisers;
5. Settled agriculturists; and
6. Industrial-urban wage earners.

Tribal communities have been coping with their physical environments for generations based on their respective cultures for eking out an existence. Their social structure and ideology are orchestrated towards this objective. Therefore, all efforts meant for their socio-economic development should be in conformity with this phenomenon. Harmony between environment and culture, which is vital for survival, has to be maintained in the process of sponsored development. For instance, food-gatherers and hunters cannot be made settled agriculturists over-night. If they are denied the right of access to the forests in their habitat for collection and gathering of food materials, they will be pushed into a state of unmitigated misery. No development initiative should aim at bringing about violent upheaval in the established socio-economic milieu of a community. Change is inevitable, but it should be gradual, smooth and beneficial. If the existing economy of a community is drastically changed, people face a great deal of hardship, because they cannot cope with the required bio-cultural adaptation, which is crucial for their survival.

Adaptation would necessitate a new set of technology and a fresh body of knowledge. Cultural adaptation[2] is the product of cumulative experience. In addition, if there is a sudden discontinuity or disruption in the socio-cultural life, people will develop a sense of insecurity. People in simple societies view the world as beneficient and predictable, except where human irresponsibility disrupts it. They believe that the universe continues its orderly unfolding of events. And if they do not carry out their functions as expected of them, there would be crop failure, famine, untimely death and all sorts of disaster would sweep over the community. Living in harsh environments, communities exhibit a typical ideological adaptation to the nature. This environmental adaptation influences their social organisation, and their techno-economic subsystem together with the social structural subsystem shapes the ideological domain of their culture. Therefore, it is incumbent on the part of development planners and executives to be acquainted with the habitat, society and culture of the beneficiaries.

If one takes a quick glance at current livelihood patterns in West Bengal, 24 per cent of tribal workers are cultivators whereas 45 per cent are agricultural labourers. It may be inferred that majority of tribal people in the State today depend upon agriculture for livelihoods, either as cultivators or wage earners. One of the most regular observations has been that many of the tribal cultivators also work in others' lands to supplement their income from own land. This is due to the relatively small size of the landholdings, because of pressure on agriculture land, to a certain extent.

Santals of West Midnapore are mostly agriculturists. They also work in others' fields as agricultural labourers. They have cattle to support their agricultural activities. Cattle also add to their income generation. Goat rearing is most common in almost all the villages and more so in the forest fringe areas of the district. As fodder is easily available, this activity is quite preferred. The number of goats owned by a family may not be too large. However, it is a common site in these villages to see the sense of possessiveness of an elderly woman clutching to her only prized possession.

In comparison, Lodhas are mostly dependent on forests for their livelihoods. They collect firewood and other forest produce for their sustenance. They also collect food from the forest. The process of shifting towards settled agriculture is happening slowly among them also. Unable to find ways and means to acquire a piece of land, they keep dreaming of that day when they also can be proud owners of land. This is in sharp contrast to their traditional way of living when the land ownership issue was non-existent. The effect of mingling with other land owning communities had impact on the Lodhas. They now feel that being landless is one of the worst forms of poverty. Moreover, in today's world, ownership of land also enhances social status of the family and gives immense confidence in oneself. These are very important changes happening in their value system, which they are imbibing through mixing with other communities.

Average Tribal Peasant and Non-tribal Peasant: Any Difference?

It may be proper here to point out that the study of tribal people and their problems need not be always done in isolation and sheer compartmentalization. This may not be appropriate also for proper appreciation of the geographic and economic ground realities prevailing in the areas being discussed. The economic condition of any non-tribal peasant does not vary much from that of a tribal peasant in the area. The problems faced are almost same. Hence, it may not be prudent to talk in watertight compartments of tribal and non-tribal peasants when we discuss the economic problems of a particular area. The problems of lack of irrigation facilities, credit support and marketing opportunities are similar for all farmers in a particular geographic context. However, it is relevant to mention that effect of poverty and deprivation on the social and cultural practices of different communities may be varied. Their response to overcome these problems will differ from one social group to another[3]. For instance, it is generally believed that a person belonging to Santal community may remain hungry and starve but will not seek alms.

Livelihood Cycle in Tribal Areas

Life in the villages is struggle for survival for the majority; it is more so for the tribal population. An effort has been made here to capture the 'livelihood cycle' of the tribal villagers throughout the year along with problems and possible solutions through the eyes of the people themselves.

Table 6.1: Tribal Life: Livelihood Cycle, Problems and Possible Remedies

Month	*Livelihoods and Problems*	*Survival Strategies*	*Possible Solutions*
Baishak (April-May)	Less work in fields, drinking water mostly available, water for irrigation is scarce	Mortgage loans, labour work in brick kilns and construction, taking *dadan* and repaying with labour at a later date, forest collections like firewood and leaves	Improving common irrigation sources and methods, skill development to make use of local markets and opportunities
Jaistha (May-June)	Availability of work in fields is less	Alternative income options like construction works, brick fields, depending on forest for sustenance	Making credit accessible to take up income generating activities, training and skill development

(*Contd.*)

Table 6.1 (*Contd.*)

Month	*Livelihoods and Problems*	*Survival Strategies*	*Possible Solutions*
Asadh (June-July)	If there is rain, agriculture work starts; incidence of fever, stomach problems and other water borne diseases	Work in brick kilns, taking *dadan* and repaying with labour at a later date, work in sand quarries	Incidence of diseases has come down after improvement in drinking water facilities and sanitation
Sravan (July-August)	A normal monsoon means some work in the fields	Same as above	Same as above
Bhadra (August-September)	Work availability in fields starts reducing	Same as above	Same as above
Aswin (September-October)	No work in fields, meaning very tough life	Same as above	Same as above
Kartik (October-November)	Potato cultivation in some areas, more investment needed, diseases, less work generally	Work in brick kilns, taking *dadan* and repaying with labour at a later date, work in sand quarries	Improving credit availability through Self Help Groups
Agrahan (November-December)	Wheat cultivation, remunerative but difficulty in harvesting	Same as above	—
Poush (December-January) and *Magh* (January-February)	No other work, cultivation of vegetables in some areas, difficult times	Same as above	—
Phalgun (February-March) and *Chaitra* (March-April)	*Boro* paddy crop gets affected due to lack of water, generally less work in fields, brief migration to other areas for work	River Lift Irrigation (RLI) and Deep Tube Wells (DTW) of Government do not work at several places, private sources are costly	RLI and DTW to function, encouraging self-help and collective efforts for investments in minor irrigation

The above Table 6.1 indicates despair, helplessness and misery of the tribal families.

Role of Traditional Moneylenders: Merciless Exploitation

As the average farmer or artisan has no easy access to credit, he has to depend upon the local moneylender for loans to fulfil his needs for small capital. This amount is needed for purchase of seeds, fertilizers, pesticides and other agriculture operations. An artisan needs small amounts of money to buy raw materials. Some of the tribal villagers buy *sal* leaves for making plates and *babui*[4] grass for making rope. This amount is taken on loan from the moneylender. It is difficult for a poor villager to approach a bank for such needs. He has little option but to walk into the trap of the moneylender (Rao, 2002). Photograph 6.1 shows Santal women stitching plates from *sal* leaves.

The story is same when it comes to exploitation of poor villagers by the moneylender. He charges interest up to rupees ten per rupees hundred per month. This means he collects rupees one hundred and twenty of interest per rupees hundred per year ! He may even insist on mortgage of valuables, to give a loan. The average villager needs money for urgent needs like medical treatment, marriage of daughter or any other unforeseen expenditure. There is no other formal system on which they can bank upon.

Once the villager fails to pay the principal, interest, or both, the moneylender appropriates his assets, whether movable or immovable. He may lose his land, livestock and even his wife's ornaments, given at the time of marriage. There are occasions when the poor peasant has to give his agricultural produce, after harvesting, to the moneylender who may be a trader or shopkeeper. The poor peasant has to pay rupees one hundred fifty per rupees hundred for the period of agriculture season. He has to give his produce to the lender alone and no one else. The lender fixes the value of the produce, which is invariably lower than the prevailing market price. Thus, the exploitation continues endlessly, making the poor victims in the hands of the middlemen. The rate of interest is even worse in villages around Belpahari and Lalgarh. The researcher met hundreds of such poor farmers, many belonging to different ethnic groups, in these remote villages. This unending misery of such a large section of people forced one as District Magistrate to look for alternative solutions so that the poor can come out of this exploitation. The message was put across to people, Panchayat representatives, officials emphasizing the need for people to organize themselves so that they get collective voice, confidence and strength. The result is formation of about thirty thousand Self Help Groups (SHGs) with nearly three lakh poor and socially disadvantaged women as members in undivided district of Midnapore including West Midnapore. Out of them, over six thousand groups belong to tribal people (Rao, 2002). Table 6.2 shows the economic condition of respondents of Bonpatna village.

Table 6.2: Ethnic Group-wise Livelihood Status of Respondents

[N = 172]

Ethnic Group	*Landless*	*BPL*	*Need to take loan from moneylender*
Santal*	31 (41.9%)	61 (82%)	54 (73%)
Lodha**	0 (0.0%)***	98 (100%)****	93 (95%)

*Santal: 74. **Lodha: 98.

*** All Lodha respondents were landless before; all of them bought about one-tenth of acre each of land through Self Help Groups during research period.

**** All Lodha households are enlisted as BPL as per Government instruction.

Problems Galore: Shortage of Water for Drinking and day-to-day Use

In Western Midnapore, there are many areas, where there is shortage of water because of the terrain. Many tribal villages face acute shortage of water for drinking and daily use. Sinking of tube wells in some places is difficult because of rocky soil. Villagers have to travel long distances for water. It is no surprise that many areas are devoid of any agriculture. The problem aggravates in summer season affecting people and cattle. Water harvesting through ponds and check dams is a viable option. As District Magistrate, the researcher came across this serious problem very often during his visits. Towards addressing this problem, the administration took initiative and hundreds of ponds were excavated during the years 2002 and 2003, mostly in tribal areas. As a result, people got work during lean season and a water source, which they needed most. On one such occasion, the discussion with the villagers in a village near Lalgarh went like this:

Dasarath Mandi (with shivering voice)	:	We do not have water for daily needs . . . (pause) . . . bathing, washing, cattle . . . very difficult to manage . . . .
DM	:	Tube-wells are inadequate, it seems.
Sitaram Mandi	:	Only one tube-well in nearby hamlet. One pond is there; it dries up before *Magh* (February).
DM	:	Then, how do you manage your needs?
Dasarath Mandi	:	Very difficult . . .
DM	:	Can we see the place?
		[*A large gathering of villagers including children followed us. The pond area was small. It appeared it was dug many years back and got silted.*]
DM	:	How old is this pond?
Dasarath Mandi	:	I see it from my childhood days . . .
DM	:	Can it not be widened and deepened? There was sudden disbelief among all there.
Sitaram Mandi	:	Will it be dug again?
DM	:	Why not? If you think it is a need, it should be done.
Dasarath Mandi (turning to the DM)	:	*Tumi ekta bidi dao* (you give me one bidi, a kind of locally made cigarette).
DM	:	I do not smoke, but let us get some for you.
Dasarath Mandi	:	When will you start the work?
DM	:	You tell us; together we need to solve the problem.
Dasarath Mandi	:	Who will do the work? Where will the workers come from?
DM (surprised at the question)	:	The community will be undertaking the work. All of you have to take full responsibility.

The villagers were in total disbelief. The plan and estimates were got prepared in next seven days and fund was sanctioned by the

District Magistrate from existing development grants and the local BDO, Mr. Rahul Majumdar, immediately initiated work. Whenever approached with such problems, the BDO was prompt in appreciating and responding to the difficulty of the villagers. The condition of rural areas and credibility of the Government machinery will be any day better with such committed officers. When work started, entire village lived there at the work site till completion of the tank excavation. A board was arranged showing the project details like amount of the work, progressive expenditure, daily wage rate and progressive work done. Whenever the non-smoker DM visited the site, he had to carry a pack of *bidi* for Dasarath Mandi. The old man spent day and night there along with the villagers.

When the villagers completed the work, there was newfound spirit in the village. The researcher sat together with the villagers and the BDO and discussed other needs of the village and ways as how to fulfil them. During discussions, it was agreed that formation of Self-Help Groups was of prime importance. This incident is one of those many the researcher came across as District Magistrate in villages across the district, during the period of work. The immense satisfaction and inner peace one felt from these collective efforts were revelation. One learnt practical lessons on how awakened people initiate action for development based on mutual trust and self-help.

Lodhas, Landlessness[5] and Livelihoods[6]

Lodhas are one of the Scheduled Tribes identified as Particularly Vulnerable Tribal Groups (PVTGs). These Groups are known for their declining or stagnant population, low levels of literacy, pre-agricultural technology, primarily belonging to the hunting and gathering stage and extreme backwardness. They were considered as a special category for support for the first time in 1979. There are 75 PVTGs spread over the country with population of 25 lakh constituting nearly 3.6 per cent of the tribal population and 0.3 per cent of the country's population.

The PVTGs live in interior pockets, which are generally inaccessible. With declining sources of sustenance, they become more vulnerable to hunger/starvation, malnutrition and ill health. Some of them are even on the verge of extinction.

After meeting hundreds of Lodha people in various villages spread across different Blocks of Midnapore (West) district, the researcher had come across time and again one strong necessity, desire and ambition of an average Lodha family; their urge to own a piece of land.

This can be possibly explained as they were traditionally staying in forest areas where their living was based on forest and they did not bother about ownership of land. However, situation started to change as they were settling down closer to towns and other villages in search of better livelihood. Due to spread of urbanization and introduction of the concept of land ownership and land records, the Lodha community started to feel the pinch and stress. This change is in contrast to their traditional living when they used to live in and around the forest. There was no necessity for 'ownership' of land as is understood in present times; nature has given plenty in the forests and there was no dearth of food. Their entire life depended on the forest. It started there and ended there. As the modern civilization spread and the other non-tribal communities started to settle down in the traditionally tribal inhabitant areas, the Lodhas started facing the heat. Their concept of life and their needs were different from the encroaching communities. As the State enacted forest laws and the forest officials, authorized and unauthorized agencies started taking interest in the forest due to huge economic interests, the Lodhas virtually had no place to go or hide! The new establishment started challenging the traditional inhabitants and questioning their legal status to stay. Some others started utilizing them as cheap labour. Some others were utilizing them for illegal transport of forest produce.

Lodhas of Asha Kathi Village: Beneficiaries or Victims of Interventions?

In Asha Kathi village of Belpahari (Binpur II) Block, residents of a Lodha hamlet have been cultivating on small parcels of land taken on lease from non-tribal people. Here, the Lodha hamlet was intermingled with other non-tribal habitations.[7] The lifestyle of Lodha and other communities do not vary much in this village. People seem to live together without any social barrier in contrast to images one often sees in many places of the district. The area cultivated by the Lodha families here is as small as one-tenth of an acre. They cultivate wheat on lands adjoining the village. They told the researcher that they did not need much land and one-tenth of an acre per family was sufficient. Compared to the demands put forward by other community people, the needs as they visualize are very simple. Any 'outsider' may even feel amused at their simplistic material needs.

When these experiences are read with an earlier episode of land purchase for the landless Lodha families of the same village, it leaves despair, disgust and even annoyance in one's mind. Nearly eight years back, some land was purchased by the local panchayat samithi for the benefit of the Asha Kathi Lodha villagers. The complaint of the villagers was that the land was unfit for any agriculture. In fact, the land is full of rocks and red hard soil, which is normally used for quarrying of stones and material useful in construction of roads. Complaint that is even more serious was that land was purchased from an influential political person at a price, which was many times higher than the prevailing market valuation. The villagers neither got the land in their possession nor did they do any cultivation! This particular incident was a cause of heartburn for the community people with the new generation leaders emerging from the Lodha community making it an issue at regular intervals. The appalling incident reminds us one of the observations made by M.N. Srinivas, several years back:

> Targets have to be achieved and it is more important to achieve them than to bother about the means of achieving them. It does not matter if in achieving them the position of the local leader is strengthened. But not infrequently there is a conflict between the interests of the leader and the rural poor. Not enough thought is given to the problem of reaching the rural poor without having to go through the rural elite. Given the present drift, the conflict between rural elite and the rural poor is bound to grow acute as the latter become increasingly conscious of the fact that they are not benefiting as much as they should from the various development programmes (Srinivas, 1962: 450).[8]

The only change one can notice from the days of Srinivas's

observation is the rural elite, in the present instance, is the elected panchayat leader.

Lodhas of Asha Kathi: Interventions can be better also

A few months later, during another visit to the village, the researcher had an absorbing discussion in the village. The thirty families living there agreed to form three Self-Help Groups (SHG). Each SHG consists of ten families. The local BDO was also present and he assured that assistance would be provided to them to buy wheat seeds and some fertilizers. In normal circumstances, the assurances are forgotten or follow up action follows much later and at times without serving any useful purpose. For a change, the villagers got the seeds and fertilizers the next day. Their confidence in the system might have increased a bit! They opened bank accounts and started saving two rupees a day from their earnings. The three Groups were provided rupees ten thousand each from tribal development fund. It was later observed that the SHG members purchased goats, individually and not as group assets. The group members found it logical to have individual assets for better maintenance. One is inclined to observe this aspect as change in preferences from community ownership and living to the modern social conditions of nuclear families and individual ownership.

Almost a year later in January 2004, some youth from Belphari came all the way to Midnapore to meet the District Magistrate. They heard about the district administration efforts in helping about hundred landless Lodha families of Bonpatna village in purchasing agriculture land for cultivation. They also wanted similar efforts to be made in their village for the benefit of poor Lodha people. It was agreed by the district administration that the three Self-Help Groups of their village would be helped to the tune of rupees six lakh out of tribal development fund, for purchasing cultivable land. The entire exercise was handled by people themselves through their Self-Help Groups, as the past experience was not encouraging.

Interface with Other Communities: Exploitation of Lodhas

In another Lodha village near Khemasuli in Kharagpur-I Block, the inhabitants of a Lodha village are sore that their homestead lands have not been recorded though they have been staying there for decades. The houses of Lodha and other communities here are almost mixed without much demarcation. Only noticeable difference is that the houses of the Lodha are mud houses and small in size. There is not much free space left beyond the house proper; one can even comment that there is not much breathing space for Lodhas in the area! They complained, "Please see our houses, the entire area surrounding our houses is occupied by bamboo plantation of *Mahatas*."[9] To the question that why they have not opposed, if not resisted, the occupation of their lands by others, the villagers said they did not have the strength to do so. One could see resignation and anguish in their faces.

Lack of Self Confidence and Apathy of the Government Machinery

A week after the experience, the researcher asked the local Revenue Officer why their records had not been recorded despite their staying there for so many years. The rules are clear that poor landless families staying in homestead lands for a continuous period would get the benefit of lands recorded in their names. In this case, they also belong to a tribe. As it happens often in a Government office, the officer had no clear reply for the inaction. He assured that he would visit the village, verify the cases and record all the eligible families. A month later, when the researcher visited the village again, the villagers were visibly elated that their long-standing problem had been resolved. That definitely did not mean that all their problems had been solved. They showed two wells from where they take water and they were in a dilapidated condition. They were at ground level. There was not any low boundary wall around the well to prevent the outside dirty water to enter into the well and pollute it. One over-zealous man brought some water showing rubbish in it. The Lodha villagers often exhibit a sense of helplessness and lack of self-confidence. It does not cost much to construct a protective wall allround the well. They can do it themselves by contributing to the cause. There was a tube well visible nearby and when asked about it, they said other community people discouraged them from using the facility. One felt shocked, embarrassed and sad as an elderly person remarked, "The scent of a Lodha's stool goes far and wide."

Observations

Incident after incident confirms that the Lodha community in most of the places has not been psychologically accepted by other communities as being equal or worthy of living together as friends or co-villagers. This is at variance from the attitude when it comes to other communities living together without much social friction. It is a fact that the situation is changing but it may take many years before the integration is achieved.

CASE STUDY 6.1

Jyotirampur Lodha Village—A Contrasting Picture

There are about 200 families of Lodha Tribe in Jyotirampur. Family size ranges from four to eight. Lodha people in this village have small pieces of land ranging from 0.1 to 0.2 acre of land. Asit Malik has been working as low paid secretary of a local cooperative society since 1985. He studied upto Class XII. He apprehends he may lose his job because change of service conditions. He is looking for some substantial employment. He takes care of the responsibility of his entire family. His mother is no more. His father is around 78 years and stays with Asit. He used to cultivate his land and also had to work as a construction labourer to supplement the meagre income from land.

Asit has a big family. He had five brothers and two sisters. The second one passed away. All of them stay in the same village. The elder one does cultivation. The third one is around 30 years old and married. He stays with Asit. Out of two sisters of Asit, the elder one is married to a Lodha person at village Rengtia near Keshiary. She along with her twelve years old daughter makes plates from *sal* leaves. Leaves are collected from nearby forest. Her husband is a landless labourer. According to Asit, not much NREGA work happened in that village. Hence, the opportunities are limited. People in that village also go to places like Contai in search of work. They stay there for about one month and come back home before they set out again in search of work. Asit's sister's daughter studied up to Class V staying with him. After that, she went to stay with her parents. Asit feels there is a serious problem for girls' education in his village. The school is up to Class V only and hence most of the girls stopped their education after that. His family feels there is at least necessity up to Class VIII. It will be even better if there is a hostel facility. Asit's younger sister stays in the same village. The couple has a son and a daughter. The boy studies in Class V in the Lodha hostel at Bidisha and the girl is in Class VIII at local High School. Asit' brother's daughter also studies in Class V at Bidisha.

Asit says, in Jyotirampur village, the earlier stigma of de-notified tribe is no longer there. In this village, all the houses of Lodha families are together and there is no other house belonging to any other community. However, situation is different in other villages like Balarampur and Doharpur, where Lodha houses and other community houses are together. They are invited to functions and programmes of other communities and they dine together.

Livelihoods and General Living Conditions

In a Lodha village of Parasia in Nayagram Block, the villagers are mostly dependent on forest for making some income. Seasonal agricultural operations give them employment for two months in a year. Life is tough beyond those two months with everyday a battle for survival. Added to these, ill health to any member of the family pushes them to situation comparable to that of a country boat caught in a cyclone in mid sea.

Some of the Lodha families own small parcels of land in the vicinity but there is problem of irrigation. They depend upon monsoon for their only one crop, which is paddy. The villagers requested for a deep tube well to be installed to solve the problem. They were convinced that they could do more crops in a year with assured water. There is no electricity in the village. Hence, the diesel pump set is the only option to pump water. It is, however, costlier to run a diesel pump than one powered by electricity.

As District Magistrate, the researcher discussed the issue with the local BDO and the required fund was arranged and a deep tube well of their dreams was installed by the villagers. The location of the tube well was left to the decision of the villagers. A month later, during our visit to the village, it was seen that the pump is in operational condition and more number of non-Lodha farmers were drawing water compared to only five farmers from the Lodha community. Better would have been to locate the tube well further down, where more Lodha lands were concentrated. The non-tribal dominant villagers whom the Lodhas could not ignore, it appeared, influenced the selection of the location. After a prolonged debate, the Lodhas came up with another proposal; one more tube well will definitely reach others who were left out. The proposal was finally agreed to and another irrigation facility came up in the location they decided.

When these discussions were happening, women stood nearby, curiously looking at the proceedings. The dress of many women, that of the children in their arms and those holding onto their mothers' saris, reflected to a greater extent, the economic condition of the village.

In Bonpatna village, and, in fact, in almost every Lodha village, people eat *pantha bhat* (watery rice) and *sag bhaja* (leafy vegetables). During the days of scarcity, many families can afford only rice without any vegetable. They eat rice with *pyaj* (onion) and *lonka* (green chili). Only during the two agricultural seasons, they take two square meals a day. For the rest of the time in a year, they struggle hard. During these days, they collect fuel wood from the forest and earn on an average rupees ten for a head load of thirty kilograms.[10] Some buy bamboo for rupees thirty a kilogram and sell cut bamboo for rupees sixty. It takes almost three days to collect, make bundle and sell the cut bamboo. Many go to Mecheda, Panskura, Egra, and Kolaghat in Midnapore (East) district to work as agricultural labourers during *boro* season (April-May). They get work for fifteen to twenty days. They get rupees fifty per day and food. During monsoon, they collect crabs, snails and small fish to eat. Some work as construction labour in nearby Kharagpur town. (Photograph 6.2 shows tribal women carrying bricks at a construction site in Kharagpur.) Some find work occasionally in stone quarry. Some find livelihood by pulling tricycle vans. Some of these activities are urban and semi-urban in nature. In other forest fringe Lodha villages, livelihood is closely linked to what they can collect from the forest. When livelihood is such an issue, thinking about education for children, leave aside higher education, has remained a distant dream for many, even today.

In Birsa Lodha village, located in Midnapore Block and about twelve kilometres from Midnapore town, most of the women go to nearby forest to collect firewood. The forest is four kilometres from the village. They go in the morning around 6 a.m. and come back around 1 p.m. A head load of dry leaves is sold at Rs. 10 and a thirty-kilogram head load of firewood is sold around Rs. 30. In a family, sometimes, wife and husband both go for collection of firewood.

Out of thirty-six families, only four families own some amount of land. Rest of them are either landless or share croppers. Either way, the land area cultivated is about 10-30 cents. There is no irrigation facility in this area. Hence, most of the farmers raise single crop. They also work as agriculture labour in others' land. They get work during sowing and harvesting season for about two and half months in a year. Some of the people go to Garbeta, Keshpur, Ghatal, Kolaghat and other adjoining areas for work. In these areas, farmers cultivate two to three crops in a year and there is demand for the agriculture labour. A person gets Rs. 40 per day as wage and he normally stays in the landowner's house during the period of work. This period ranges from fifteen days to one month. In Birsa village and surrounding areas, the daily wage is Rs. 30. They go to work around 8 a.m. and work till 4 p.m. Some of them also go to Midnapore town to work as construction labour. They go by cycle or on foot. The average daily wage is Rs. 60 for construction labour. Once the harvesting season is over in January, the only alternative livelihood for most of the families is to go to the nearby forest and collect dry leaves and firewood. In many houses, they can eat only after they sell these and buy daily provisions. This situation continues till June when sowing season starts normally.

Out of thirty-six families in this village of Birsa, only two of them got Below Poverty Line (BPL) cards. Others are treated as Above Poverty Line (APL). The BPL families are eligible for many facilities under various government programmes. The newly elected Panchayat member, a young man, from the Lodha community says he is still new and he is unable to understand why other families of his village are not getting the BPL benefit though their economic condition is very poor. One elderly person remarked that he heard over the radio that power was now with the Panchayat and if that was so why the Panchayat was unable to solve this problem.

There is a tube well in the village for drinking water but it is not functioning at present. They take water from a well, which has no built platform. There is all likelihood that the water is polluted from run off and drainage from the adjoining area. They feel that they cannot repair the well themselves as they do not have the means. There is a general sense of helplessness and excessive dependence on the Government and Panchayat for all issues.

Most of the elderly persons felt that lack of agriculture land was the biggest challenge for their livelihood. They say they also need bullocks, plough and help in the form of seeds and irrigation facility. They feel that their life would be better if these needs were met.

Bishnupriya studied up to Higher Secondary in Sarada Ashram School near Jhargram. She, however, could not pass the examination. She is from Baghjhapa village, near Jhargram town. She stayed in hostel during her studies. She is married to a person in Birsa village. She says she cannot work in the field. It is also not possible for her to go to the forest to collect firewood or dry leaves. She is not accustomed to such works as she stayed in hostel and studied. She will be happy to get some Government job. Her husband completed ITI course as welder from Midnapore. He studied up to Class 10 staying in a tribal hostel at Chandra, a place about thirty kilometres from Midnapore. He is in search of a job. He currently does agriculture in the land he got from his father.

Another young man from the village has been trying for a loan for the last four years under Prime Minister Rozgar Yojana (PMRY), one of the many self-employment programmes supported by the Government. The Bank is not sanctioning the loan.

CASE STUDY 6.2

Livelihoods in Transition

Akshay Pramanik (70) is from *uttar* Bonpatna Lodha village. A person not in good health, he receives old age pension of Rs. 750 per month. This amount is credited to his account in Post Office. Payment of pension is not regular and he gets it once in three to four months together. He becomes ill frequently and goes to Khelar Primary Health Centre which is nearby. Akshay has 0.8 acre of land. Out of this, 0.3 acre is his own whereas 0.5 acre has been given as *patta* by the Government. This *patta* land is located about one and half kilometre from his home. As this land falls within Gopalbandh area, half of the land is mostly under water and not available for cultivation.

Akshyay has four sons and a daughter. His sons are in the age group of 24 to 45. All are married and stay independently. Akshay and his wife Subhashi live together. They prefer not to stay with any of their sons, as they are apprehensive that their stay will not be liked by sons and daughters-in-law. Akshay feels that daughters-in-law look at them as additional burden. Only the youngest daughter-in-law frequently enquires about their health and well-being. According to Akshay, his sons are not generally bothered about parents. His second son got a house under Indira Awas Yojana. There is no electricity in the entire village. His youngest son is 28 years now and was married about twelve years back. By inference, his son got married at the age of 16. He has a son and a daughter. His son studies in Class VI at Khelar High School and the daughter is in Class II at primary school. His sons cultivate their land and also work in building construction during off season. Building works are normally in and around Kharagpur and Bankura town. They stay with the contractor for about a month and half till the completion of the building and come back home. Again, they look for new work. They get around Rs. 100 to Rs.120 per day as construction labourers. Except the younger one, other three daughters-in-law are members in Self Help Groups formed during the campaign launched in the year 2000. All three of them got around 0.1 acre of agriculture land, purchased in a group with the assistance of district administration. His daughter was married about eight years back. She has three daughters and a son. Before that, they lost two children at the age of twenty one days and three days. They were always apprehensive about this. The couple now opted for family planning operation. His daughter studied up to class IV whereas his son-in-law has no formal education. He works as a construction labourer. His son-in-law's father worked in railways at Kharagpur. Akshay regrets that his son-in-law did not inherit any of these qualities from his father. Akshay feels many of the Lodha youth idle away time and are habitual drinkers.

Lodha Village of Bagh Jhapa: Perils of Planning from Above

In Lodha village of Bagh Jhapa, literally meaning a 'tiger's leap', near Jhargarm, the story is familiar. One always finds a community hall built out of Government funds in a Lodha village. The idea is that they can have social occasions and celebrations in the hall. There is no problem with the idea and intention; only the hall is constructed without any imagination. The area of the hall is so small that most of the villagers may have to sit outside the hall. It is invariably a concrete structure and not uncommon to see such vignettes flowing from centralized planning methods. People "above" tend to decide the so-called "schemes" and "model" estimates without taking into account the villagers' needs. May be a less costly but more spacious structure would have been appropriate. It is difficult to expect the junior engineers or bureaucrats, who never stayed in a village, leave alone in a tribal village, will have better understanding of the needs of tribal people like Lodhas.

The small portion of families owning some land here also have irrigation problem. Many said a deep tube well was a necessity. One person needs vegetable seeds. Some would like to cultivate wheat and need seeds and fertilizers. The researcher came across a former *Upa-Pradhan* (Vice President) of the local Gram Panchayat belonging to the Lodha community. He owns some land and his house condition was definitely better than that of most other houses. One always finds one or two houses in every Lodha village with shining tin roof; they are the lucky recipients of housing assistance under the Indira Awas Yojana (IAY), a scheme for providing houses to the poor and homeless. It was winter time and there was demand for blankets from villagers. The researcher advised the BDO, who was also present to arrange the required blankets and one hundred pieces were arranged in a week time. It was found later that blankets were distributed and people were happy with the arrangement. The former Upa Pradhan was also one of the recipients. The deep tube well was also sunk with fund arranged from the district and water started irrigating the lands. The location was even better this time; it is adjoining the former Panchayat Upa Pradhan's plot of land! At least his plot is assured of water irrespective of others at a distance, getting it or not! Then, there were some angry voices. They said it was fine that some development was happening in the village. However, they were landless. They needed land. There was a piece of cultivable Government land adjoining the village, which could be allotted to them. The BDO promised to initiate action. He said he would request the Panchayat Samithi, who could legally deal with the issue, to consider their request. With all good intentions of everyone, the land was not distributed even after three months. Only solace was that the process in that direction had started.

For their own benefit, many landless and poor families of the village took initiative and formed thirteen Self-Help Groups (SHGs). They started saving small amounts daily, from their nominal earnings[11] . The Government and banks would provide the SHG with revolving fund of rupees twenty-five thousand rupees after six months.

The group members could use this money for income generating activities. Only road block, on many occasions, is the attitude of banks and apathy of field level officials who process the cases. But the battle has to be carried forward as there are not many options for survival and better living of rural masses, in general, and tribal population, in particular.

Repayment of Loans

If an amount of rupees one hundred is taken on loan for a period of six months, the borrower has to pay back rupees one hundred and fifty. In case of rice, one has to return one and half quintal for one quintal for the same period. If the loan is returned in the form of labour, the wage rate is rupees five less than the standard rate. In case of rice, two kilograms of rice amounts to one day of labour. It may be mentioned that standard wage rate consists of rupees twenty in cash, one kilogram of rice and 250 grams of puffed rice. There is no difference in wage rate paid to men and women.

It is observed that the poor and, particularly tribals, have to struggle hard to survive in times of lean agriculture seasons and in times of any crisis like death and disease in a family. They have to take loans and repayment is tough because of the harsh terms of the moneylender. They fall into this vicious cycle and start working almost like bonded labour to repay the debts. The suffering of the poor and especially, tribal people seems to be similar across districts and even States! As observed by Behera and Nath in the context of indigenous people of Kalahandi district of Orissa :

> Especially in the lean months when their stocks get exhausted and no other food is available and also in crisis they knock the door of the *mahajan*, who waits eagerly to bounce on such opportunity. They even mortgage their lands in certain cases. They borrow in cash or kind . . . . . .For borrowing one kg of *kosla*/paddy/*mandia*, one has to pay an interest of half kg per season and, therefore, he has to return 1.5 kg after the harvest . . . . In a situation when the harvest is very poor and the forest collection is less and the person has nothing to repay the loan, he has no way out but to lose the household articles . . . .The higher interest charged by the moneylender

> made the repayment of the loan impossible on the part of the poor indigenous people. Finally, he takes away their land. As a result, more often than not, indebtedness itself is followed by land alienation (Behera and Nath, 2004 : 14).

There are lean periods in a year when life is really tough for any average villager and Lodhas cannot be an exception. These periods are *Baisakh*, *Jaishtha*, *Ashadh* and again *Bhadra*, *Ashin*, *Kartik*. Normally *dadan* is taken in the months of *Baisakh* and *Jaishtha*, the summer time, when the agriculture fields in these areas are vacant without any cultivation due to lack of irrigation. Life also becomes tough and it is struggle for survival in the months of *Bhadra, Ashin* and *Kartik*. After sowing is complete in *Sravan*, the Lodhas will not have much work to do.

Taking loan to be repaid in the form of agriculture labour is called *dadan*. One *dadan* is equal to one day agriculture labour, normally repaid during the month of *Sravan*, when agriculture season is on. One has to work from 9 am to 5 pm in the field. The cash wages are rupees twenty-five per day, whereas in *dadan* one has to give a day's labour in lieu of two kilogram of rice. A kilogram of rice costs ten rupees in market. That means, the wage is rupees five less when repayment of *dadan* is made. For a period of nearly two to three months, the Lodha will be paying rupees five of hidden interest on a loan of rupees twenty! This works out to a rate of interest of over 100 per cent. It is pertinent to point out here that any poor villager normally pays similar or even higher interest rate anywhere in the district, whatever community one may belong to. This situation is also true in respect of many other places in the country. Poverty seems to be a great leveller and equalizer transgressing regional and ethnic boundaries. Kalpana Mallik says, "*Amra dadan shodh korte korte shesh hoye jachi*" meaning "we are dying repaying our loans." She says sadly, "We wait up to seven in the evening for *dadan* to be given by the lender. Then only, we can buy rice and cook food for the night." When the researcher wanted to know who the lender was, she said, "We have the houses of *Sen, Kar* and *Bhunia*."[12]

Livelihoods in Lean Periods

In Khelar, Lodhas depend upon the Dhangori forest across the river *Keleghai* to collect food and firewood. When the river is full, they cannot cross it and they face enormous difficulty without any livelihood. The river, of course, is a shallow one and remains dry or with less water, most of the year. Many also go to Mecheda, Tamluk and Contai in search of work. These areas are rich in agriculture and work is available better as compared to situation in Khelar and most other parts of western Midnapore.

From the forest, they collect edible roots, fruits and tubers. These include tubers like *shakalu, dhanalu* and *panalu.* During the months of February to May, thirty-five families of the Lodha village of Khelar, depend upon fishing from the Gopal *bandh*, huge water body of the village. It is easy fishing during these months as water in the reservoir is less. Men and women both go to catch fish. Their catch ranges between half a kilogram (kg) to one kg in a day. They sell fish for rupees thirty a kilogram in the market. (Photograph 6.3 and Photograph 6.4 capture the scene of local people at this water reservoir catching fish).

When they fail to hunt any animal, they collect snails and tuberous roots and eat these to manage the day. It happens quite often for them that while wandering in the forest, they feel hungry and they make fire with the help of two pieces of wood. They roast their catch or tuberous roots in the fire and satisfy their hunger. These scenes are familiar in the forest areas of Belpahari, Nayagram and Gopivallabhpur. They also catch cranes by the side of water reservoirs, with a trap net. They eat the flesh when no other food is available. At times, they earn their living by selling the skins of Snakes.

Clothing

Children, especially boys, below five years normally do not wear any clothes in many Lodha houses. This results in their remaining unclean as they play around, soiling their bodies. One mostly finds a child in a Lodha mother's lap without clothes. Bhushan Dandapat, a former Upa Pradhan (Vice President) of Khelar Gram Panchayat says due to poverty, they cannot afford to buy clothes. When having two meals a day is a problem, clothing comes next on priority for a family. Photograph 6.5 shows the belongings of a Lodha family in Uttar Bonpatna village. They hardly have any materialistic assets.

Lodhas and Malnutrition: Constant Companions

As there are minimum opportunities available, the Lodha family constantly befriends hunger and malnutrition[13]. They have little choice. They wait untiringly, and with resignation, for the tide to turn and hope for 'better days'. The word 'better' here is relative and means minimum livelihood opportunities so that the entire family can eat twice a day.

Lodhas : Easy Prey for the Predators

As the Lodha people are simple, innocent and gullible, they are an easy prey to constant exploitation by others. They can be given loans at ridiculously high rate of interest. Their assets, whatever little they may have, can be seized for non-payment of dues. They can be engaged as labour at any rate and on most exploitative conditions.

The onslaught of modern materialistic civilization has left the average Lodha way behind in the rat race. He has not learnt the modern art of machinations and managing situations. He will remain unfed and undernourished without even questioning. He will be stoic and detached even in penury and misery. There are opportunities galore for the fast moving 'others'. When it comes to a Lodha, he remains a bystander to happenings around. He may not even know what is due to him lawfully. (Photograph 6.6 symbolises the evening time of a typical Lodha family in Bonpatna village).

An Educated Lodha dreams only about a Government Job

Like any other educated youth, one will come across a Lodha boy with education qualification up to class ten, longing for a Government job. He cannot think of any other alternative career. Whatever may be his education, he looks it as a job provider. He has to struggle hard to complete the studies, coming from the environment in which he is born and reared. Despite strong desire of parents, the journey is tough. There are certain facilities for the children provided by the Government in the form of free education, books, stipend, and hostel facilities. The reservation quotas in the jobs are normally availed by other advanced and forward groups in the ST category. Hence, it is rare that a Lodha boy or a girl finds any Government job bracing the competition within the ST quota. Situation may change slowly in times to come but the present day scenario is bleak.

The researcher met representatives of the *Lodha Sabar Kalyan Samiti* [14] who carry a list of boys and fewer girls, requesting for some opportunity in the government jobs.[15] They feel sure about the entire affair that their boys rarely get a chance to land in a job. The number of Lodha men and women in Government offices is limited. Mostly, they were taken in casual capacity and later on confirmed in their posts.

Modern Day Entrepreneurship is New to Lodhas

If one asks a Lodha boy why he does not try for a bank loan and become self-employed, the response is negative. He is averse to taking any such venture. He would say "*cholbe na* and *parbo na*" meaning "it will not work" and "I cannot". The reason could be lack of self-belief and confidence. They must not have seen any such entrepreneur in their community. There is hardly any successful entrepreneur to emulate for the youth. The journey, perhaps, has to begin some day. It may be harsh to say but is true that the Lodhas are easy targets for other adventurous entrepreneurs of their neighbourhood.

As mentioned in another context, the loans sanctioned from various poverty alleviation programmes like IRDP, SCP and TSP were not much successful. There had been tendency on part of the bankers not to disburse the entire sanctioned loan amounts. Sometimes, the subsidy portion alone was disbursed and the loan portion was kept in fixed deposit after showing as disbursement. The bank manager would have definitely got promotion as he increased deposits and loans with great efficiency! Only sufferer was the borrower. His project would have been underfinanced and ended in unnatural death. In many cases, the meagre amount sanctioned was used for consumption needs. One cannot find fault with the borrower as he has needs and problems ready for any extra money to absorb. The result is that the poor tribal gets the title of a defaulter, which will haunt him and his successors for many years to come.

Procurement of *Tasar* Cocoons

Many people living in forest fringe areas depend upon *tasar* (a form of silk) cultivation. They collect *tasar* cocoons from forest, which are occurring naturally. Some of these forest areas are in Nayagram, Gopivallabhpur, Lalgarh and Belpahari Blocks.[16] There is a serious problem of marketing these cocoons collected by thousands of villagers, predominantly belonging to the Scheduled Tribes. There are a number of traders and middlemen operating in these areas who buy these cocoons at very low prices. These traders are from adjoining places like Chakulia in Jharkhand State and Baripada in Orissa State. These intermediaries collect huge quantities of cocoons cheaply and sell at a very high price to weavers. In this process, the poor tribal villagers do not get proper remuneration for their labour. Weavers in other places of the district like Anandapur in Keshpur Block also do not get cocoons at reasonable prices for weaving *saris* and other materials. This vicious circle has been operating for ages.

Various Self-Help Groups, which were formed and have been working in these areas since 2000, have been undertaking diverse economic activities. Some of the groups have been motivated by the district administration and Panchayats to buy *tasar* cocoons at reasonable prices from cocoon collectors and sell to weavers of the district after keeping profit margin. The *tasar* cocoons used to be bought by intermediaries at the rate of 50 paise per cocoon. On the other hand, weavers used to buy at a rate varying from Rs. 1.20 to Rs. 2.00 per cocoon. During the year 2002 and 2003, the Self-Help Groups bought cocoons at price ranging from 80 paise to rupee 1. The weavers could procure cocoons in the range of rupee 1 to rupees 1.5 rupees depending upon prevailing market situation. As a result, the cocoon collectors got 100 per cent additional price and the weavers could procure raw materials at 40 per cent of the price they paid earlier.

There are four Self-Help Groups of Lodha women in Jyotirampur village under Makrampur Gram Panchayat. Group members said they had received Rs. 25,000 as revolving fund from the bank and Government. They used it mostly for purchase of livestock. They contribute Rs. 2 per day to the group savings. Because of Self-Help Groups, they got some relief from poverty. The groups were formed in the year 2003.

It is pertinent to mention about the efforts made in the district of undivided Midnapore in mobilizing poor women to form self help groups. The researcher—District Magistrate was impressed by similar efforts made in the State of Andhra Pradesh around that time. During field visits, it was felt that the experience can be replicated in Midnapore district with necessary changes to suit local conditions. What followed was a huge social mobilization campaign to reach out to the socially and economically disadvantaged women of hundreds of villages. Entire development machinery and Panchayat representatives participated in the exercise which was to become role model for the entire State of West Bengal. Nearly three lakh women became members of about thirty thousand self help groups. They included close to sixty thousand women belonging to tribal communities. These women are residents of remote tribal villages and the experience gave them confidence and courage to address their social and economic problems. In addition to creating micro enterprises for women, the larger benefit was in the social sector where together they could address hitherto formidable challenges like sanitation for all, early marriage of girls, immunization of children, adequate spacing between two children, child delivery in hospitals under medical supervision and primary school enrolment. Through their own savings, Government assistance and bank credit, women challenged the bane of extreme poverty and dependence on moneylenders. The self help groups created a solid foundation and platform for several other initiatives to be taken up by the people themselves with the help of district administration.

Through empowerment and support, the Self-Help Groups have successfully proved that they are capable of bringing a significant change in their living conditions. Though it is a fact that traders and intermediaries continue to operate and the intervention of the Self-Help Groups in the whole volume of trade is not remarkable, a beginning has been made in the right direction.

The Reasons for Economic Backwardness[17]

Lodhas traditionally stayed inside or in the fringes of forest areas. Most of them did not have any agricultural land. They used to depend on forest for livelihood. From the childhood, young girls tend to go to forest to collect dry leaves and fire wood. In Western Midnapore, agricultural lands in adjoining areas where Lodhas live do not have proper irrigation facilities. Hence, opportunity for labour work in agricultural sector is limited to one main season only, which is *aman* or kharif. This forces some of the labour to migrate to other areas in search of work. Some of them living in villages close to towns have adapted to new forms of livelihood like construction labour. Some also work as labourers in the quarry activities for extraction of morrum and boulders. Because of the distance from main land, almost all the Lodha villages do not have electricity. Hence, modern day amenities like television are beyond their reach and scope. The entire life cycle of a Lodha revolves around scarcity, inadequate food and disease. Added to this, the historical element of branding them as criminal tribe has caused sense of inferiority and insecurity in the minds of earlier generation. The new generation is trying to come out of this mindset and stigma by education and looking for opportunities. Nevertheless, it is still a long way before they make significant progress. The benefits offered by the Government in the form of residential schools are helping some of the Lodha children to access modern education. This has not been matched by availability of Government jobs for the small number of educated youth in the community. This creates frustration among them as education is primarily seen and believed to be the means to get Government employment. Their enterprising skills are very limited when compared to other community people living in the vicinity. Hence, if any Lodha youth tries to venture into some business or trade, which is very rare, the chances of success and survival are limited. The situation may change gradually when the youth of the community mixes more and more with the outside world and learns various skills, may be even guile!

The Lodhas seem to have been caught in web of poverty. Alcoholism drains away whatever meagre earnings they make. Their dependence on intermediaries, traders and moneylenders increases because of their liquor addiction. Their health also suffers in the process. The conditions on which they take informal loans are quite exploitative and leave little room for a Lodha person to come out of the debt trap. He has to work mostly for a lower wage to pay back the loan and extravagant interest on it. Some of the benefits they receive from Government are also frittered away because of their daily needs including consumption of alcohol. For example, if a Lodha family gets cattle, goats and roofing material, these are sold at a pittance to the hawks, waiting for such an opportunity in their neighbourhood. Most of the loans given to them through banks cannot be repaid because of poor selection of schemes, lack of adequate support, training and follow-up. They cannot hold on to the assets given to them because of the environment in which they live and work. Constant support, guidance, confidence building and real empowerment of the community can make difference in their lives over a period.

If the Lodhas themselves could buy the Land they Liked !

Studies after studies pointed out the wrong implementation of the Government plans and programmes. These reviews and papers put the blame on the Government machinery and at times, the local Panchayats. However, they stop there; they do not suggest or provide any alternative method of implementation of programmes. One sincerely feels the authors of these reports of reviews are not greatly helping the cause until and unless they come up with better implementation models.

The discussion with the Lodha people of Bonpatna on a typical day went like this:

DM : With all these difficulties, can you ensure two meals everyday for you and your family?

Basanti Kotal : No, it is very difficult.

DM : So, what needs to be done? Which is the critical issue?

Basanti Kotal : We are landless. That is the main problem. If we have some agriculture land, that will solve our livelihood problem.

DM : But, will it ensure livelihood throughout the year?

Bhushan Dandapat	:	It will take care of our daily food for six months, at least. Rest six months, we will work in others' fields and go to the forest.
DM	:	Is land available nearby? These efforts often fail because of reasons like wrong identification of lands or lands situated far away from villages.
Bhushan Dandapat	:	Yes, we will find land nearby. Then, we can take care of the cultivation easily. We will be grateful if you arrange some land for us.
DM	:	There is no need to be thankful to me. If the plan becomes successful, I will be only doing my duty. And, believe me, all development money is your money; it is people's money. We are all honest trustees, or you can say, priests of the process.
Bulbuli Layek	:	Nobody ever came to us and talked like this in our lives.
DM	:	I feel sad and sorry about it. The entire exercise has to be handled by you only. We will only facilitate to the extent you ask for.
Bhushan Dandapat	:	Kindly, explain clearly how we can go about the task.
DM	:	What I am saying is that, land identification and price negotiation has to be done by your community. We will not be in the picture. I request the *Pradhan* also to be an observer to the process. I am confident that you will collectively negotiate the correct market price with the prospective landowners. We propose to transfer the fund directly into the bank accounts of your Self-Help Groups.

After this, in Bonpatna village, we could provide assistance to 113 Lodha families for purchase of agricultural land. These families belong to ten Self-Help Groups. Before this, we had several meetings with the families' alongwith the local *Pradhan* to form these SHGs. The members of these SHGs purchased 10.08 acres of private land in the same village. Nearly ten lakh rupees were arranged by the district administration from a rural development programme, *Swarna Jayanti Gram Swarozgar Yojana* (SGSY) for purchase of land and cultivation of vegetables. The land was selected by the Lodha families themselves as discussed unlike what is normally done in Government programmes. In a normal routine Government programme, the villagers are kept out of the selection and determination of land price. There is hardly any "participation" by the villagers in such "development process." The elite of the area handles this part; whatever may be the name and style of such elite. One may ask, is it not sufficient if the elected Panchayat representatives are involved in such decision-making? With due respect to them and recognition of their role, one would say that decision-making by representatives alone does not constitute and guarantee participation of people for whom the development is proposed. There has to be active and direct involvement of the persons and families when it comes to selection of schemes or decision-making which affects them. Table 6.3 gives details of Self-Help Groups belonging to Lodha people of Bonpatna mouza.

Table 6.3: Details of Self-Help Groups of Women belonging to Lodha Tribe of Bonpatna Village

Sl. No.	*Name of the SHG*	*Bank Account No.*	*Date of Opening*
1.	Bonpatna Ma Tilottama SHG	4210	06.05.2003
2.	Bonpatna Ma Jugini SHG	4211	06.05.2003
3.	Bonpatna Joy Ma Chandi SHG	4209	06.05.2003
4.	Bonpatna Joy Ma Tara SHG	4208	06.05.2003
5.	Bonpatna Ma Durga SHG	4207	06.05.2003
6.	Bonpatna Joy Ma Kali SHG	4206	06.05.2003
7.	Dakshin Bonpatna Joy Ma Laxmi SHG	4479	09.07.2003
8.	Dakshin Bonpatna Joy Ma Sitala SHG	4480	09.07.2003

Note : Name of the Bank: Mallabhum Gramin Bank, Elasai Branch

The villagers were very clear about the change the land would bring in their lives. Their children would be definitely assured of two square meals a day for six months in a year. One would ask, what would happen for the remaining six months. Basanti says they would manage from the earnings from the forest. Does it mean that, at present, are they not assured of two meals daily? Sadly, may be shocking even, the situation is just that in many homes for some parts of the year.

The Lodhas have their dreams woven around the land. They have many ideas. They would like to cultivate *aman* paddy. This would be followed by *sorsa* (mustard) or vegetables. Of course, they were stuck in the age-old problem faced by an average Indian farmer; the land needs some irrigation help. Water is available but some money is needed to install shallow tube wells to tap underground water. What has happened to the Bank credit, one may wonder. The manager will be the last to sanction agriculture loans to such small farmers. The amount involved is too small and the workload is too huge. It does not merit consideration in his scheme of things. The average bank manager will be too happy and inclined to sanction any such loan to a farmer with reasonable landholding. He will welcome people who can afford to give any guarantee or offer property for mortgage on loans to be sanctioned. The *Pradhan* made efforts to arrange some method of irrigation of land. The constraint is always availability of funds for a Panchayat to take up such useful schemes; even bigger constraint in most cases is lack of imagination, dependency mind-set and inability to motivate them towards action based on collective self-help.[18]

In the year 2003, during one of those many visits to the area, villagers highlighted the problem and we arranged a mini deep tube well in Jyotirampur Lodha village for cultivation. Thanks to that, nearly thirty families can do cultivation. However, problems continue for these poor villagers. In the year 2009, Lodha villagers paid Rs. 25,000 for electrification charges to the electricity board for one tube well. The connection amount was paid on a temporary basis for a period of three months of cultivation. In 2010, the amount has gone up to Rs. 33,000. This amount was huge for them. They could not afford to pay the money and no cultivation could happen from the tube well. This shows that there is no convergence of development activities. The tube well was given but electricity is not there in the village. Cost of operating the tube well through diesel pump set is costlier and may not be remunerative for the villagers. It was possible that from various schemes existing for tribal development and particularly for Lodha development, the Government could have arranged this.

Under Lodha Development Scheme, 33 houses were constructed in Makrampur Gram Panchayat in the year 2009. Out of those, eleven Lodha families got benefit in Jyotirampur village. Each house was built at a cost of rupees one lakh. The construction work was given to an agency from Midnapore. Villagers feel the quality of construction has been good.

Works under NREGA

Households who applied were provided job cards under NREGA[19] (National Rural Employment Guarantee Act) in Bonpatna and other villages. This has been a significant intervention to provide minimum hundred days of manual work on demand in rural areas. Before start of NREGA works, villagers including those belonging to Santal, Lodha and other tribal communities had to depend upon forest for collection of food and wood. Many of them find work under NREGA. As a result, poor people including tribal families got a new opening hitherto unavailable to them on this scale. Significantly, getting hundred days of manual work per household on demand is a legal entitlement.

Work under NREGA was started at Gopal bandh where local Lodha, Santal and other villagers could get work. As a result of this, families started getting up to 60-70 days of work in a year. Wage seekers from Bonpatna, Kata Bani, Bolla and Nischintapur got work at Gopal bandh. The work normally starts at 7.00 AM and is over by noon. The normal wage rate is Rs. 100 which is significant compared to the situation before start of NREGA. Wages are paid through accounts of the villagers kept with the local cooperative society. They do not face any problem in withdrawing money from their accounts. However, they faced hardship due to enormous delay in getting their wages even after nearly two months of working. As these are poor people, they are forced to take loans from *mahajan* and shopkeepers at interest rates ranging from Rs. 5 to Rs. 10 per cent per month, depending upon the urgency. This is again a throwback to earlier times for people who had to depend upon moneylenders for loans for consumption.

Bakul Naik says, thanks to NREGA and Antyodaya, people of Jyotirampur and other villages under Makrampur Gram Panchayat are getting big relief. Their migration to places like Contai and Tamluk, in search of agriculture work, has reduced. This is certainly a significant change after introduction of Antyodaya under which they get rice and wheat whereas work is provided under NREGA programme. However, in the year 2010, the rains were delayed and as a result sowing in the fields suffered. As a result, there was not much work for labourers from agriculture operations and nearly twenty persons of Jyotirampur Lodha village went for railway line laying work under a contractor near Balasore in Orissa. They got about Rs. 150 per day. This is the period when NREGA works would have provided employment to villagers. However, inadequate planning and system deficiencies come in the way.

Reported Starvation Deaths

Huge controversy was generated in and outside West Bengal when sections of media reported death of at least six persons in Amlasole village near Belpahari, reportedly due to malnutrition.[20] These deaths took place during April and May 2004. The victims belonged to Lodha community. The State Government directed the district administration to go into the details of the cases and take immediate remedial measures. The researcher collected details leading to these unfortunate incidents. The researcher visited the village in 2006 as part of the research work. Lodha community people inhabit Amlasole. The Lodha families here live in extreme poverty. Their main source of livelihood is collection of sal leaves and firewood from the adjoining forest. It has been noted that the local police, imposed several restrictions on movement of the villagers for some time, to check the influence of left wing extremism in the areas. As a result, the source of livelihood dried up for the villagers.

The local administration differed from the reported cause of deaths and they maintained these were due to disease. It may be purely academic discussion whether the persons died because of hunger, disease, or both. The truth of the matter, which is admitted by most of the people, is the people are helpless and they have hardly any effective livelihood opportunities. Their lives precariously vacillate between starvation and two square meals a day. The question is, whether these people get to lead life of human beings with dignity and honour. When the villager is asked for reaction about the prevailing abject poverty, normally there is no answer. The person in question, unfortunately, shows the silence and resignation of a dead man. He has no anger or frustration on anyone. He is philosophical.

Rise of Leftist Extremism[21]

Many parts of the remote forest areas of the district have been operating zone for leftist extremists. The comparative lack of amenities and poverty gives rise to growth of these forces. Lack of communication and road network makes it easy for their activities. They tend to organize poor people on various problems being faced by the people. A sizeable proportion of people in these areas belong to tribal communities. Sometimes, the people become sandwiched between the extremists and the police. Raids and arrests in the area follow any extremist incident against the police. Many a time, poor tribal people become scapegoats and get trapped in these arrests. The main charge against these people is that they give shelter to the extremists. The poor tribal families live in fear and men sometimes leave homes leaving their families behind. Once arrested, the poor tribal may not have the means to prove his innocence and come out of the jail. As a result, he may have to languish in jail. This also puts his family back home in the village, in stress and distress. It is a paradox that the actions of the administration intended to curb the problem may actually spur such tendencies in the minds of people out of sheer anger and helplessness. Moreover, for the administration, it is a very tough task to strike the right balance. The following Case Study highlights one such situation where the administration could successfully reach out to the people.

CASE STUDY 6.3

The Changing Patterns in Mahadeb Soren's Life

Mahadeb Soren is from Kashmar village near Belpahari. Life has been tough for this middle-aged person and many others in the area. The village has a Santal habitation and Mahadeb belongs to the same tribe. One finds him as an innocent, straightforward and simple person.

The area has not seen much development. There is problem of

> rocky and unfriendly terrain, which does not help agriculture. Irrigation facilities are scarce in the area. In fact, drinking water itself has been a problem for many years. Life has been frustrating for people of the area with hardly any economic activity to talk about. Not many efforts have been there from Government to alleviate the problems. The region has been grossly underdeveloped and neglected because of many geographic and complementary reasons.
>
> The situation is just ripe for any individual or group to orchestrate the age-old difficulties of the people and provoke them against the administration and system. Mahadeb was one of those who used to lead angry protests, highlighting the underdevelopment of the area and their problems, when the researcher used to visit tribal villages as District Magistrate in connection with assessing development needs and aspirations of people. The researcher discussed the problems with the local BDO and both together visited the village and held discussions with villagers. Mahadeb was doubtful, like many others in the village, about the efforts of the administration to improve the livelihoods of the people. We realized the need to take up development schemes like creating minor irrigation facilities in the area. Over a period, Mahadeb became active member of villagers, who themselves implemented works like tank excavation and vegetable cultivation in the arid zone. The participative development process bridged, to a large extent, the psychological gap between the administration and the tribal people.

The problem repeatedly attracts the attention of the Government and the areas get additional funds for undertaking development programmes. As the needs are too many and the funds are not always unlimited, the impact takes time to get reflected on the lives of people. In the interregnum, the impression gains ground in the minds of people that enough is not being done to uplift the condition of the poor.

The whole issue developed into what is now known as Lalgarh problem where the central paramilitary forces and state police are conducting operations to check the leftist-extremist influence. As a result of the series of incidents, many areas in West Midnapore district have become 'law and order hot spots'. Natural consequence of these prolonged operations, though inevitable, is the turbulence in the areas, which are mostly forest, and forest fringe areas where thousands of tribal populations live. The debate continues as to what is the best course of action to contain influence of such tendencies; development of people and areas need to be addressed first or the issue is tackled from law and order angle and 'peace' is restored so that development work can be initiated without any interruption. There is also the 'middle path', which advocates that both strategies should happen simultaneously.

Due to the attention the area and incidents attract, funds are not an issue any more. Only problem is how to reach out the benefits to the people. Various Government departments like health, animal resources, education, tribal welfare, drinking water supply and power are working overtime to tackle the deficiencies in infrastructure and meet the demands of people. These have been long standing issues, which resulted in disenchantment of people with the systems. In addition, NREGA is in operation from 2006 across the country. However, there was not much concerted effort in the initial years as a result of which needy and tribal people could not get the expected benefit out of this statutory programme. Government wants immediate redressal of people's grievances and fulfilment of their needs. However, the process has not been found to be that easy. There are multiple reasons for this slow pace of achieving objectives of development. Some of these include lack of awareness and capacity of people to take benefit from various programmes, periodic law and order incidents disrupting the work of development and traditional and cultural ethos of people not being taken into account while designing and implementing programmes.

Self-Help Groups and Tribal Development[22]

Formation of Self-Help Groups of women benefited Santal, Lodha and other social groups who were suffering poverty and deprivation for a long time. This initiative has come as a boon to the families. Their confidence has been low so far and they have exhibited such a sense of helplessness as if they are incapable of changing their lives in their lifetime. Normally, there is no concept of savings among them. They tend to spend whatever they earn or make loan whenever there is a need. They were not in a position to look beyond today or at most tomorrow. Through formation of Self-Help Groups, the district administration and the local Panchayat motivated them to save small amounts in a group. That slowly grew into a sizeable amount, which provided immense confidence and enthusiasm to the members of the groups and the families who were initially reluctant and doubtful of the initiative. There are several instances, when the group withdrew money from their savings from the bank and helped their members' families to come out of immediate needs and emergencies. One example was saving a boy when a snake bit him and the family was in need of urgent money to shift him to hospital. The boy could be saved with the money from the group. Likewise, in times of marriage and illness, the groups came to the rescue of the member families and those in the neighbourhood. The entire exercise brought self-belief and refreshing hope for the future, which was unthinkable in a normal Lodha village. Through the help from Government and bank, these group members started getting assistance for acquiring income-generating assets.

1. Self-Help Group of Tribal Youth

Name and address of SHG	Mulunia Adibasi Unnayan Prakalpa, Vill. Dhabani, P.O. Dhadika, GP : Dhadika, Dist. West Midnapore
Date of formation	13.3.2000
Savings as on 15.1.2008	Rs. 29,710
Amount of revolving fund and assistance received	Rs. 25,000 One transport vehicle (three wheeler) from development fund
Activities taken up	Rice processing, Vegetable cultivation, Rearing of Goats, Poultry, Vegetables business, Piggery
Members of the group	(1) Gobinda Murmu, (2) Kali Charan Soren, (3) Jadunath Mandi, (4) Chana Hembram, (5) Kebal Saren, (6) Rabin Saren, (7) Satyanarayan Soren, (8) Sanatan Hansda, (9) Sunil Murmu, (10) Jiten Mandi
Average additional monthly income after formation of SHG	In the range of Rs. 940 to Rs. 1,150 per member

Some of the male members bought trolleys and rickshaw vans for livelihood. Some of them opted for cattle and goats.

2. Self-Help Group of Tribal Women

CASE STUDY 6.4

Self-Help Groups as Means of Tribal Development and Economic Growth

Social and economic development through Self-Help Groups became almost a movement in the undivided district of Midnapore. Some examples have been selected out of thousands of such Self-Help Groups functioning in West Midnapore.

Name and address of SHG	Chhireama Jaher Ayo Swa-Sahayak Dal, Village Chhireama, P.O. Pathartora, District West Midnapore
Date of formation	20.9.2001
Savings as on 15.01.2008	Rs. 26,980
Amount of revolving fund received	Rs. 25,000 Rs. 10,000 from development fund
Activities taken up	Poultry and rearing of cows
Members of the group	(1) Chintamani Soren, (2) Bijali Charon Saren, (3) Tunu Soren, (4) Nilmani Soren, (5) Malati Soren, (6) Mungli Soren, (7) Balmani Soren, (8) Ludi Mandi, (9) Kajal Soren, (10) Sudhamani Soren
Average additional monthly income after formation of SHG	In the range of Rs. 542 to Rs. 708 per member

NOTES

1. Corbridge's (2004) work systematically analysed the tribal economy and society during the period of 1950—1980 of tribes of Jharkhand. For detailed explanation and analysis on tribal economy and shifts and fluctuations of tribal economy, *see* Gaiha *et al.* (2009), Kumar (2006), Shah (2006), Meher (2003), Parry (2003), Rogaly *et al.* (2003), Singh (2003), Sinha *et al.* (2002), Rao (2001), Bapat (2000), Fernandes and Raj (1996), Sarkar and Sarkar (1996), Nanda (1992), Mahalingam (1990), and Prasad and Sen Gupta (1973).
2. See Steward (1986) Mosse *et al.*, (2002), for more anthropological and sociological analysis.
3. Related argument and analysis can be found from the studies of Kasi (2011a), Sengupta *et al.* (2008), Sundaram and Tendulkar (2003), Pathy (2003), Mosse *et al.* (2002) and Meenakshi *et al.* (2000).
4. Sal trees are common in forests and along the main roads. The leaves are traditionally used to make plates for use in festivals and other social occasions. *Babui* grass grows naturally in forests. It is used to make rope, which has wide use. The economies of *babui* rope are startling as the researcher understood that big traders and intermediaries are involved in this business. They procure the rope from mostly tribal people for pittance and sell in different parts of the country. The end price is, not surprisingly, many times more than what the primary producer in a forest gets. Similar situation prevails with regard to *sal* leaf plates.
5. Landlessness is a serious problem for the poor and the marginalized and it is even precarious for tribal communities of India. For related literature, *see* Ambagudia (2010), Reddy and Reddy (2007), Rao *et al.* (2007), Purushothaman (2006), Sharan (2005), Rao (2003), Gaiha and Kulkarni (2002), Sharma (2001), Dalvi and Bokil (2000), Karuppaiyan (2000), Patel (1998) and Haimendorf (1982).
6. Livelihoods of tribal communities are receiving increased attention among academicians and scholars. For instance, *see* Suykens (2011), Agnihotri and Mazumdar (2009), Gardner (2009), Meher (2009), Sahu (2008), Arya (2007), Rao *et al.* (2007), Kasi (2007), Prasad and Kasi (2007), Federici (2004), Phansalkar and Verma (2004), Xaxa (2004), Krishna (2003), Krishna (2001), Ramdas *et al.* (2001) Singh (2001), Sudarshan (2001), and Thamizoli (2001).
7. The BDO and the researcher visited the village to speak to Lodha families about the failed misadventure of land purchase many years back. We were almost escorted, from the village entry point, by some non-tribal villagers. With great difficulty, we could get detached from them! The innocent and gullible Lodha people are constantly shadowed (or

overshadowed!) by other well-wisher non-tribal neighbours from dawn to dusk!

8. The researcher, however, hold a different view from that of what P.K.Bhowmick expressed repeatedly in his study, *Primitive Tribal Groups in Eastern India.* Bhowmick often refers to the 'siphoning off money' by Panchayats and officials, which is meant for the tribal people. My view after working in the system for many years is that the problem is more of non-participation and non-involvement of tribal people in the development process because of the top-down approach to development, whereas what is needed is "development for the people, by the people and of the people." When people own the plans and programmes, implementation will be better.
9. *Mahatas* are mostly agriculturists. They are found in reasonable numbers in West Midnapore villages. The researcher met many of them who felt they deserved to be identified as Scheduled Tribe. Those belonging to *Kurmi* caste among the *Mahatas* are recognized as Other Backward Class (OBC).
10. When one drives through Jhargram, Garbeta and Salboni areas, one picture is constant: a stream of women and girls carrying head loads of firewood. If ever one tries to lift the bundle, even out of sheer curiosity, as the researcher tried to do on several occasions, the chances of success are limited. It is sad that these women have to go miles after miles to collect firewood and sell it to earn living. No woman or girl will be wearing footwear; and every one of them is thinly built. The picture will be repeating endlessly. One wonders when the scenario will change for these people.
11. SHG movement became very popular among the rural and tribal people of India in post 2000 era. For instance, *see* Tagore (2011), Thomas *et al.* (2010), Ghosh (2009), Kasi (2009), Rao (2007), Vasimalai and Narender (2007), Dasgupta (2005), Kannabiran (2005), Kalpana (2005), Varman (2005), Harper *et al.* (2005), Galab and Rao (2003), Vatta (2003), Gaiha and Kulkarni (2002), and Mishra (1999) .
12. Kalpana Mallik is referring to the comparatively well off families of the village from whom they take loans for survival.
13. For detailed analysis on women's malnutrition in India, *see* Bisai *et al.* (2008), Jose and Navaneetham (2008). For related literature on malnutrition or undernutrition and diseases in tribal societies, *see* Chowdhury *et al.* (2008), Jena (2008), Sethuraman and Duvvury (2007), Ghosh (2006), Mane (2006), Alderman (2005), Rao *et al.* (2006), Rao *et al.* (2005), Radhakrishna *et al.* (2004), Rana and Johnson (2002), Baru and Sadhana (2000), and Prasad (2000).

14. *Lodha Sabar Kalyan Samiti* is an organization working for betterment of Lodha community and acts as a pressure group to highlight their problems and seek remedy. Many eminent persons are associated with the organization; most notable among them is Mahasweta Devi, renowned writer.
15. In a society, where educated children are rare to find so far, two Lodha boys who completed B.A., used to meet the researcher seeking guidance for job opportunities. Though Lodhas belong to PTG, they have to compete for Government jobs in the quota fixed for the Scheduled Tribes. This puts them at a disadvantage *vis-à-vis* other more progressive tribal groups. One could arrange books and admissions in computer courses at Midnapore for needy students of Lodha community pursuing college studies. However, the need is for sustainable long-term solutions.
16. The researcher came across many Lodha people collecting these cocoons across the forest areas. The researcher could spot suddenly a person sitting on top of an *Arjun* tree. In most of the times, the person happened to be a Lodha. Frail and with hardly any clothes on his body, he gives a picture of an altogether different world.
17. Sundaram (2005) in his paper examined the criteria of backwardness among the different social groups in India. For related studies and information, *see* Makwana and Pais (2011), Barua (2010), Seth (2009), Kathuria and Khan (2007), Pai *et al.*, (2005), Stewart (2005), Gudavarthy (2004), Jodhka (2002), Baru (2002), Dahiwale (2000), and Srinivasan and Kumar (1999).
18. The researcher must admit here, with humility and honesty, that people considered him their well-wisher and this trust and confidence of people provided the additional strength and courage so that the researcher could suggest workable ideas and make requests on behalf of the people.
19. NREGA was renamed as MGNREGA on 2nd October, 2009, in honour of Mahatma Gandhi.
20. Electronic and print media of the country prominently carried the news of reported starvation deaths in Amlasole village for a considerable period. The focus remained on the village with prominent political leaders and Government officials making series of visits to this otherwise 'anonymous' village, inhabited by Lodha people. Typically, such villages can be found across regions and districts. The social and economic indicators mirror the living conditions of the village and people. Consequent to this incident and adverse publicity it generated, the West Bengal State Government directed the District Magistrates of all districts to identify livelihood problems of such underdeveloped villages. The information was to be drawn from the Census 2001 data.

21. Sunder (2006) paper looked at the sociological and empirical intricacies involved in the rise and spread of Maoism in Bastar region.
22. Rao *et al.* (2006), paper critically examined the impact of developmental interventions in the Scheduled Areas with special focus on Andhra Pradesh. For related sources and analysis *see* Chavan (2008), Ray (2008), Ramesh (2007), Jakimow and Kilby (2006), Galab and Rao (2003), Rao (2003), Karuppaiyan (2000), and Mishra (1999).

7

Tribal Health[1] : Tradition and Modernity[2]

The Santals and Lodhas of Bonpatna and many other villages believe in *ojha, gunin* and priest. Though they avail modern medicines and treatment, they also believe in treatment using medicinal herbs. In case of different ailments of women, they prefer traditional methods for their treatment. If children suffer from measles or chicken pox, many worship *Ma Sitala,* the goddess, for relief and cure. They believe in the rituals and methods followed by the local priest.

Their beliefs and concepts have changed over a period. However, many still believe in witch, ghost and evil influence. If a child cries continuously, they think it is due to evil influence. In such cases, they visit the *ojha* or *gunin* for help and they believe they get good results. In present times, their perception about *ojha* or *gunin* has undergone change. Less people tend to believe in their powers. Consequently, their number is also dwindling steadily. The researcher met Jhapat Singh, a *gunin*, aged about 45 years at Bonpatna village. People go to him in times of need.

Now-a-days, Lodha and Santal people consult a doctor in times of fever or other ailments. However, if the medicine fails to improve the condition, they take the help of the *ojha,* who provides charms like *maduli* and *tabij.* He also performs other magical activities like *jharfuk*[3]. Nevertheless, the medicine is also continued simultaneously. However, it is rare that, in present days, anybody relies completely on the *ojha*. Most of the people take the patient to the hospital in case of snakebite. It is not infrequent that a snakebite patient is first taken to the *ojha*. When there is no result and the patient's condition starts deteriorating, he is taken to the hospital. In some cases, it is observed that patients even die because of the inordinate delay in treatment.

During the period of pregnancy, Lodha women are not allowed to go for agricultural works or fuel collection from the forest when they reach ninth month of pregnancy. They are not allowed taking fish that are caught by *pata,* a bamboo made instrument to catch fish, and *tanga,* a kind of fish wheel. It is so because there is a belief that if the expecting women eat fish caught by *tanga* and *pata*, their newborns will suffer from tetanus and epilepsy. They also have a superstition that if the newborns are given onion, they will not develop clear eyesight. Otherwise, there is no taboo regarding consumption of any other type of food, unless they are suffering from any physical problem.

About fifteen years back, Budhi Bhakta (19), wife of Gurupada Bhakta belonging to the Lodha community of Bonpatna village, died while giving birth to a child. After six or seven hours, the newborn also died. After that incident, for next fifteen years, no woman died during childbirth. In most of the Lodha houses, women deliver children in their homes. If need arises, they are taken to the hospital. Women in the neighbourhood and the *dais* (experienced, elderly women of village) take care of the expectant mothers. During the study, the researcher observed that the average family size of tribal population is decreasing due to improved education and health awareness, as is the case with other non-tribal population. In Bonpatna village, many tribal married couples are taking recourse to family welfare measures after two or three children.

As they use potable water, incidents of stomach ailments have come down. Consulting professional doctors and taking medicines have become the rule than exception in Bonpatna village. This could be because of proximity to Kharagpur town and urban influence. Earlier in this village, the life expectancy of a Lodha person used to be around fifty-five years. Now-a-days, many live beyond 65 years. The researcher met Ram Mallick, Bhupati Mallick, Sushila Kotal and Sarada Kotal who are past seventy years.

Bishnupriya of Birsa Lodha village has a two years old son and a two months old daughter. She does not want a third child. The first child was born in hospital. As a prevailing custom, she was staying with her parents before childbirth. The second one was born at home, as the vehicle got delayed in coming. Most of the parents go for family planning operation after two or three children. Large families were common in earlier generation. Elderly persons could not tell their age in years. One of them said, by way of gesticulating, he was three feet tall when the severe cyclone hit the area in the Bengali year, long ago.

In one such incidents, a dog bit an eighteen years old boy. He was shown to the *gunin* or priest. Situation became worse after a few days and he was taken to the Midnapore hospital. The boy died in the end. They believe that many people were cured by the *ojha* for snakebite. He applies paste and extracts from selected herbs at the affected place. The *ojha* has learnt the treatment from his ancestors. One of the villagers feels that modern medicine is also made from traditional knowledge and medicinal plants for preparation of drugs for many diseases.

A tribal youth from a forest village of Salboni Block was admitted, during the course of the research, in the Midnapore district hospital for treatment of snakebite after long delay. He was taken to the local *ojha* and situation only became worse. Unfortunately, response of the hospital was also slow causing further delay. The doctor had already concluded that the patient would die. He advised the patient's relatives to take him to a big and well equipped hospital in Kolkata as he needed dialysis and there was no such facility in Midnapore. The patient's relatives had to run from pillar to post to arrange for rupees one thousand to pay for the ambulance service to take the patient to Kolkata. They almost lost three hours in the process. The hospital authorities will not attend the patient unless the fee is deposited in advance as per their norms. The researcher got a call around midnight from an onlooker explaining the situation. He requested the Superintendent of the Hospital over phone to get the patient transferred to the hospital by an ambulance immediately. To everyone's relief and joy, the person survived after treatment in Kolkata.

The incident highlights many issues:

- tribal people tend to believe in superstitions and traditional methods even in cases when scientific treatment is the need of the hour;

- the response of the government hospitals, at times, tends to be callous and irresponsible to the people's needs;
- lack of sensitization among the government set-up to the needs of the poor, particularly tribal people; and
- blind application of rules without solving the problem when a human being is dying before one's eyes.

Diseases[4] : Malaria and Leprosy

The remote villages in Jhargram sub-division are proclaimed endemic zones for malaria disease. Together with the adjoining forest areas of Jharkhand and Orissa States, the areas present a challenge to the health officials in eradication of malaria. People, mostly belonging to tribal communities, suffer from both normal malaria fever and the more deadly version of malignant malaria or cerebral malaria. People suffer endlessly, as the health facilities are grossly inadequate to meet the challenge. The preventive measures planned to check malaria are hardly implemented and without much impact. The patients become weak and bed ridden. The hospitals and health sub-centres, which are not, in any case, in the reach of many remote villagers, are full of such patients. Those who cannot afford to go long distances to reach the Government facilities, depend upon local quacks. They have to spend considerable money either way. Some patients even die of lack of adequate and timely treatment.

Incidence of leprosy is one of the highest in these areas and tribal people cannot be outside such huge number of affected people. Belpahari, Jamboni, Keshiary in West Midnapore district figure prominently in leprosy prevalence. These areas have sizeable tribal population. Lack of awareness and social stigma inhibits these people from seeking timely treatment. The health department, supported by the Central Government, has been conducting detection and treatment programmes regularly, as part of leprosy eradication campaign. As a result, many new patients get detected and are given treatment to come out of the disease.

Immunization[5], Mother and Childcare : Or Lack of these

Lack of adequate facilities and inaccessibility also adversely affect ensuring that all children are vaccinated timely. As more than half of childbirths take place at home, there is always the risk of maternal and infant mortality. Awareness has definitely grown over the years and coverage of immunization has gone up in these areas. The problem, however, is quality of such immunization. The entire immunization cycle needs to be completed and vaccines need to be given in time. Many pregnant mothers also do not get the facility of regular check ups by the doctors and health workers. It is safe to conclude that immunization coverage of mother and child tends to be weak in case of home deliveries. In absence of proper medical advice, they tend to depend upon elders and local quacks for help. Superstitions also play adverse role in proper handling of pregnant mothers and infants.

Initiatives and Innovations in spreading Health Facilities

During extensive visits, the researcher got an opportunity to know and understand the sufferings of the villagers due to lack of health amenities. The district administration planned and organized several mobile health camps with the help of health officials. Doctors attended to patients and provided medicines to various ailments. Common problems were malaria, fever, stomach disorders, skin infection and some cases of leprosy.[6]

The district administration started mobile health units to cover the remote areas, which are not served by the regular health facilities. The doctor and his assistants go around the villages as per pre-announced routine. They also distribute essential medicines to the patients. The exercise was started by the administration from November 2001. It was of immense use to the people of the areas it served. The problem is that the effort may not be just enough to reach all the needy people of these areas. It is again a paradox that the formal set up cannot fulfil the needs and gaps in the working though it is aware of the problem. Sheer bureaucratic systems and lack of initiative sometimes come in the way of rising to the occasion.

During one of the visits as District Magistrate to Parasia Lodha village of Nayagram Block, the researcher was discussing local people's livelihood issues. As discussions were on, women stood nearby, curiously looking at the proceedings. The dress of many women and that of the children in their arms as well as those holding onto their mothers reflected the poor economic condition of the village. One could also see an old woman sitting in front of a house nearby virtually remaining unmoved. To the enquiry, the villagers told that her eyesight was not good probably because of cataract. There were many such elderly persons in the village of about hundred families. There is an eye hospital in Baripada, in adjoining Orissa State, which is located about forty kilometres from the village. The Government hospitals in Midnapore and Jhargram are comparatively far off. Some people get their eyes tested and operated in the Baripada hospital. These villagers of Parasia could not afford any such dream. A week later, we could organize an eye check-up camp in that remote forest village with the help of an NGO of Midnapore district. Almost all in the village — children, young and old people — got their eyes tested! Thirty-five persons belonging to Lodha community were detected with cataract after screening done at the village. The patients were taken by a small bus and were operated upon in the NGO's eye clinic at Daspur of the district. A few days later, again on a visit to the area, the researcher was touched by an incident. The less confident and almost blind elderly woman came as if she was running! She caught the researcher's hand firmly and started leading towards their house. The family members said that she had been very active ever since she got back her vision after the operation. She would look at every person coming to her house and escort him or her! The elderly woman got new vision in her life. Now, she does not feel burden for herself and others.

Voluntary Health Workers : Self Help is Better

The district administration started another initiative in the form of voluntary health workers in the month of August 2003 in selected areas of the district, including tribal inhabited Gram Panchayats of Baspahari and Kakrajhar near Belpahari[7]. Nearly fifty women from these villages were trained in preventive health care and treatment of commonly occurring diseases in the areas. They were also given medical kits containing essential medicines to supply to the people. One such volunteer served each village of about one hundred families. No Government remuneration was announced, as it might degenerate into another typical government programme. The health workers became extremely popular in the villages; they almost were treated like doctors in these remote areas where treatment was a distant dream. The volunteers also got highly motivated and spurred to help the villagers. The new assignment brought them immense status and respect in their villages. There was regular supply of medicines to these workers as the stock got over quickly.

Arati Pramanik (23) of Bonpatna village has been trained as Voluntary Health Worker. She was given training in first aid and day-to-day health problem management. She was provided a medical kit with essential medicines. Her services were found extremely useful to the Lodha people. She is the doctor at hand. They need not run here and there for small health problems. Their expenditure on the treatment has also come down considerably. There are twenty-five such health workers in Khelar GP and about thousand in West Midnapore district. This is a significant initiative of the district administration to provide community managed low cost health solutions and strengthening preventive health framework in villages to reduce disease burden and consequent difficulties faced by the villagers. It is heartening to note that the idea of voluntary health workers of West Midnapore found acceptance and became a policy option in the form of ASHA under the National Rural Health Mission.

CASE STUDY 7.1

Experiences and Achievements of a Tribal Voluntary Health Worker

Malathi Hembram is from Amkopa village. She is the group leader of Pandit Raghunath Murmu Self-Help Group. She studied up to Class VIII. There are 92 families in Amkopa, which is predominantly a tribal village. Total population is 312 (men 151, women 161). The villagers are dependent on agriculture. There are many small farmers and day labourers. Literate persons are less in number among tribal population. Sanitation facilities and safe drinking water were not adequately available. The surroundings were unclean and not healthy. Consequently, they were suffering from various diseases. Many tribal people still believe in prayers and exorcise. After joining as a health worker, Malathi made efforts to make them health conscious though she knew that it would take time. At first, they ignored her due to their superstitions. People used to go to local religious priests for their treatment. She visited every house of the village. She tried to mingle with them, explaining to them that she was a *swasthya sahayika* (voluntary health worker) and she could help them to address their routine health problems by giving medicines and advice. As time passed by, they were very pleased and started thinking as if a doctor had come to their doorstep. She told them that they could save themselves from many diseases by undertaking simple but effective preventive measures. She arranged for vaccination of pregnant mothers and children. She advised the women to adopt family planning and she noticed good results.

She talked them about superstitions that concern health issues. She explained to them the harm if there is delay in treatment or improper treatment was given. She advised them to contact the hospital or health centre for their treatment. One villager, Suren Murmu was suffering from fever for a long time. They did not admit him in any hospital. They depended on a priest and the patient nearly died. She arranged to admit him in the hospital. He was suffering from cerebral malaria. Hospital authority took care of him and he recovered soon. After this incident, the villagers' confidence in her had gone up and their attitude became very cordial towards her. Ten families of the village decided to build latrines in their homes. She always told them to wash their hands with soap after going to toilet and to use footwear to prevent worm infection. She disinfected water sources by adding bleaching powder. She kept close watch on pregnant mothers and told them to get admitted in hospital at the time of delivery. She took initiative so that every child took part in pulse polio and vaccination programme. She along with four other women opted for operation at a family welfare camp at Garbeta Rural Health Centre. She takes her duties sincerely and does her best in spite of many limitations. She thinks she needs more training, help and cooperation from health officials, Panchayat representatives and district administration. In her opinion, to improve the health status of the villagers, these are necessary:

— Improve the condition of health sub-centre and provide medicines to them;
— Assistance to build latrines;
— Arrangement of vehicle for admission of pregnant mothers at hospital or health sub-centre;
— Safe drinking water;
— Vaccination programme for pregnant mothers and children; and
— Arrangement for periodic visit of an M.B.B.S. doctor to health sub-centre.

Positive Impact of Sanitation and Hygiene on Health of Tribal People

Traditionally, rural India is not known for having toilets in houses and open defecation is the only option for majority of the people (around 70%) in the country[8]. Bonpatna is no exception but things are changing fast. As Midnapore district has been pioneering rural sanitation in the entire country, it is naturally expected that the initiative reaches every village of the district including Bonpatna. Whenever the researcher asked them, women members of both Santal and Lodha families were unanimous that sanitation was one of the basic requirements for all of them and the only issue was affordability. As innovative low cost designs have been popularized in the district, that problem is also mostly taken care of. As Jharna Paramanik says, "It is a nightmare for us, particularly for ladies, to go out for attending the nature's call everyday. For elderly and sick persons, it is even worse. Then, there is rainy season and night time." After talking to many tribal housewives, it proved to be a gross misconception that tribal people do not need 'formal' sanitation facilities in homes. This wrong notion feeds on the idea that they live near forest areas where space is no problem, compared to an urban or semi-urban habitation with dense population. The problems are same for an elite house wife or one belonging to a tribal family. The families happily accepted the administrative and Panchayat's proposal to have sanitation facilities installed in their houses. There are various models available and the cheapest model costs Rs. 375 without the superstructure. If the family belongs to Below Poverty Line (BPL) category, they get Rs. 200 as subsidy from the Government. Along with toilets, change in hygiene behaviour is seen, with people using soap or soil to wash their hands after using the toilet. All these have resulted in significant reduction in diarrhoeal diseases in the village. Children have less health problems after the installation of the toilets. Table 7.1 shows the response of Santal and Lodha respondents regarding availability of toilets at home on one hand and lack of adequate health facilities on the other. This perceptible change has come about in about six months after their adopting improved hygiene practices, including use of toilets. It is a matter of great satisfaction for the researcher, the District Magistrate, that the district of Midnapore became a role model

Table 7.1: Ethnic Group-wise Health Status of Respondents

[N = 172]

Ethnic Group	*Toilet facility at home*	*Spending over 30 per cent income on health problems*	*Child birth at home*
Santal*	74 (100%) ***	54 (72%)	90% ****
Lodha**	98 (100%) ***	79 (81%)	85% ****

* Santal: 74.
**Lodha: 98.
*** Due to successful Total Sanitation Campaign, entire Khelar Gram Panchayat achieved 100 per cent coverage of sanitation facilities.
**** Main reason for such low institutional delivery is no facility at Khelar PHC.

for the entire country in rural sanitation. The success has been well documented by the Government of India and UNICEF as replicable models for the country. The district used to be frequently visited by various State Government representatives to study the success story. Photograph 7.1 epitomises the remarkable progress in achieving total sanitation in hundreds of villages in West Midnapore. In this picture, a Santal woman is seen at the improvised sanitation facility in her home.

NOTES

1. For further discussions on tribal health, *see* Acharya and McNamee (2009), Dhargupta *et al.*, (2009), Karlsson (2009), Hardiman and Raje (2008), Jena (2008), Hardiman (2007), Rani *et al.* (2007), Barnes (2007), Reddi *et al.* (2006), Prakash (2005), Maharatna and Chikte (2004), Rao (2003), Rana and Johnson (2002), Tiwari *et al.* (2001), Basu (1996), Ray and Basu (1996), and Sharma (1970).
2. Tradition and modernity is a never ending theme in the readings of anthropology and sociology. For related references, *see* Rodrigues (2011), Vajpeyi (2009), Ghosal (2006), Heredia (1999), and Skaria (1999).
3. *Maduli* or *tabij* is a piece of copper tied to the body of a person with a thread to ward off evil forces and ill health. It is tied normally to the wrist, neck, or waist. *Jharfuk* is chanting and rituals done to rid a person from the influence of ghost or any external evil force.

4. Bhattacharya's (2008) paper gives details on diseases in South Asian societies. Also, *see* Bhate and Acharya (2005) for related information on social medicine.
5. In their impressive essay '*Communicating Immunisation*', Singh and Bharadwaj (2000) have systematically analysed communicating mechanisms of immunization, particularly in the context of tradition and modernity. Also, *see* Patra (2008), Addlakha (2000), and Das and Dasgupta (2000) for further related sources.
6. The seriousness of the shortage of medical facilities can be understood from one statement of the MLA of Binpur, Mr. Sambhunath Mandi: *Ajke era jibone protham bar doctor ke dekheche!*" (These people saw doctor for the first time in their lives!)
7. The initiative is a result of an interesting incident. During the visit to Amkopa Gram Panchayat under Garhbeta-I block, villagers at a work site narrated how the existing three health sub-centres were inadequate to cater to the needs of forty villages of the Gram Panchayat. They were requesting that the number of sub-centres should be increased. During the interaction that day, the idea of voluntary health workers was born. The researcher told them, to their initial disbelief, that they would have health workers in each of their villages!
8. For more analysis and information on the issue, *see* George (2009), Purohit and Purohit (2009), Abraham & Kavi Kumar (2008), Mehrotra and Patnaik (2008), Gupta and Pal (2008), Ramanna (2004), Devaranjan and Shah (2004), and Bose (2000).

8
State Interventions and Resultant Changes

Tribal Development[1] : Existing Strategy of the Government

The Tribal Sub-Plan strategy, adopted at the beginning of the Fifth Five Year Plan, seeks to ensure adequate flow of funds for tribal development from the State Plan allocations, schemes and programmes of Central Ministries and Departments, besides financial and developmental institutions, in proportion to their population. The Ministry of Tribal Affairs is also implementing several schemes and programmes for the benefit of the STs.

Special Assistance

Special Central assistance is given to the States and Union Territories (UTs) to supplement their efforts in tribal development through the Tribal Sub-Plan, meant for family-oriented income generating schemes in various sectors. Grants are also given to States/UTs under the first proviso to article 275 (1) of the Constitution to meet the costs of projects for tribal development and for raising the level of administration of Scheduled Area therein at par with the rest of the State/UT. A part of the funds is utilized for setting up of residential schools to provide quality education to the tribal students.

Particularly Vulnerable Tribal Groups (PVTGs)

Based on the pre-agricultural level of technology, low level of literacy, declining or stagnant population, 75 tribal communities in 17

States/UTs have been identified and categorized as Particularly Vulnerable Tribal Groups[2]. A new Central sector scheme has been introduced for an all-round development of these groups from 1998-99 under which financial assistance is made available to the Integrated Tribal Development Projects (ITDP) , Tribal Research Institutes (TRIs) and Non Governmental Organisations (NGOs) for undertaking projects and activities not covered by any of the existing schemes.

Fourteen Tribal Research Institutes (TRIs) have been set up in different States. They are engaged in providing planning inputs to the State governments, conducting research and evaluation studies, collection of data, codification of customary laws and the conduct of training, seminars and workshops. Some of these Institutes are also having museums exhibiting tribal artifacts.

A scheme for tribal girls' hostel was started in the Third Five Year Plan with the aim of providing residential facilities to them while pursuing education. The Centre provides assistance to the tune of 50 per cent cost of construction to the States, and cent per cent to the Union Territories under the scheme. The boys' hostel scheme was started in 1989-90 under the same pattern as the girls' hostels. Photograph 8.1 is a visual of a room in a girl's hostel at Belpahari.

The Central sector vocational training scheme for tribal areas, introduced in 1992-93, aims at developing the skills of the tribal youth for providing them employment or self-employment opportunities by setting up of Vocational Training Centres (VTCs).

Cooperatives

The Tribal Cooperative Marketing Development Federation of India (TRIFED) was set up by the Centre in 1987 with the prime objective of providing marketing assistance and remunerative prices to the STs for their minor forest and surplus agricultural produce and to wean them away from exploitative private traders and middlemen.

A Central sector scheme of grain banks in tribal villages was launched in 1996-97. The scheme provides for food security to prevent starvation in remote and backward tribal areas. Funds are channelised through the Tribal Cooperative Marketing Development Federation of India (TRIFED). So far, 534 Grain Banks have been set up in the country till 2001.

The Ministry gives grant-in-aid to voluntary organisations working for the welfare of the scheduled tribes for projects like residential schools, hostels, medical units, computer training units, shorthand and typing training units, balwadis/ creches, libraries and audio-visual units.

Scholarships

Students of Scheduled Castes (SCs) and Scheduled Tribes (STs) get financial assistance for pursuing recognized post-matriculation courses including professional, technical as well as non-professional and non-technical courses at various levels, correspondence courses and distance education. The scheme is implemented by the State governments, which receive full financial assistance from the Government of India. Photograph 8.2 shows some girls belonging to Santal tribe in a classroom at Jhargram. The dress pattern of tribal girls at Belpahari School is shown in Photograph 8.3 can be compared with that of any other girls.

The Ministry of Tribal Affairs provides National Overseas Scholarship for higher studies abroad, book banks, coaching and upgradation of merit for the benefit of ST students. The purpose of these efforts has been to improve social and economic condition of the Scheduled Tribes.

Interventions and Resultant Changes

Land Distribution

Throughout the State of West Bengal, nearly two lakh landless people belonging to Scheduled Tribes (ST) have been given *pattas* or ownership rights of Government land.

Provision of Funds in the District Plan

In addition to funds provided under the heads of backward classes welfare department and W.B.S.T. and S.C. Development and Finance Corporation, various rural development programmes provide scope for welfare of tribal people through components, known as individual beneficiaries' schemes. These include schemes like Swarnajayanti Gramswarojgar Yojana and Indira Awas Yojana.

Table 8.1 provides information on assistance planned by Government to students belonging to tribal communities in the district of West Midnapore in the year 2010-2011. Tables 8.1 and 8.2 also provide benefits planned for development of Scheduled Tribes in the district by the Government:[3]

Table 8.1: Government Assistance for Welfare of STs in 2010-2011 in West Midnapore District
Name of the Department: Backward Classes Welfare, Paschim Medinipur

(Rs. in lakh)

Sl. No.	Proposed Schemes for the year 2010-11	Amount provided by Government		Bank credit
		2009-10	2010-11	2010-11
1.	Merit Scholarship S.C. / S.T. IX-X & XI –XII	5.28	5.28	
2.	Special Merit Grant for S.C. / S.T. Girls	3.69	3.69	
3.	Maintenance of Ashram Hostel S.C. / S.T.	132.00	162.00	
3.	Book Grant to S.T.	150.00	165.00	
4.	Hostel Charges to S.T.	804.00	804.00	
5.	Maintenance Charges to S.T.	200.00	220.00	
6.	Compulsory Charges to S.T.	12.51	12.70	
7.	Post Matric Scholarship to S.T.	264.25	265.00	
8.	Lodha Development	771.78	850.00	
9.	Community Development S.C.A. to S.C.P.	30.00	45.00	
10.	Community Development S.C.A. to T.S.P.	211.71	350.00	
11.	1st Proviso Article 275/1	402.44	500.00	
12.	Training facility to SC & ST	0.57	0.57	
13.	Vocational Training Centre	17.00	17.00	
14.	Hul Festival	1.00	1.25	
15.	Old age pension for S.T.	2269.83	2790.90	
16.	One Act Drama	3.00	3.00	
17.	Feeder School	23.75	25.00	
18.	JBY for PTGs	0.00	2.68	

Education

1. Grants for purchase of books, hostel charges, maintenance charge for the scholars, special merit scholarships for tribal girls and additional assistance to the meritorious students.
2. Nearly two lakh ST students are getting book grants
3. Twenty eight thousand ST students are provided hostel charges for pursuing studies staying in hostels.

4. Maintenance charges for one lakh twenty nine thousand ST students who pursue secondary education from home.
5. Two hundred sixty Ashram Hostels for ST children studying in primary and high schools.
6. Post-School final scholarships for various courses for thirteen thousand students.
7. Vocational Training Centres to train youth in various trades.
8. Pre-examination training centres for recruitment to various services.

Table 8.2: District Annual Plan [2010-11]: West Bengal SC and ST Development and Finance Corporation

(*Rs. in lakh*)

Sl. No.	*Proposed schemes for the year 2010-11*	*Amount provided by Government*		*Bank Credit*
		2009-10	*2010-11*	*2010-11*
1.	SCA to SCP	223.52	251.46	480.06
2.	SCA to TSP	404.70	404.70	
3.	N.S.T.F.D.C.	31.50	31.50	
4.	A.M.S.Y. (for ST Women)	86.00	87.60	
5.	M.K.Y.	0.00	10.00	

How are the Development Programmes being implemented ?

Self-employment Programmes : The Right Intent

Self-employment schemes[4] are in operation for many years. It is observed that the names of these poverty alleviation programmes keep changing often though the contents remain nearly same. Under these schemes, selected families are provided bank loan and subsidy for taking up income generating activities. There is an element of margin money also in the project cost, which is provided by the Government on the premise that the poor tribal family cannot afford to arrange it. The objective is that tribal families will benefit from Mid-Term lending programme under Tribal Sub-Plan. This is popularly known as MT loan in the district. In a district like Midnapore (West), the 'target' is to assist around 7,000 tribal families in a year.

Problems observed in Actual Implementation

- The projects are selected from the shelf of "model projects" without paying attention to the physical condition of the village, the interest and capabilities of the target family. The person is not treated as a dynamic individual with own opinions and preferences. 'Others' do the selection of the project for him with sheer apathy and detachment. The marketing part of the product is also not given proper thought. As a result, the project is less likely to succeed. This is like trying to put a square peg into a round hole. The major 'offenders' here are the official at the Block level, local Panchayat representatives and, at times, the bank manager.

- The bank does not finance the full project cost; only the subsidy portion is released and the bank loan portion is shown as disbursed but put into a savings account in the name of the borrower. As a result, the project, whatever be its merit, suffers from the day one for lack of fund.
- There is delay at every level; the Panchayats and the Block sponsor current year's cases at the end of financial year in the months of February and March. This is partly due to pressure on achieving targets. As there is hurry in the process, one finds lack of proper scrutiny and application of mind in selection of the target family and scheme. Because of the same financial year pressure, the bank normally does not even touch the applications. The bankers are generally a busy lot in March. They will only take up the cases in May and afterwards. There are rejections and queries in the process. By the time he sanctions, the subsidy is released and the disbursement is made, three to four more months will be gone. There is often delay in receiving subsidy from the Government at the district level. As the Chairman of the District Consultative Committee of Bankers at the district level, one had these painful experiences while monitoring and pursuing these schemes with bankers and officials.

Are the Desired Results achieved ?

As a result of bureaucratic and flawed handling, starting from wrong selection of family and economic activity and subsequent delay at the offices and banks, the project is less likely to succeed on many occasions. As a consequence of wrong selection of the project and/or inadequate loan amount sanctioned, the project 'withers away', leaving the family with the loan burden. At the end of story, we have tribal and poor families becoming defaulters of bank loans for no fault of their own. History of implementation of these programmes is full of many such examples everywhere in the country. This experience matches with the following observation of the Planning Commission:

> The strategy of TSP, as is implemented, has also become very much routinized. Thus, its impact on improving the conditions of STs is not being felt.
> (Planning Commission, 2001: *Indian Planning Experience: A Statistical Profile*)

This is the scenario from the days of the proverbial IRDP and its descendant schemes of the new millennium. One always comes across so many poor families in the villages, having the tag of defaulter tied around their necks. Their fathers and fore-fathers might have taken such unintelligent loans, only to default in repayments later. The bank religiously treats the family head, his or her sons and dependents as defaulters. They will not be sanctioned any loan unless the old dues are cleared.

We find many tribal women asking,

> "*Amra kono bhool kori nai, to amaderke saja deva hoche keno? Hote pare, amaar sashur loan niyechen kudi bochor aage. Ekhun uni nai. Bank bolche ota shodh na hole notun loan ekhun deva jabe na*."
> "Why are we being victimized for no fault of ours? My father-in-law might have been given a loan twenty years back, but he is no more and the bank says it needs to be cleared before fresh loan is granted now."

As Robert Chambers rightly observed

> Ignorant and stupid poor people are often the creation of ignorant and stupid outsiders...The evidence speaks for

itself. Again and again, observers have remarked on the toughness, application and ingenuity of the poor[5] (Chambers, 1983).

Hostels for Tribal Students: The Neglect Shows

The researcher found one common feature in almost all the hostels of tribal children: their condition is poor, even appalling in many cases. The building, if one may call it, is in bad condition. The problems are plenty. These include roof leakage, broken toilets, insufficient drinking water facilities and general poor condition of buildings. There is neglect and apathy on the part of the school authorities, 'tribal welfare' officials and local elected representatives. There is always shift in responsibility when it comes to improving hostel conditions. The school authorities feel it is the Government's responsibility. The Government, despite best intentions, cannot provide enough funds to all the schools and hostels. For the local Panchayat, there are 'other priorities' which always take precedence. There is a general feeling among them that the main responsibility rests with the line department dealing with backward class welfare. The irony is that one finds a large expansive school building built at a huge cost and adjoining it, one finds the pitiable hostel. Table 8.3 indicates the dissatisfaction of student respondents belonging to Santal and Lodha communities about hostel facilities and irregular payment of scholarship.

Table 8.3: Ethnic Group-wise Responses of Student Respondents

Ethnic Group	*Timely payment of scholarship*	*Satisfaction about hostel facilities*
Santal*	25: No (65.8%)	22: No (57.9%)
Lodha**	21: No (77.8%)	18: No (66.7%)
Total	**46: No (70.8%)**	**40: No (61.6%)**

*Santal: 38. **Lodha: 27.

In a school in Nayagram Block, the researcher was shown the hostel building by the headmaster and the teachers. The condition needs no description. It is unfit for human residence. The structure may fall any time, by teachers' own admission. When asked why they can't improve the hostel a bit, pat comes the reply: the Government never provides any assistance despite many requests. One persists, saying that if they could construct such a palatial school building, they could also do something to this hostel along with it, as same children will be staying here. One also suggested that they could give two or three rooms from the school building for hostel purpose, as children spend sixteen hours there compared to school where the time spent is only half of that. All these suggestions yield little; one gets another petition at the end of the day, asking for Government fund.

The story is similar in Kapgari, Ranarani, Khemasuli and many other places. In Ranarani High School, the condition of adjoining hostel for boys and girls was very discouraging. There was no electricity. Snakes were often found inside the rooms during the night; the children slept on the floor, which was fully broken. The girls' hostel windows had no doors. A grown up person could enter from outside creating serious security risk. In all these hostels, children from far-flung areas and adjoining districts used to come and stay for studies. There was only one well for drinking water and other purposes, which was insufficient. The accommodation itself was insufficient with children staying in overcrowded conditions.

Interventions Consequent to Field Visits

These scenes shook the researcher conscience as an administrator, researcher and above all, as a human being. The researcher discussed these various development needs and gaps with officials and Panchayat representatives at Block and district level and could convince them about the deplorable conditions and, after some time, fund for Kapgari and Ranarani Hostels was released from Paschimanchal Unnayan Parshad. The Ranarani hostel got totally transformed. The headmaster was so inspired and enthused that he almost stayed day and night in the school till the works were completed. It was insisted that the community, including the guardians of children, should contribute for the improvement in the conditions. This was necessary to make it participatory and increase involvement of the community. A generator was provided for better study environment, as electricity connection was uncertain to reach the village in near future. Another drinking water source was established. Additional rooms were built for children. The floor and the windows got repaired. Toilets were added. In short, the entire ambience was changed. There was a social function after the works were completed. The children, teachers and local people were very happy and the researcher also joined them in celebrating the new hope for the institution, neglected so far. It also demonstrated that involvement of local people in managing public institutions is always necessary. These experiences provided the researcher practical examples in participatory development.

The High School at Andharia, about ten kilometres from Jhargram, has majority of students hailing from tribal families. The teachers told the researcher that classrooms were so overcrowded that the children had to be sent out literally once in thirty minutes to breathe fresh air. Otherwise, they may get suffocated. The school authorities pleaded helplessness, as they did not get any grant from the Government. One of the teachers remarked that the school did not get any assistance from any source due to political reasons. Whatever may be the political affiliations, the students deserved a better environment, one thought.

With rupees two lakh assistance from Paschimanchal Unnayan Parshad funds and local contributions, the teachers got additional classrooms constructed. A Class 10 girl, belonging to Santal community, aptly inaugurated the new building.

One is reminded of the following words of Gerald D. Berreman

> . . . . empathy—the ability to put one's self in the place of others, to experience the world as they experience it. Empathy is insurance against narrow complacency, ethnocentrism and sterile scientism. Only through empathetic ability can the scientist hope to understand the phenomenal world of the people he studies, to comprehend their motives, their hopes, joys, and fears, and their reactions to himself . . . He must be liked and trusted as an individual to win the trust and confidence of those with whom he works (Berreman, 1968: 162).

Malnutrition and Hunger[6]

Due to poverty and lack of opportunities arising out of change in tradition mode of living, many Lodha families are among the poorest of the population. Their lack of entrepreneurship and guile to survive in the so-called modern civilized world makes them pawns in the hands of the oppressors who are not very far off from them. Lack of own land and opportunities in other economic activities make them very susceptible to hunger, malnutrition and disease. The children in any remote Lodha village give the onlooker an unhealthy look due to lack of proper food, nutrition and clothing. The pregnant women also do not get proper food needed leaving the mother and prospective child victims of malnutrition. Throughout the year, the families will not get enough food to eat. Their capability to raise loans is limited. If they succeed to get some loan, it will be at horrifying terms and conditions. They have little option but to remain hungry and wait for better days in utter resignation.

In June 2004, the village of Amlasole near Belpahari hit the national headlines, as there were allegedly deaths because of starvation. Despite denials and interpretations that followed the reporting saying that the deaths could have been due to other diseases, almost everyone agreed that the area in question is remote and inaccessible. The area is underdeveloped and devoid of opportunities for the people living there. Consequent to this incident, the Government announced packages for the village and similar other areas of Midnapore (West), Bankura and Purulia districts which have significant tribal population.

Difficult Terrain and Barren Lands

As pointed out on several occasions in the study, the land in many parts of district is hard, rocky and laterite soil. Hence, agiculture is difficult. Suitable irrigation facilities are grossly inadequate though efforts are made by the Government machinery to build check dams, excavate ponds and other water harvesting structures. As the general trend is to go for paddy cultivation irrespective of land conditions and water availability, local people do not get much benefit out of the exercise. Even if paddy is grown near water sources, it is mostly limited to *kharif*. There is immense scope for cultivating fruit crops with appropriate technology and methods. However, such efforts by local people and the Government efforts are sporadic. Added to the topography is general poverty which goes with it due to lack of economic activities. Bank credit is negligible as an average banker is not inclined to give loans to poor farmers and particularly tribal communities. There are issues of lack of trust from the bankers on one hand and lack of knowledge and information among tribal people on the other. The result is virtually lack of any economic activity in many areas. The poor have to look for opportunities to work as agriculture labour in other areas or construction labour.

Efforts were made through existing programmes and through mobilizing tribal people to take up need based water conservation efforts, promoting horticulture and other less water intensive crops like maize, mustard, sesame, blackgram and greengram. Seeds for these crops were distributed among needy tribal families in several areas of the district during 2002 and 2003. There was tremendous enthusiasm among tribal people and they had a good harvest of these crops. This shows both the need and opportunity, which is enormous.

CASE STUDY 8.1

The Mango Plantation of Murari

Strategy Undertaken

In April 1994, the district administration and Midnapore *Zilla Parishad* (ZP) selected dry land horticulture with intensive plantation as a strategy in selected areas of the region. Mango plantation was taken up, as it was not only suitable but also easy for people to appreciate and accept the idea for adoption. As income from mango crop will start only from the fourth year, it was necessary to plan for suitable intercropping like papaya, ginger, turmeric, elephant foot yam, vegetables, etc. This would give immediate income to the farmers and also increase total income from the land.

New Cultivation Methods followed

Traditionally, mango plants are planted at a distance of 30 ft. In an acre of land, only 54 plants can be provided in this method. It has been observed that the density of plants can be increased in dry land horticulture. Distance between two plants has been reduced to 15 ft. As a result, 196 plants can be provided in an acre of land. Additional number of plants results in more income for the farmer. As the landholding is mostly small and marginal, additional income will benefit and enthuse the farmers. The pits also serve as small reservoirs of rainwater and moisture. During summer, farmers themselves dug pits in many cases. Some of them took assistance of labourers. Each pit was one metre long, wide and deep. Dry leaves, compost or cow dung, adequate fertilizer and pesticide were added to the soil.

The farmers with the help of Panchayat collected local mango seeds. These seeds were planted in the pits before rains. In each pit, three mango seeds were planted. The idea behind planting three seeds was that not all of them might germinate. Secondly, the plants have to survive one year before grafting is done. After one year, as the plants grew, *in situ* grafting was done with better quality mango varieties like *Amrapali*, etc. In this method, grafting is done in the field itself. As a result, the root of the local mango variety is retained and better and desired quality variety is grafted on the plant.

Farmers' Motivation

It was initially difficult for the farmers to visualize the dream of reaping mango crop after four-five years. They were hesitant as they had little faith in the utility of the barren land. Repeated meetings with villagers and Panchayat representatives were made explaining the concepts.

The district administration of Midnapore made arrangements for a study tour of representatives of the area to Khammam and Krishna districts of Andhra Pradesh[7]. We visited horticulture plantations in dry land areas and studied the techniques. We also interacted with farmers and officials in those areas.

Video shows were organized in the village explaining the methods of plantation and showing the visit of the representatives to Andhra Pradesh. Easy to understand literature was prepared in Bengali and the farmers were given these leaflets. As a result of these, they could be motivated to take up this project.

As they were mostly *pattadars* (assignees of Government surplus land) and marginal farmers, they themselves worked in their lands and they were paid wages from existing rural development schemes like Employment Assurance Scheme (EAS). Some of them were trained in grafting methods. Two tanks were excavated to preserve rainwater, which will be useful for minimum irrigation in post monsoon period.

Hurdles Faced

It was difficult to protect the plants from cattle, as all farmers could not do fencing as it was found costly. Trenches were cut on the boundary, but cattle still managed to enter the area. Not all of the farmers were equally convinced about the dream being projected to them. Papaya seedlings were planted as inter-crop, but a lot of them could not survive the first year summer heat.

From Dependence to Self-reliance

Initially, the tribal farmers mostly used to give the impression of onlookers. Their wholehearted participation was limited. This was mainly because they were not sure about the benefits of the exercise being undertaken. When asked whether pesticides were sprayed, the reply was that nobody came from Block office and sprayed. It was also the case with weeding and other works, which the plants needed.

It took a lot of time and efforts from the Panchayats and Block officials to motivate them that it was their project and others could only assist them in their efforts. The task became easier as the plants grew well and the area developed greenish colour from the red and dry features. Their involvement and interest grew as time passed. They started realising the potential of the work they were doing. As plants started growing, the farmers got attached to the plants. They started putting fencing and guarding the area by turn.

Sweet Success

As nearly 196 pits of one cubic metre each were cut in one acre, the soil started retaining moisture. As *in situ* grafting was done instead of opting for grafted plants, the plants could withstand the summer heat even without proper irrigation. The barren land slowly started turning green. The farmers also widened and deepened the tanks. They started intercropping of vegetables in the area. From fourth year, the small mango plant started giving fruits and the farmers were thrilled. They started weeding the area more rigorously and spraying pesticides to protect the crop. During fifth, sixth and seventh year, they had a good harvest of mango crop. Today, the area has turned into a beautiful orchard. When one visits places like Murari, one finds very refreshing and proud farmers telling how they have transformed the desert into an orchard.

Positive Impact of Joint Forest Management (JFM) Committees on Tribal Livelihoods

Joint Forest Management[8] is a concept of developing partnerships between fringe forest user groups and the Forest Department (FD) on the basis of mutual trust and jointly defined roles and responsibilities for forest protection and development. In JFM, local communities and the Government manage the resources and share the costs. Arabari experiment in West Midnapore has been the pioneer in JFM and won national and international recognition for participatory forest management and development.

In West Midnapore, there are 1109 registered Forest Protection Committees (FPCs) with a membership of 1,25,521 covering an area of 14,184 hectares. There are three Forest Protection Committees (FPCs) in the Khelar Gram Panchayat. These are Kesuria, Nachana and Gaighata committees. These are generally known by the village name in which the forest is located. Of these, Nachna FPC has sixty-two Santal community members. The Committee recently got rupees one lakh twenty-one thousand from felling of trees. The money was deposited in the bank account of the Committee. This amounted to 25 per cent share of the produce and the remaining 75 per cent would go to the Government. The committee decided that the money would be used for electrification of their village. There is also one SHG, *Sagan Salta*, formed with ten members of Nachna FPC.

JFM is slowly emerging into a form of sustainable forestry with processes for rapid adaptation to changes in what people need, want, and can do. JFM has increased popular understanding about what the forest is about and should be.

As these developments have significant impact on the lives of tribal people who traditionally lived in the forest and fringe areas, an attempt has been made to understand and present the important features of this evolving system of participatory development.

Some of the achievements and evolving features of JFM over the years are:

1. The State did not allow any rights or share for people from forest products like NTFP, timber and other intermediary products in the past, which has, however, changed with JFM.

All NTFP, barring few nationalized products, are now available to the people free of royalty in all States. People have a right to collect even the nationalized products like *kendu* leaves, *sal* seeds, etc., but have to deposit these with the agency responsible for procurement and earn a prescribed wage. In South-West Bengal, people get 25 per cent of the net profit from items like cashew. Income accruing to members is substantial notwithstanding the poor infrastructure for marketing or processing of NTFPs.

2. Marketing of timber and poles was done by the FD during pre-JFM period. Currently, VFC members receive 25 per cent of the net sale proceeds of the final harvest sold by the Forest Corporation in open auctions attended by concerned VFC. As per available data with the FD, additional income that accrues per family varies from as low as Rs 50 to as high as Rs 13,000 across different sites in West Midnapore.
3. Women are able to save considerable time thanks to increased access and supply of fuel wood and fodder. Some of the time saved is spent in income generating activities.
4. Three types of products are available to communities in JFM areas. These are: (i) immediate products like NTFPs, grass, fuel wood which are available almost immediately or after a time period depending upon the state of degradation of the forest that is being managed jointly; (ii) intermediate products from operations like thinning, other cultural operations; and (iii) final products like timber from fellings.
5. Fuel wood is the most important commodity that people access from forest areas. With JFM, there has been an increase in the availability of fuel wood to villagers. However, fuel wood is supplemented with dry leaves, particularly during December to May. Most cultural and intermediate operations like bush cutting, culling and thinning undertaken by the FD also provide fuel wood to people. There have been attempts by the FD to raise fuel wood plantations and also distribute improved *chullahs* to a limited extent. However, there is immense scope and also necessity to integrate rural energy component with JFM programme.
6. Forest protection has been provided by communities through

patrolling on a rotational basis or through a paid watcher to guard against grazing, fires and illicit felling. The effect of years of protection is reflected in positive trend with respect to various forest and ecological parameters such as grass productivity, tree count, basal area, and regeneration of trees and shrubs. There have also been several examples of VFC members fighting organized gangs of timber smugglers at great risk. However, system of reward to VFCs from such efforts is yet to be worked out and implemented in many cases.

The primary objective of the JFM programme is rehabilitation of degraded forest lands with people's organizations (Village Forest Committees—VFCs). In the course of evolution, approaches like village resource development, micro watershed development have got integrated into JFM to improve the socio-economic status of forest-dependant communities to reduce pressure on forests.

The issues which need mention here are traditional rights and privileges of communities for accessing fuel wood, fodder, timber, NTFP, etc., and the conflicts arising out of restrictions on these with the implementation of JFM.

Considerable community funds have been generated by VFCs from voluntary contributions, money obtained in lieu of protection, membership fees, voluntary labour contributions, sale of surplus forest produce and of timber harvests, fines generated through social fencing activities and revenue generated against the use of the committee's forests.

Ensuring equity in functioning of JFM institutions is crucial though it is a difficult task. Making provisions for representation of Scheduled Castes, Scheduled Tribes, the landless, women and the marginalized sections, in the General Body and Management Committee will be a step in this direction. The FD and NGOs have a major role to play in solving equity issues as they could ensure participation of all sections of the society in meetings, and decision-making process, impartial functioning, equitable benefit-sharing mechanisms for forest produce and other indirect benefits like wage employment.

Wherever Self-Help Groups have been formed and functioning in West Midnapore, dependence of women on moneylenders has come down. This is mostly because of their savings. Additional income opportunities led to some decrease in seasonal out-migration from villages. Increased agricultural productivity owing to investments in agricultural inputs and irrigation infrastructure has resulted in comparatively increased incomes for people. However, there is unmet need for skill development and market access in all these areas.

Major areas of conflict are demarcation of forest boundaries, forest ownership, and tenure rights and responsibilities. With evolution and maturity of JFM institutions, issues that are seen to take precedence are sharing of benefits from wage employment, usage of the forest, political interference, inter- and intra-village conflicts related to interests, lack of transparency in account keeping, equity issues in distribution of gains, leadership issues, representation of marginalized sections of the village in the Management Committee, functioning norms of the committees and inter-departmental conflicts.

Impact and Adequacy of Interventions

It is observed that the interventions planned and implemented are inadequate to ameliorate the plight of poor sections of the tribal population. Tribal people share the burden of poverty with other disadvantaged groups. The proportion of scheduled tribes below poverty line is substantially higher than the combined average. The so-called integration of tribal people with the mainstream economy, society, political and cultural systems has been forced upon them by the outside world. This made them vulnerable and they were unable to negotiate and cope with these impositions. This "mainstreaming" did not happen on the terms of the tribal people.

Efforts seem inadquate to build the knowledge, skills and confidence of the needy tribal people, which will also enable them to assert their rights. Same is the case with creation community assets, which can benefit both the community and the environment. The problem is "top-down interventions" whereas the need is for "community driven initiatives". It is only occasional where one can find the community identifying, implementing and managing the interventions for their good. It is difficult to find ownership of the community when it comes to the development programmes. These are mostly centrally planned and designed. There is no problem with ideas being shared. However, the experience shows that actual planning and implementation of the initiatives does not rest with the people for whom they are meant. The Panchayats work towards these objectives to some extent; and it is not just sufficient. It is a long way before the tribal communities get formal recognition, authority and responsibility to plan and implement development initiatives with technical inputs and guidance from resource persons.

NOTES

1. Tribal development received focus and emphasis during different plan periods. For related sources of information, *see* Elwin (1960), Haimendorf (1960), Thapar (1977), Boon (1982), Mohanty and Bailey (1984), Aurora (1985), Hardiman (1987), Chaudhuri (1990), Bedi (1992), Malhotra (1992), Varma (1996), Bandyopadhyay (1999), Bhengra *et al.* (1999), Krishna (2000), Louis (2000), Okongwu and Mencher (2000), Sankaran (2000), Bokil (2002), Das (2003), Heredia (2003), Krishna (2003), Pathy (2003), Rao (2003), Sarangi (2003), Chaudhury (2004), Phansalkar and Verma (2004), Rao (2004), Sah and Sisodia (2004), Jenamani (2005), Mohanty (2005), Shah (2005), Vira (2005), Xaxa (2005), Barik (2006), Behura and Panigrahi (2006), Purushothaman (2006), Padhi and Adve (2006), Rao *et al.* (2006), Rath (2006), Sen and Lalhrietpui (2006), Guha (2007), Menon (2007), Chaudhury and Patnaik (2008), Sharma (2008), Srivastava (2008), Karlsson (2009), Patnaik (2009), Sachchidananda and Srivastava (2009), Behera and Basar (2010), Sabar (2010), Nongkynrih (2010), Patnaik and Mehrotra (2010), and Maharatna (2011).
2. For the welfare of the PVTGs, Government of India initiated various schemes and programmes. For related literature, *see* Hsu (1964), Fuchs (1992), Varma (1996), Guha (1998), Das (2006), Sharma (2006), Sengupta *et al.* (2008), Khera (2009), and Sarkar (2009).
3. Source: Project Officer, Backward Classes Welfare, West Midnapore.
4. In order to support the poor and the marginalized, Government has initiated several self-employment programmes in India, for example *see* Bhargava (1987), Ravinder (1999), Gate (2001), Pal (2002), Jakimow and Kilby (2003), Ghose (2004), Narayana (2006), Costa (2007), Jeffery and Jeffery (2008), Ghosh (2009), Kumar (2009), Shariff (2009), .
5. In Gopali of Kharagpur block, disgusted over repeated denials and rough treatment of a bank manager, hundreds of women members of Self-Help Groups, many of them belonging to Santal tribe, went *en masse* to the manager and protested. The approach of many managers and staff,

not necessarily all of them, in villages is not conducive to proper implementation of schemes and ideas. There is general mistrust among the bank machinery about the Government officials and Panchayat representatives. They tend to believe that Government schemes are projected as doles to the loaners and the bank might never get their money back. To conclude the story, the affected manager disbursed long pending and genuine loans of many groups. It may be mentioned here that the officials could not make the manager see reason after many requests. The needy women got their due after sustained struggle.

6. The condition of tribals and the marginalized with reference to malnutrition and hunger is severe due to lack of awareness and their vulnerable condition. For instance *see* Gluckman (2009), Radhakrishna (2009), Gopaldas (2006), Mane (2006), Sharma (2005), Dreze (2004), Gupta and Rhode (2004), Gaiha (2003), Pathy (2003), Jha (2002), Pfeffer (2002), Steward (1986), and Singh (1982).
7. The researcher was working as Additional District Magistrate of Midnapore at that time, looking after development administration. During visit to Andhra Pradesh, one could see the progress made in dryland horticulture in districts like Khammam, Krishna and West Godavari districts. Impressed by the innovative practices, the researcher could convince the District Magistrate and Zilla Parishad for a study visit to those areas to see and visualize the experience.
8. JFM, as a process of developmental intervention in the tribal areas of India, has received academic and research prominence in recent times. For more details, *see* Pattnaik and Dutta (1997), Dhanagare (2000), Jodha (2000), Khare *et al.*, (2000), Agarwal (2001), Singh (2001), Kumar (2001), Kumar (2002), Ballabh *et al.* (2002), D'Silva and Nagnath (2002), Sarkar and Das (2002; 2006), Agarwal (2003) Edmunds and Wollenberg (2003), Ghose and Jha (2004), Gupta *et al.* (2004), Tiwari (2004), Agarwal *et al.* (2006), Sarkar (2006), and Mukhopadhyay (2007).

9
Findings and Recommendations

Intensive study and observation of tribal issues in West Midnapore has brought out several problems faced by people and inadequacies in the response to meet the challenges. Lodhas in many parts of the district still put up with the historical stigma as 'criminal tribes', though the tribe has been 'de-notified' after India achieved independence. In the process, their human and constitutional rights are getting violated, though the conditions have been improving slowly, over the years. Education and adequate opportunities alone can limit the damage suffered by these innocent people, generation after generation. Awareness generation among people is necessary about their rights and legal aid has to be provided when needed. It is worthwhile to recall the *Punchsheel* or five fundamental principles for upliftment of tribal communities, enunciated by the first Prime Minister of India, Pandit Jawaharlal Nehru:

People should develop along the lines of their own genius and we should avoid imposing anything on them. We should try to encourage in every way their own traditional arts and culture;

Tribal rights to land and forest should be respected;

We should try to train and build up team of their own people to do the work of administration and development. Some technical personnel from outside will, no doubt, be needed, especially in the beginning.

We should not over administer their areas with a majority of schemes. We should rather work through their own social and cultural institutions and;

We should judge results, not by statistics or the amount of money spent, but by the quality of human character evolved.

It is ironical that these principles are relevant even today after many decades.

One would like to point out some suggestions which if implemented will redress the grievances of tribal communities and salvage the situation from damage, already done over decades if not centuries.

Tribal communities must have the collective and individual right for preventing and redress in these situations:

- Any action which has the aim or effect of depriving them of their integrity as distinct peoples, or of their cultural values or ethnic identities;
- Any action which has the aim or effect of dispossessing them of their lands, territories or resources;
- Any form of population transfer which has the aim or effect of violating or undermining any of their rights;
- Any form of assimilation or integration by other cultures or ways of life imposed on them by legislative, administrative or other measures;
- The State need to take positive steps and allocate necessary resources so that rights and entitlements of tribal communities are ensured and protected.

Tribal communities should be able to:

- preserve and develop their identities and characteristics which are distinct to them;
- identify themselves as indigenous and also to be acknowledged ;
- belong to an indigenous community as per their traditions and customs without any hardship being experienced;
- develop and pass on to future generations their languages, traditions, philosophies, literature;

- establish and control their educational institutions and structures and to provide education in their languages and manner suitable to their culture;
- protect and pursue traditional medicines and health practices including intellectual property rights; and
- advance and uphold their distinct institutional structures, juridical customs, traditions, procedures and practices.

In addition to these observations, one would also like to record the specific needs of tribal people of the research area and the possible steps needed to improve their social, cultural and economic development.

Education

The Human Development Indicators (HDI) of the tribal population are much lower than the HDI of the rest of the population in terms of all parameters, such as, education, health, employment, income, etc. Tribal population also suffers from geographical and cultural exclusion, aspects that are not captured in the HDI. Similarly, lack of capacity to make choices is not accounted for. Education is the most crucial requirement for the sustained growth of a developing society. The dropout rate among tribal school going children is alarming. Various steps taken by the State to check dropout, including free distribution of books and stationery, scholarship, reimbursement of examination fee, free bus travel and mid-day meal have had an impact but still fall short. The performance in many areas in providing matching grant and maintenance of service and management of hostels is not encouraging. The pace of construction of hostels has been very slow and the basic amenities provided therein are not up to the mark. Low literacy, especially among tribal girls and high dropout rates at elementary and higher levels are areas of serious concern.

During the course of the study, one always felt the need for fine-tuning the existing programmes and schemes to focus on the specific needs of education of tribal people in the study area. These may also hold good for other districts and areas with tribal habitations. Some of the specific suggestions based on observations after looking at the running programmes are:

- The higher number of dropouts from schools defeats the goal of universalisation of primary education. There are many reasons for this and these are complementary too. Some of the reasons are poverty, lack of schools in neighbourhood and girls taking care of younger ones. It is important to focus on achieving 100 per cent enrolment of tribal children and reduction of dropouts, especially tribal girls.
- Education of tribal girls requires special focus. This will call for innovative interventions keeping specific situations into consideration. One such idea is to link Anganwadis/creches with schools, which will reduce girls' dropout from schools to take care of the younger children in the family. Sustained education initiatives and drives are to be launched in low female literacy tribal pockets of the district, particularly in Jhargram sub-division, to raise the literacy levels among Scheduled Tribe girls.
- On several occasions, teachers in schools in ST areas are non-STs and some of them tend to have bias and pre-conceived notions about tribal language, culture and social practices. This can have a negative impact on children, which again contributes to their dropping out of school. To enable comprehension of lessons taught, tribal children need to be taught in their mother tongue at least in the Classes I to III. For this, it is necessary to develop primers in major tribal languages for the students up to Class III. Textbooks will acknowledge the role of tribal leaders and people in the struggle for Indian independence and their contribution in other areas.
- Primary, secondary and high schools with proper school buildings, hostels and other essential infrastructure facilities need to be created in all tribal areas. It is generally accepted that there has to be atleast one residential high school for ST boys and one residential high school for ST girls in each block in the tribal areas, and at least one primary school and one girls' hostel at primary level in every Gram Panchayat. The idea is to ensure primary schools for boys and girls within a radius of one kilometre of tribal villages.
- The Ministry of Tribal Affairs has an existing scheme of

Eklavya Model Residential Schools. These need to be set up and made functional ensuring high quality.

- The scope of scholarships needs to be widened to include higher studies. Suitable scholarships and special training to outstanding tribal sports persons need to be considered to develop their talent in line with international standards.
- Appropriate infrastructure for sports in schools has to be created from primary stage. Specific annual grant for schools may be provided for development of sports and sports events.
- Suitable incentives need to be given for parents to send their daughters to schools until secondary level.
- Absenteeism of teachers is high in schools in tribal areas as teachers tend to view the places as remote with inadequate facilities for stay at village. There is lack of proper supervision also. To prevent teacher absenteeism in tribal areas, the teaching and non-teaching employees of primary schools need to be placed under the control of the village management committee appointed by the Gram Sabha or Gram Panchayat.
- It is a fact that number of literate among the tribes has increased over the years. The literacy programmes also contributed to increase in the adult literacy levels. However, it is still a long way as the literacy levels are about 30 per cent among tribal people when compared to the overall level of literacy of 70 per cent in the district. The female literacy among tribal people is further low at 20 per cent. The levels are not uniform with people in remote areas still languishing in illiteracy due to lack of suitable facilities. Increase in literacy levels for both men and women in tribal areas have to get priority. Innovative strategies have to be developed to reach these vast sections of population. The content and methods may have to take into view the cultural and social aspects of tribal people.
- Vocational education needs to be given priority to provide the tribal youth with the necessary technical knowledge and upgradation of skills. It is the need of the hour to make education relevant and suitable to their setting, background, local situations and functional needs;

- Special skills development programmes are necessary to meet the demands of livelihoods of thousands of tribal youth, particularly those who could not finish schooling. The field level institutions offering training must have freedom to prepare courses that are relevant, based on requirements of the community. Tribal candidates must have access to recognized different vocational training institutions so that they can acquire certificate and diploma, which have acceptability in the public as well as private sector.
- Present formal educational system is unable to cater to the needs of tribal children and youth. Hence, innovative and refreshing structures and institutions need to be developed to benefit the large number of youth.
- Each tribal community is distinct and no community is identical to another. Their social, cultural and historical conditions are different. Hence, no uniform policy or system will meet the needs and aspirations of all communities.

All these suggested steps and processes can also simultaneously help in fostering and protecting rich tribal culture from extinction. The whirlwind of materialistic culture and modern means of living have severely endangered the diverse mosaic of tribal culture in various parts of the research area.

Health Issues: Inadequate and Inaccessible Health Services

In course of the research process, one repeatedly realized that the tribal people are prone to poor health and nutritional deficiency. Detection and treatment of endemic diseases affecting tribal people continues to be weak as the facilities are inadequate and inaccessible. The major contributors to the increased disease risk amongst tribal communities include:

- Poverty and resultant undernutrition;
- Poor environmental sanitation, poor hygiene and lack of safe drinking water leading to increased morbidity from water and vector-borne infections;

- Lack of access to health care facilities resulting in the increased severity and duration of illnesses;
- Social barriers and taboos preventing utilization of available health care services; and
- Vulnerability to endemic diseases like malaria.

As tribal population in the district is heterogeneous, there are wide variations in their health status, access to and utilization of health services.

Nutritional Deficiencies and Diseases

As already observed earlier, malnutrition is common amongst the tribal people; especially children and women. This weakens their physical condition and lowers their resistance to disease, leading at times even to permanent brain impairment. Most tribal women suffer from anaemia, which lowers resistance to fatigue; this affects their working capacity and increases susceptibility to disease. This is particularly true for those women having frequent pregnancies. The nutritional status of tribal women directly influences their reproductive performances and the birth weight of their children, which is crucial to the infant's chances of survival, growth and development. Most of the tribal people of the research area do not have a satisfactory dietary pattern, as their diets are frequently deficient in calcium, vitamins and proteins. They are thus caught in a vicious cycle of malnutrition and ill health. It needs to be re-emphasized here that behind all the word play of starvation deaths or otherwise remains a grave reality of severe malnutrition and hunger in several tribal inhabitations.

Possible Remedial Action

As the health care delivery system in the district is inadequate and mostly inaccessible to the tribal communities because of geographical limitations and bureaucratic approaches, the community needs to be trained and oriented towards preventive care and immediate management of health problems like diarrhoea and fever. Taking care of pregnant mothers and children can be better managed with community participation and orientation. West Midnapore has shown workable ideas in this direction; trained women of villages have been able to achieve what the formal system found it difficult to address for years. The voluntary health workers contributed to drastic reduction in disease incidence in remote areas. It reduced suffering of the poor villagers and saved them sizeable amounts of hard-earned money; which was in many cases up to thirty per cent of their income.

Culture and Development

Development has to result in economic growth and progressive social mobility. It also implies harmonious upward mobility with social justice. Economic development and social development are complementary to each other. In the context of tribal communities, development has to strike a balance between economic and social domains and has to be culture specific. However, right from the inception of planned tribal development in 1952 until now the approach mostly has been influenced by the macro culture of the country. The planners, project executives and the field level workers generally tried to address tribal development programmes with the spirit of macro culture. The reason for such an approach emanates from an uncanny sense of ethnocentrism. Hence, efforts in respect of tribal development have not yielded desired results. During the past few decades, the district of West Midnapore achieved significant growth, but the levels of living and quality of life of the masses including most of the tribals, in many parts remained gloomy.

Development is being now conceived as a multidimensional process involving major changes in socio-economic domains. The objectives of development can be threefold, namely :

(1) To ensure smooth life sustenance;
(2) To bestow self-esteem on persons; and
(3) To ensure freedom from servitude.

These goals are universal for all people but graphically apply to the Lodha community of the district.

All these goals are to be realised within the framework of the culture of the people. Cultural knowledge is critical for socio-economic development, because anything worthwhile we do depend on critical cultural information. Knowledge is required to use the resources to fulfil the human needs. The living standards of the household, community and society have to be raised while conserving the resources and preserving common environment. It has to be more than simple transformation of resources, which are scarce and limited. These resources need to be used in a manner that generates ever higher returns for the efforts without destroying the traditional cultural matrix. For example, agricultural knowledge has to be tuned to local conditions and culture of the beneficiaries for acceptance and to get better results. Adaptation of higher and better technology requires study of indigenous culture.

Over the years, every culture has accumulated a body of technical and pragmatic expertise, which has scope for further enrichment. Societies receive such knowledge, which are more or less compatible with their cultural values. Though traditional societies have closed social boundaries, they have open systems. In other words, they are static to certain measure yet dynamic, and moderately open. They are slowly evolving. Simple societies are more tradition-bound. However, tradition cannot be understood as absolute, exclusive and inflexible. Every tradition is prone to change, but the rate of change is slow as it gradually evolves. Traditional societies accept change selectively and slowly. Traditions are strongly linked with the notion of cultural heritage, social identity and historical continuity of a society. On the other hand, economic activities, material traits and livelihood styles are more prone to change. Every tradition and culture is subject to reinterpretation in course of interaction between inter-cultures. In the process, an apparently static society may develop more or less heterodox initiatives and innovations and prepare the course for integrative pluralistic advances.

From this viewpoint, development has to be seen as an evolutionary process involving holistic approach in a society. However, approach to planned development need to be through the culture of the community. Development approach, which is not compatible with the traditional knowledge and culture of the society, in the long run, may prove to be unsustainable. For this reason, generation of information on cultural parameters is a prerequisite condition in the process of planned development. Traditions and customs need to be respected, preserved and incorporated in development programmes. Rituals, taboos and ceremonies have to be kept in mind during operation and implementation of a project. Creativity and innovative ideas of the beneficiaries need recognition encouragement. Myths, riddles, proverbs and anecdotes of the community can offer insights about situations and behaviour patterns. Resource utilisation plans need to take traditional practices into account. Traditional authority structures have to be utilized for solving problems and involving community members in development. It is important that ethnic and cultural identity of the community should be respected and not interfered in the process of planned development.

Creating Livelihood Opportunities : Action Points

Improving livelihoods of tribal people on a sustainable basis is perhaps the biggest challenge of current times. The researcher would like to suggest some action points, which will immensely help the tribal communities to improve their living conditions.[1]

- Skill development, upgradation and training for youth to create opportunities for livelihoods.
- Easy availability of credit facilities for income generation through micro enterprises.
- Experience shows regulation of moneylenders is not easy and has not been effective in most of the areas. Availability of consumption loans on easy terms is necessary in areas inhabited by tribal and poor people to save them from the devastation of indebtedness.
- Formation and promotion of Self-Help Groups among tribal population, particularly women, to fight the perennial problems of poverty and indebtedness. This will help redress issues of credit availability for income generating activities, consumption needs and developing leadership among tribal communities.
- Encouraging marketing networks of Self-Help Groups for procurement of agricultural produce and forest collections.
- Encouraging and forming Forest Protection Committees for participatory forest protection and management; wherever these committees are existing, democratic functioning and

participation of the stakeholders, especially women, needs to be promoted.

- To arrest migration of people from villages to towns and cities in search of low paid jobs; they are only adding to the swelling numbers of slum dwellers. If reasonable livelihood opportunities are available in villages, people will not like migration, which involves tremendous social, cultural and psychological stress. Effective implementation of MGNREGA and other programmes will help to address this problem to a large extent.
- Quick disposal of tribal land alienation cases and restoration of land to people.
- Encouraging minor irrigation projects in mono crop areas through community ownership and management.
- People know their needs best and hence they only should decide their plans with relevant and practical technological inputs from outside.
- Selection of development functionaries with right attitudes and concern and reorientation of existing machinery is vital for success of various schemes in operation. Present arrangements existing for service delivery are not adequate and up to the mark. There is a need to get over bureaucratic approaches in planning, thinking and implementation of development schemes for tribal welfare. Community participation has to be strengthened to improve planning efficiency and reduce leakages.
- In case of Lodhas who are identified as Vulnerable Tribal Group (VTG), an effective strategy for their survival, protection and development is necessary. For this to happen, different set of development machinery is needed from what we find presently. Appreciation, concern and identification with tribal people and their needs is sadly missing in the present set-up.
- The opportunities of reservations and facilities offered by the State are seen to be utilized by a small section of tribal society. At present, there is no way to restrict a person or family who has benefited and got raised socially and economically, from further accessing these facilities. As a

result, the deprived among the tribals continue to suffer whereas the cream among them continue to benefit from the State largesse. Though it is a sensitive issue, it is time to think and devise methods so that the objectives of providing social justice to the deprived sections are achieved quickly and efficiently. The point becomes clear when one looks at the glaring example of the continuing suffering of Lodha tribe of West Midnapore.

- Tribal people possess invaluable traditional knowledge of medicinal plants and herbs, which is the nature's gift to them; it is necessary to harness their knowledge and protect their intellectual property rights in the context of patent regime.
- Proper collection and marketing arrangements are needed for procuring medicinal plants and herbs collected by tribal people. Intermediaries who exploit them by paying very less amounts compared to the market price normally corner the gains. Again, empowered Self-Help Groups are the possible answer to save people from exploitation of the intermediaries and to ensure commensurate returns.

Huge area has been distributed to thousands of *pattadars* belonging to tribal and other poor people in this part of the district. It must be the endeavour of the officials and Panchayats to motivate these farmers to make effective use of their invaluable asset of land. Many people are forced to migrate to other places in search of work, as their land mostly remained unused.

Success stories like Murari encourage more and more farmers to take up fruit crops. Efforts need to be made to replicate such successful experiences in many other areas of Western Midnapore. Extension projects must be taken up in new areas following similar methods. However, there needs to be a definite action plan to make any impact on the socio-economic condition of the people of the area. Some of the areas needing attention are training, extension, improvement of credit facilities and market linkages. This appears to be one of the practical solutions in developing the wastelands of Western Midnapore, Bankura and Purulia and to improve the economic condition of thousands of people, particularly the disadvantaged sections of the society.

It may be possible for some entrepreneurs to procure land legally or otherwise and develop it with capital infusion. However, that may turn the present landowners, including tribal farmers, into workers in their own lands. Logical alternative would be to provide training and credit support to the farmers to take up horticulture and other less water intensive crops.

Ray of Hope

The Self-Help Groups could bring light of hope in the lives of Lodhas, Santals and other social groups silently suffering poverty and deprivation from a long period. The efforts need continuity and upgradation of strategies from the lessons learnt from the working of these groups. It is necessary to resist the temptation and easy option for the officials and Panchayat representatives to take over the reins of peoples' lives as the concerns and voice of people may eventually be drowned.[2]

Empowerment through Participatory Development

Whether it is the traditional bureaucracy of officials or the local political leaders, people holding power find it difficult to shed it for fear of losing importance. It is pertinent that the tribal community participates in their development process. It provides sense of ownership to people in what they do. They also take responsibility for the consequences of their actions. It also presents opportunity for leadership development among tribal people. Space and opportunity need to be provided for tribal people to know their potential and requirements so that they can draw plans for their future.

In conclusion, one can say from the study and understanding of the research area that tribal communities need to get back their 'original freedom' that they enjoyed for centuries. The avalanche of modernization has caught them unaware and left clueless. They lost, in many cases, their originality, culture and ingenuity, which are 'their own'. Half-hearted and half-cooked solutions prescribed by outsiders, alien to their milieu, have aggravated the situation. It is definitely not the researcher's idea that they should be 'replaced in their original abode.' The fruits of modern science and education must not be denied to tribal population. The only precaution and prerequisite is that they only should hold the steering of the ship. What 'others, experts and well wishers' can do is to put forward the available options and allow the people to decide what is best for them.

NOTES

1. The researcher is humble enough to mention that some of the suggestions made here are not new. The need is for "pointed action on the action points".
2. It has been the repeated experience during the period of work as well as study that elected representatives of people like Panchayat members at different levels, tend to get caught in the web of procedures and formalities. Bureaucratic approach is not necessarily the prerogative of officials alone; it can overtake public representatives too.

Photographs

Photograph 3.1: Agriculture is the main livelihood activity in Bonpatna and many other tribal villages of West Midnapore district

Photograph 3.2: Collecting firewood is a daily routine for these tribal women

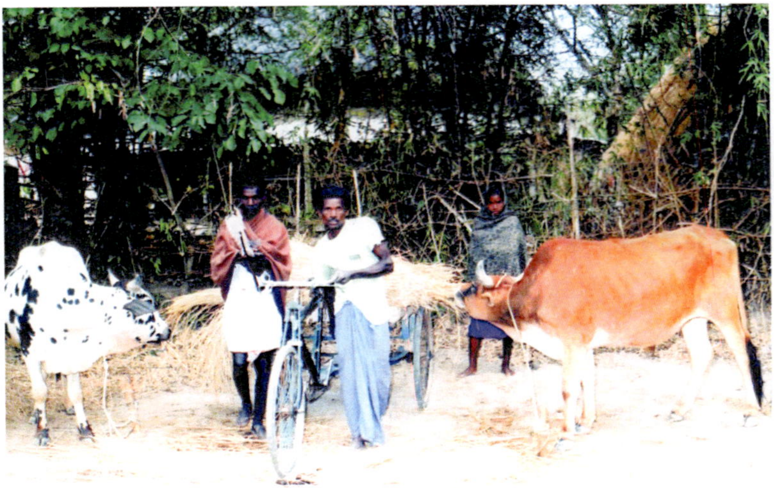

Photograph 3.3: While bullock-carts play important role in earning livelihood, this three-wheeler has changed transportation mode for Montu Soren

Photograph 3.4: Changing occupations among Santals: Readymade dress shop of Badal Murmu in Bonpatna village

Photograph 3.5: A Lodha couple painstakingly rebuilding their mud house

Photograph 3.6: A Lodha man before his simple hut, which he can call his own

Photograph 4.1: Tribal beliefs and customs: These statues of horses and elephants are believed to be carriers of Bongas by Santals

Photograph 4.2: Culture is an integral part of life: Lodha men and women participating in dance on the day of Sitala *puja*

Photograph 4.3: When tradition meets modernity: As the elderly Lodha members dance to the beat, a young boy watches wearing goggles

Photograph 4.4: Tradition passes on: A Lodha child trying his hand on the traditional drum

Photograph 6.1: Common sight in tribal villages of West Midnapore: Santal women making plates from *sal* leaves

Photograph 6.2: Tribal men and women depend upon construction activity to supplement income from forest and agriculture

Photograph 6.3 : Waterbody in Bonpatna village: Intricately linked with lives of local Lodha and Santal people

Photograph 6.4: Happy with the catch

Photograph 6.5: An average Lodha house has little material possessions to talk about

Photograph 6.6: Not much worry about tomorrow: A symbolic evening in Bonpatna Lodha village

Photograph 7.1: Changing lifestyles of tribal villages: Sanitation is accessible to all

Photograph 8.1: A hostel room of tribal girls at Belpahari

Photograph 8.2: More and more tribal girls are able to access formal schooling: Santali girls attending a class in Jhargram school

Photograph 8.3: Altering dress code: Young girls at Belpahari tribal school

Bibliography

Abraham, A. Rosa and K.S. Kavi Kumar. 2008. 'Multidimensional Poverty and Vulnerability, *Economic and Political Weekly*, 43 (20), pp: 77-87.

Acharya, Akash and Paul McNamee. 2009. 'Assessing Gujarat's 'Chiranjeevi' Scheme', *Economic and Political Weekly*, 44 (48), pp. 13-15.

Addlakha, Renu. 2000. 'Global-Local Dialectic in Medico-Administrative Practice', *Economic and Political Weekly*, 35 (8), pp. 676-683.

Alderman, Harold. 2005. 'Linkages between Poverty Reduction Strategies and Child Nutrition', *Economic and Political Weekly*, 40 (46), pp. 4837-4842.

Agnihotri, Indu and Indrani Mazumdar. 2009. 'Dusty Trails and Unsettled Lives: Women's Labour Migration in Rural India', *Indian Journal of Gender Studies*, 16 (3), pp. 375-399.

Agrawal, Anuja. 2004. "The Bedias are Rajputs': Caste Consciousness of a Marginal Community', *Contributions to Indian Sociology*, 38 (1-2), pp. 221-246.

Agarwal, Arun. 2001. 'Common Property, Forest Management and the Indian Himalaya', *Contributions to Indian Sociology*, 35 (2), pp. 181-212.

Agarwal, Arun. 2003. 'Sustainable Governance of Common-Pool Resources: Context, Methods, and Politics', *Annual Review of Anthropology*, Vol. 32, pp. 243-262.

Aggarwal, A., R.S. Sharma, B. Suthar, and K. Kunwar. 2006. 'An Ecological Assessment of Greening of Aravali Mountain Range through Joint Forest Management in Rajasthan, India', *International Journal of Environment and Sustainable Development*, 5 (1), pp. 35-45.

Ali, Ashan. (N.D). *Santals of Bangladesh*. Bidisha, West Midnapore District: Institute of Social Research and Applied Anthropology.

Ambagudia, Jagannath. 2010. 'Tribal Rights, Dispossession and the State in Orissa', *Economic and Political Weekly*, 45 (33), pp. 60-67.

Arya, Swarn Lata. 2007. 'Women and Watershed Development in India: Issues and Strategies', *Indian Journal of Gender Studies*, 14 (2), pp. 199-230.

Aurora, G.S. 1985. 'Tribal Studies', *Contributions to Indian Sociology*, 19 (2), pp. 359-365.

Barua, Joydeep. 2010. 'Towards a Programmable Index of Backwardness', *Economic and Political Weekly*, 45 (6), pp. 27-31.

Bailey, F.G. 1960. *Tribe, Caste and Nation: A Study of Political Activity and Political Change*, Manchester: Manchester University Press.

Bailey, F.G., 1961. 'Tribe and Caste in India', *Contributions to Indian Sociology*, (Old Series), 5, pp. 7-19.

Bailey, F.G., 1969. *Stratagems and Spoils: A Social Anthropology of Politics.* Philadelphia: Westview Press.

Bailey, F.G. 2001. *Treasons, Stratagems and Spoils, How Leaders Make Practical Use of Beliefs and Values*. Philadelphia: Westview Press.

Ballabh, V., Balooni, K., and S. Dave. 2002. 'Why Local Resources Management Institutions Decline: A Comparative Analysis of Van (Forest) Panchayats and Forest Protection Committees in India', *World Development*, 30 (12), pp. 2153-2167.

Bandyopadhyay, D. 1999. 'Where Assertion is Insurrection', *Economic and Political Weekly*, 34 (10), pp. 576-578.

Bandyopadhyay, D. 2001. 'Tebhaga Movement in Bengal: A Retrospect', *Economic and Political Weekly*, 36 (41), pp. 3901-3907.

Bapat, Jyotsna. 2000. 'Globalisation, Environmental Protest, Locality and Modernity', *Contributions to Indian Sociology*, 34 (2), pp. 221-242.

Bara, Joseph. 2010. 'Alien Construct and Tribal Contestation in Colonial Chhotanagpur: The Medium of Christianity' *Economic and Political Weekly*, 44 (52), pp. 90-96.

Barik, B.K. 2006. 'Faulty Planning in a Tribal Region: The Dandakaranya Development Authority', in Rath, Chandra, Govinda. (ed.) *Tribal Development in India: Contemporary Debate*, New Delhi, Sage Publications.

Barnes, Lindsay. 2007. 'Women's Experience of Childbirth in Rural Jharkhand', *Economic and Political Weekly*, 42 (48), pP. 62-70.

Baru, V. Rama and G. Sadhana. 'Resurgence of Communicable Diseases', *Economic and Political Weekly*, 35 (40), pp. 3555-3556.

Baru, Sanjay. 2002. 'Strategic Consequences of India's Economic Performance', *Economic and Political Weekly*, 37 (26), pp. 2583-2592.

Basu, Salil. 1996. 'Health and Socio-Cultural Correlates in Tribal Communities', in R.S. Mann (ed.), *Tribes of India: Ongoing Challenges*, New Delhi, MD Publications, pp. 207-220.

Bates, Crispin. 1995. 'Race, Caste and Tribe in Central India: The Early Origin of Indian Anthropometry' in Peter Robb (ed.), *The Concept of Race in South Asia*, New Delhi: Oxford University Press.

Bedi, M.S. 1992. 'Nehru and Tribal Development Policy', in R. Malhotra (ed.) *Anthropology of Development: Commemoration Volume in Honour of Professor I.P. Singh*, New Delhi: Mittal Publications.

Behera, D.K. and George Pfeffer. (eds.). 2008. *Contemporary Society: Tribal Studies* (Vol. 7) Identity, Intervention and Ideology in Tribal India and Beyond), New Delhi: Concept Publishing Company.

Behera, Deepak Kumar and Satyanarayana Ratha. 1986. *Socio-economic responsibility of tribal women: A Micro-study of the Kissan of Western Orissa, Tribal Women and Development,* Agenda Papers, Theme I, p. 15.

Behera, Deepak Kumar and Nibedita Nath. 2004. "Impact of a Mega Dam Project on the Land Resources of the Project Affected Indigenous People of Kalahandi District, Orissa," *Man and Life,* 30 (1 & 2): 1-18.

Behera, M.C. and Jumyir Basar. (eds.) 2010. *Interventions and Tribal Development: Challenges before Tribes in India in the era of Globalisation*, New Delhi: Serial Publications.

Behura, N.K. 2002. 'ILO Convention: Indigenous and Tribal People—An Analysis', in R.N. Pati and Jagannath Dash (eds.). *Tribal and Indigenous People of India: Problems and Prospects*, pp. 29-38; New Delhi: S.B. Nangia and APH Publishing House.

Behura, N.K. 1997. "Economies of Tribal Communities in India", in *Anthropological Economics, Substantivism* versus *Formalism*. Bidisha: Samaj Sevak Sangha.

Behura, N.K. 1996. 'Planned Development and Quality of Life among Indian Tribes', in R.S. Mann (ed.), *Tribes of India: Ongoing Challenges*, New Delhi: MD Publications, pp. 1-16.

Behura, N.K. and N. Panigrahi. 2006. *Tribals and the Indian Constitution: Functioning of Fifth Schedule in the State of Orissa*, Jaipur and New Delhi: Rawat Publications.

Berremen, Gerarld D. 2004. "Ethnography: Method and Product," in Vinay Kumar Srivastava (ed.), *Methodology and Fieldwork*. New Delhi: Oxford University Press.

Beteille, Andre. 1996 (1965). *Caste, Class and Power: Changing Patterns of Stratification in a Tanjore Village*. New Delhi: Oxford University Press.

Beteille, Andre. 1986. *Six Essays in Comparative Sociology*, New Delhi: Oxford University Press.

Beteille, Andre. 2000. *Teaching and Research*. Accessed from internet, Source: http://www.india-seminar.com/2000

Bhargava, Ashok. 1987. 'Indian Economy during Mrs. Gandhi's Regime', *Journal of Asian and African Studies*, 22 (3-4), pp. 194-217.

Bhate, Kamaxi and Shrikala Acharya. 2005. 'Preventive and Social Medicine', *Economic and Political Weekly*, 40 (18), pp. 1870-1875.

Bhattacharya, Sanjoy. 2008. '*Introduction: Epidemics in South Asian History. Economic and Political* Weekly, 43,(12 & 13), pp. 39-78.

Bhengra, R.; C.R. Bijoy and S. Luithui. 1999. *The Adivasis of India* Report of the Minority Rights Group, London: Minority Rights Group International.

Bhowmick, A.C. 2004. 'Santhal', in Prakash Chandra Mehta (ed.). *Ethnographic Atlas of Indian Tribes*, pp. 371-380; New Delhi: Discovery Publishing House.

Bhowmick, P.K. 2004. 'Lodha', in Prakash Chandra Mehta (ed.). *Ethnographic Atlas of Indian Tribes*, pp. 335-345; New Delhi, Discovery Publishing House.

Bhowmick, P.K. 1981. 'Rehabilitation of a 'Denotified Community': The Ex-Criminal Lodhas of West Bengal', *Rain*, 44, pp. 6-8.

Bhowmick, P.K. 1963. *The Lodhas of West Bengal, A Socio-Economic Study*. Calcutta: Institute of Social Research and Applied Anthropology.

Bhowmick, P.K. 1994. *Primitive Tribal Groups in Eastern India*. New Delhi: Gyan Publishing House.

Bhowmick, P.K. and S.K. Jana. 2008. 'Community in Search of a New Identity: The Santal of West Bengal', in Deepak Kumar Behera, & George Pfeffer. (eds.), *Contemporary Society: Tribal Studies* (Vol. 7: Identity, Intervention and Ideology in Tribal India and Beyond), pp. 94-103; New Delhi: Concept Publishing Company.

Bisai, S.; K. Bose; and A. Ghosh. 2008. 'Nutritional Status of Lodha Children in a Village of Paschim Medinipur District, West Bengal', *Indian Journal of Public Health*, 52 (4), pp. 203-206.

Biswas, P.C. 1956. *Santals of the Santal Parganas*. Delhi: Bharatiya Adimjati Sevak Sangh.

Bodding, P.O. 1925. *Studies in Santal Medicine and connected Folklore*. Calcutta: Asiatic Society of Bengal.

Bokil, Milind. 2002. 'De-notified and Nomadic Tribes: A Perspective', *Economic and Political Weekly*, 37 (2), pp. 148-154.

Boon, James. A. 1982. *Other Tribes, Other Scribes: Symboloc Anthropology in the Comparative Study of Cultures, Histories, Religions and Texts*, Cambridge: Cambridge University Press.

Bose, Ashish. 2000. 'Reaching the Unreached in Uttarakhand: Demography, Drinking Water and Technology', *Economic and Political Weekly*, 35 (25), pp. 2090-2092.

Breman, Jan. 2009. 'The Actuality of Tales from the Past', *Contributions to Indian Sociology*, 43 (1), pp. 135-147.

Campbell, Andrew. 1915. "Superstitions of the Santals," *Journal of the Bihar and Orissa Research Society*.

Census of India, 1901. Source: District Magistrate's Library, Midnapore.

Census of India, 1951. Source: District Magistrate's Library, Midnapore.

Census of India. 2001. Accessed from the internet site, censusindia.

Carrine, Marine. 2008. 'Santal Religious Discourse and the Assertion of Adivasi Identity', in Deepak Kumar Behera, & George Pfeffer. (eds.), *Contemporary Society: Tribal Studies* (Vol. 7: Identity, Intervention and Ideology in Tribal India and Beyond), pp. 24-37; New Delhi: Concept Publishing Company.

Carrine, Marine. 2002. 'The Santal Conception of Time', in George Pfeffer and D.K. Behera (eds.), *Contemporary Society: Tribal Studies* (Vol. 5, The Concept of Tribal Society), pp. 139-159; New Delhi: Concept Publishing Company.

Chakravarty, P.; S. Palit; M. Desai; and M.K. Raha. 2005. 'Family among Lodhas of West Bengal', in S.K. Chaudhari and S.S. Chaudhari (Eds.). *Primitive Tribes in Contemporary India*, pp. 229-246; New Delhi: Mittal Publications.

Chambers, Robert. 1983. *Rural Development: Putting the Last First,* Essex: Longman Group Limited.

Chaube, S.K. 1999. 'The Scheduled Tribes and Christianity in India', *Economic and Political Weekly*, 34 (9), pp. 524-526.

Chaudhuri, Buddhadeb, 1990. *Tribal Development in India: Problems and Prospects*, Delhi: Inter-India Publication.

Chaudhury, S.K. 2004. *Tribal Identity: Continuity and Change among Kondhs of Orissa*, Jaipur and New Delhi: Rawat Publications.

Chaudhury, Sukant K. and S.M. Patnaik. (eds). 2008. Indian Tribes and the Mainstream, Jaipur and New Delhi: Rawat Publications.

Chavan, Pallavi. 2008. 'Gender Inequality in Banking Services', *Economic and Political Weekly*, 43 (47), pp. 18-21.

Chowdhury, S.D.; T. Chakraborty; T. Ghosh. 2008. 'Prevalence of Undernutrition in Santal Children of Puruliya District, West Bengal',. *Indian Pediatrics*, 45 (1), pp. 43-46.

Claerhout, Sarah and Jakob De Roover. 2005. 'The Question of Conversion in India', *Economic and Political Weekly*, 40 (28), pp. 3048-3055.

Corbridge, Stuart. 2004. 'The Ideology of Tribal Economy and Society: Politics in the Jharkhand, 1950-1980', in Stuart Corbridge, Sarah Jewitt and Sanjay Kumar (eds), *Jharkhand: Environment, Development, Ethnicity*, New Delhi: Oxford University Press.

Costa, Dia Da. 2007. 'Tensions of neo-liberal development: State discourse and dramatic oppositions in West Bengal', *Contributions to Indian Sociology*, 41 (3), pp. 287-320.

Crossley, Nick. 2009. *Making Sense of Social Movements*, Jaipur and New Delhi: Rawat Publications.

Culas, Richard J. 2006. 'Debt and Deforestation: A Review of Causes and Empirical Evidence', *Journal of Developing Societies*, 22 (4), pp. 347-358.

Culshaw, W.J. 2004. *Tribal Heritage: A Study of the Santals,* New Delhi: Gyan Publication.

Dahiwale, S.M. 2000. 'Identifying'Backwardness' in Maharashtra', *Economic and Political Weekly*, 35 (37), pp. 3293-3297.

Dalvi, Surekha and Milind Bokil. 2000. 'In Search of Justice: Tribal Communities and Land Rights in Coastal Maharashtra', *Economic and Political Weekly*, 35 (32), pp. 2843- 2850.

Daly F.C. 1916. Manual of Criminal Classes operating in Bengal, Calcutta

Das, A.K. and S.K. Banerjee. 1962. *Impact of Industrialisation on the Life of the Tribals of West Bengal*. Calcutta: Cultural Research Institute, Tribal Welfare Department, Government of West Bengal (Special Series no. 1).

____, 1964. *Impact of Tea Industry on the Life of the Tribals of West Bengal*. Calcutta: Government of West Bengal.

Das, R.K. and Purnamita Dasgupta. 2000. 'Child Health and Immunisation: A Macro-Perspective', *Economic and Political Weekly*, 35 (8), pp. 645-655.

Das, Debojyoti. 2006. 'Demystifying the Myth of Shifting Cultivation: Agronomy in the North-East', *Economic and Political Weekly*, 41 (47), pp. 4912-4917.

Das, Vindhya. 2003. 'Democratic Governance in Tribal Regions: A Distant Dream', *Economic and Political Weekly*, 38 (42), pp. 4429-4432.

Dasgupta, Rajaram. 2005. 'Microfinance in India: Empirical Evidence, Alternative Models and Policy Imperatives', *Economic and Political Weekly*, 40 (12), pp. 1229-1236.

Derne, Steve. 1985. 'Religious Movement as Rite of Passage: An Analysis of the Birsa Movement', *Contributions to Indian Sociology*, 19 (2), pp. 251-268.

Devaranjan, Shantayanan and Shekhar Shah. 2004. 'Making Services Work for India's Poor', *Economic and Political Weekly*, 39 (9), pp. 907-919.

Dhanagare, D.N. 2000. 'Joint Forest Management in UP: People, Panchayats and Women', *Economic and Political Weekly*, 35 (37), pp. 3315-3324.

Dhargupta, Antara; A. Goswami; M. Sen; and D. Mazumdar. 2009. 'Study on the Effect of Socio-economic Parameters on Health Status of the

Toto, Santal, Sabar and Lodha Tribes of West Bengal, India', *Studies of Tribes and Tribals*, 7 (1), pp. 31-38.

District Gazeteer Midnapur, 1931. Source: District Magistrate's Library, Midnapore. *District Plan of Paschim Medinipur District* for the Financial Year 2006-2007.

Dove, M.R. 2006. Indigenous People and Environmental Politics, *Annual Review of Anthropology*. p. 35:191-208.

Dreze, J. 2004. 'Democracy and Right to Food', *Economic and Political Weekly,* 39 (17), pp. 1723-1731.

D'Silva, E. and B. Nagnath. 2002. 'Behroonguda: A Rare Success Story in Joint Forest Management', *Economic and Political Weekly,* 37 (6), pp. 551-557.

Dube, S.C. 1958. *India's Changing Villages: Human Factors in Community Development.* London: Routledge and Kegan Paul.

Duyker, Edward. 1987. *The Tribal Guerillas: The Santals of West Bengal and the Naxalite Movement*, Delhi: Oxford University Press.

Edmunds, David and Eva Wollenberg. (Eds.) 2003. *Local Forest Management: The Impacts of Devolution Policies*, London: Earthscan.

Elwin, Verrier. 1960. 'Issues in Tribal Policies Making', *Seminar*, 14 October.

Elwin, Verrier. 1942. *The Agaria*. Calcutta: Oxford University Press.

Elwin, Verrier. 1943. *The Aboriginals*. Bombay: Oxford University Press.

Elwin, Verrier. 1950. *Bondo Highlander*. Bombay: Oxford University Press.

Evans-Pritchard, E.E. 1937. *The Witchcraft*, Oracles and Magic among the Azande, London: Oxford University Press.

Evans-Pritchard, E.E. 1940. *The Nuer*. Oxford: Clarendon Press.

Evans-Pritchard, E.E. 1962. *Essays in Social Anthropology*. London: Faber & Faber.

Federici, Silvia. 2004. 'Women, Land-Struggles and Globalization: An International Perspective', *Journal of Asian and African Studies*, 39 (1-2), pp. 47-62.

Fernandes, Walter and S. Anthony Raj. 1996. 'The New Economic Policy and GATT: Their Impact on the Tribals', in R.S. Mann (ed.), *Tribes of India: Ongoing Challenges*, New Delhi: MD Publications, pp. 295-324.

Fried, M. 1968. 'On the Concept of 'Tribe' and 'Tribal Society'' in L. Helm (ed.), *Essays on the Problem of Tribe*, Washington: American Anthropological Society.

Fuchs, Stephen. 1992. *The Aboriginal Tribes of India*, New Delhi; Inter-India Publications.

Fuchs, Stephen. 1973. *The Aboriginal Tribes of India*. New Delhi: Macmillan India.

Gaiha, R. 2003. 'Does the Right to Food Matter?', *Economic and Political Weekly*, 38 (40), pp. 4269-4276.

Gaiha, Raghav, Katsushi Imai, and Mani Arul Nandhi. 2009. 'Millennium Development Goal of Halving Poverty in Asia: Progress, Prospects and Priorities', *Journal of Asian and African Studies,* 44 (2), pp. 215-237.

Gaiha, Raghav and Vani Kulkarni. 2002. 'Panchayats, Communities, and the Rural Poor in India', *Journal of Asian and African Studies*, 37 (2), pp. 38-82.

Gaiha, Raghav, Vani S. Kulkarni, Manoj K. Pandey, and Katsushi S. Imai. 2010. 'National Rural Employment Guarantee Scheme, Poverty and Prices in Rural India', *Journal of Asian and African Studies*, 45 (6), pp. 645-669.

Galab, S. and Rao, N. Chandrasekhara. 2003. 'Women's Self-Help Groups, Poverty Alleviation and Empowerment', *Economic and Political Weekly*, 38 (12), pp. 1274-1283.

Gardner, Katy. 2009. 'Lives in Motion: The Life-Course, Movement and Migration in Bangladesh *Journal of South Asian Development*, 4 (2), pp. 229-251.

Gate, Smita. 2001. 'Empowerment of Women in Watershed Management: Guraiya Panchayat, Madhya Pradesh', *Indian Journal of Gender Studies*, 8 (2), pp. 247-256.

George, Benny. 2009. 'Sanitation Programmes: A Glass Half-full', *Economic and Political Weekly*, 44 (8), pp. 65-67.

George, Somen E. *The Dynamics of Santal Traditions in a Peasant Society*, New Delhi, DK Publishers.

Ghosal, Chandikaprosad. 2006. 'Kolkata's Changing Puja Ethos', *Economic and Political Weekly*, 41 (46), pp. 4727-4729.

Ghose, Abhijit and A.K. Jha 'Paryavaran Pathshalas: Education in the Desert', *Economic and Political Weekly*, 39 (41), pp. 4507-4508.

Ghosh, Biswajit. 2011. 'Early Marriage of Girls in Contemporary Bengal: A Field View', *Social Change*, 41 (1): 41-61.

Ghose, K. Ajit. 2004. 'The Employment Challenge in India', *Economic and Political Weekly*, 39 (48), pp. 5106-5116.

Ghosh, Shanti. 2006. 'Food Dole or Health, Nutrition and Development Programme?', *Economic and Political Weekly*, 41 (34), pp. 3664-3666.

Ghosh, Sujay. 2009. 'NGOs as Political Institutions', *Journal of Asian and African Studies*, 44 (5), pp. 475-495.

Ghurye, G.S. 1963. *The Scheduled Tribes*. Bombay: G.R. Bhatkal.

Gluckman, Max. 2009 (1965). *Politics, Law and Ritual in Tribal Society*, Oxford: Basil Blackwell.

Godelier, M. 1977. *Perspectives in Marxist Anthropology*, Cambridge University Press, Cambridge.

Gopaldas, 2006. 'Hidden Hunger', *Economic and Political Weekly*, 41 (34), pp. 3671-3674

Gudavarthy, A. and G. Vijay. 2004. 'Andhra Pradesh: Some Contemporary Trends', *Economic and Political Weekly*, 39 (16), pp. 1571-1574.

Guha, Ramachandra. 2007. 'Adivasis, Naxalites and Indian Democracy', *Economic and Political Weekly*, 42 (32), pp. 3305-3312.

Guha, Sumit. 1998. 'Lower Strata, Older Races, and Aboriginal Peoples: Racial Anthropology and Mythical History Past and Present', *The Journal of Asian Studies*, 57 (2), pp. 423-441.

Gupta, and Rohde. 2004. 'Infant and Young Child Undernutrition', *Economic and Political Weekly*, 39 (49), pp. 5213-5216.

Gupta, R.; S.K. Srivastava; A.K. Mahendra; P. Ira; and D. Kumar, 2004. 'Impact of Participatory Forest Management on Socio-Economic Development of Rural People: A Case Study in Kodsi and Talaichittor Villages of Dehra Dun District', *Indian Forester,* 130 (3), pp. 243-252.

Gupta, Vikas and Mahi Pal. 2008. 'Community Sanitation Campaign: A Study in Haryana', *Economic and Political Weekly*, 43 (33), pp. 20-23.

Hackenberg, Robert A. 1967. 'The Parameters of an Ethnic Group: A Method for Studying the Total Tribe', *American Anthropologist*, 69 (5), pp. 478-492.

Hardenberg, Roland. 2009. 'Categories of relatedness: Rituals as a form of classification in a Central Indian Society', *Contributions to Indian Sociology,* 43 (1), pp. 61-87.

Hardiman, David. 1987. *The Coming of the Devi: Adivasi Assertion in Western India*, New Delhi: Oxford University Press.

Hardiman, David. 2007. 'Healing, Medical Power and the Poor: Contests in Tribal India', *Economic and Political Weekly*, 42 (16), pp. 1404-1408.

Hardiman, David and Gauri Raje. 2008. 'Practices of Healing in Tribal Gujarat', *Economic and Political Weekly*, 43 (9), pp. 43-50.

Harper, Malcolm, Andreas Berkhof , R.V. Ramakrishna. 'SHG-Bank Linkage: A Tool for Reforms in Cooperatives?', *Economic and Political Weekly*, 40 (17), pp. 1720-1725.

Heredia, C. Rudolf. 2003. 'Interrogating Integration: The Counter-Cultural Tribal Other', *Economic and Political Weekly*, 37 (52), pp. 5174-5178.

Heredia, C. Rudolf. 1999. 'Interpreting Gandhi's *Hind Swaraj*', *Economic and Political Weekly*, 34 (24), pp. 1497-1502.

Hsu, Francis. L.K. 1964. 'Rethinking the Concept "Primitive"', *Current Anthropology*, 5 (3), 169-178.

Inayatullah, Sohail. 1999. 'Leadership, Evil and Future-Generations Orientation: Towards a Global Conversation of Cultures', *Journal of Asian and African Studies*, 34 (2), pp. 178-198.

Jakimow, Tanya and Patrick Kilby. 2006. 'Empowering Women: A Critique of the Blueprint for Self-Help Groups in India', *Indian Journal of Gender Studies*, 13 (3), pp. 375-400.

Jana, Shyamal K. 2010. 'Economic Life of the Lodhas of West Bengal: Past, Present and Future'', in M.C. Behera and Jumyir Basar (eds.), *Interventions and Tribal Development: Challenges before Tribes in India in the era of Globalisation*, New Delhi: Serials Publications.

Jeffery, Patricia and Roger Jeffery. 2008. ''Money itself discriminates': Obstetric emergencies in the time of Liberalisation', *Contributions to Indian Sociology*, April 2008; Vol. 42, 1, pp. 59-91.

Jena, Manipadma. 2008. 'Food Insecurity among Tribal Communities of Orissa', *Economic and Political Weekly*, 43 (6), pp. 18-21.

Jenamani, Suvendra. 2005. *Poverty and Underdevelopment in Tribal Areas: A Geographical Analysis*, New Delhi: Concept Publishing Company.

Jha. 2002. 'Rajasthan: Hunger and Starvation Deaths', *Economic and Political Weekly*, 37 (52), pp. 5159-5163.

Jodha, N.S. 2000. 'Joint Management of Forests: Small Gains', *Economic and Political Weekly*, 35 (50), pp. 4396-4399.

Jodhka, S. Surinder. 2002. 'Nation and Village: Images of Rural India in Gandhi, Nehru and Ambedkar', *Economic and Political Weekly*, 37 (32), pp. 3343-3353.

Jogdanand, P.G. and S.M. Michael (Eds.). 2003. Globalization and Social Movements: Struggle for a Humane Society, Jaipur and New Delhi: Rawat Publications.

Jose, Sunny and K. Navaneetham. 2008. 'A Factsheet on Women's Malnutrition in India', *Economic and Political Weekly*, 43 (33), pp. 61-67.

Judge, Paramjit S. 2005. Religion, Identity and Nationhood : The Sikh Militant Movement, Jaipur and New Delhi: Rawat Publications.

Kalpana, K. 2005. 'Shifting Trajectories in Microfinance Discourse', *Economic and Political Weekly*, 40 (51), pp. 5400-5409.

Kannabiran V. 2005. 'Marketing Self-Help, Managing Poverty', *Economic and Political Weekly*, 40 (34), pp; 3716-3718.

Karlsson, G. Bengt. 2009. 'Nuclear Lives: Uranium Mining, Indigenous Peoples and Development in India', *Economic and Political Weekly*, 44 (34), pp. 43-49.

Karuppaiyan, E. 2000. 'Alienation of Tribal Lands in Tamilnadu: Panel Data Analysis', *Economic and Political Weekly*, 35 (37), pp. 3343-3350.

Kasi, E. 2007. *An Anthropological Study of Livelihoods: The Case of Two Sugali Settlements from Anantapur District of Andhra Pradesh*, An unpublished PhD Thesis Submitted to Department of Anthropology, Hyderabad: University of Hyderabad.

Kasi, E. 2007d. 'Development and Change among *Sugalis*: An Ethnographic Account from a NGO Based Village', *Journal of the Indian Anthropological Society*, 42 (3), pp. 259-275.

Kasi, E. 2009. 'Role of NGO in the Development of *Sugalis*: A Case Study of a Settlement in Andhra Pradesh', *Journal of Human Ecology*, 27 (2), pp. 115-122.

Kasi, E. 2009b. 'Poverty and Vulnerability among Tribal People: A Case of *Sugali*', in Kasi Eswarappa and Ramesh C. Malik (eds) *Theory and Practice of Ethnography: Readings from the Periphery*, pp. 337-354; Jaipur and New Delhi: Rawat Publications.

Kasi, E. 2011a. 'Poverty and Development in a Marginal Community: Case Study of a Settlement of the *Sugali* Tribe in Andhra Pradesh, India' *Journal of Asian and African Studies*, 46 (1): pp.5-18.

Kathuria and Khan. 2007. 'Vulnerability to Air Pollution: Is There Any Inequity in Exposure?', *Economic and Political Weekly*, 42 (30), pp. 3158-3165.

Khare, A.; M. Sarin; N.C. Saxena; S. Patil; S. Bhatia; F. Vania; and M. Satyanarayana. 2000. "Joint Forest Management: Policy, Practice and Prospects", Policy that works for Forests and People Series No. 3. New Delhi: Worldwide Fund for Nature—India and London: International Institute for Environment and Development.

Khera, Reetika. 2009. 'Starvation Deaths and 'Primitive Tribal Groups', *Economic and Political Weekly*, 43 (52), pp. 11-14.

Kochar, V.K. 1966. 'Village Deities of the Santal and Associated Rituals', *Anthropos*, 61, pp. 241-257.

Krishna, Daya. 2000. 'The New Tribal States: Can they Survive in the Modern World?', *Economic and Political Weekly*, 35 (46), pp. 3997-3998.

Krishna, Sumi. 2003. 'Light Shines through Gossamer Threads: Inside-Outside Political Spaces', *Economic and Political Weekly*, 38 (17), pp. 1691-1696.

Krishna, Sumi. 2001. 'Gender, Tribe and Community Control of Natural Resources in North-East India', *Indian Journal of Gender Studies*, 8 (2), pp. 307-321.

Kumar, Ashutosh. 2009. 'Disconnect between Economic Reforms and Electoral Democracy in India: Explaining Why Indian Political Parties Do What They Do', *Journal of Asian and African Studies*, 44 (6), pp. 719-739.

Kumar, D. (ed). 2008. Proselytisation in India: The Process of Hinduisation in Tribal Societies, New Delhi: Aakar Books.

Kumar, Pushpesh. 2006. 'Gender and procreative ideologies among the Kolams of Maharashtra', *Contributions to Indian Sociology*, 40 (3), pp. 279-310.

Kumar, Sanjay. 2001. 'Indigenous Communities' Knowledge of Local Ecological Services', *Economic and Political Weekly*, 36 (30), pp. 2859-2869.

Kumar, S. 2002. 'Does Participation in Common Pool Resource Management Help the Poor? A Social Cost-Benefit Analysis of Joint Forest Management in Jharkhand, India', *World Development*, 30 (5), pp. 763-782.

Kumar, Sanjeeva. 2005. State 'Simplification: Garo Protest in Late 19th and Early 20th Century Assam', *Economic and Political Weekly*, 40 (27), pp. 2941-2947.

Laidlaw, James. 2004. "Informal Colloborations as an Aspect of Urban Anthropological Fieldwork: Experiences from Jaipur City," in Vinay Kumar Srivastava (ed.), *op. cit.*

Lee, Su H. 2010. *Debating New Social Movements: Culture, Identity and Social Fragmentation*, Jaipur and New Delhi: Rawat Publications.

Lindner, Rudi P. 1982. 'What Was a Nomadic Tribe?' *Comparative Studies in Society and History*, 24 (4), pp. 689-711.

Louis, Prakash. 2000. 'Jharkhand: Marginalisation of Tribals', *Economic and Political Weekly*, 35 (47), pp. 1487-1491.

Macfarlane, Alan. 2004. "To Contrast and Compare," in Vinay Kumar Srivastava (ed.), *op. cit.*

Macdougall, John. 1977. 'Agrarian reform *vs.* religious revitalization: collective resistance to peasantization among the Mundas, Oraons and Santals, 1858-95', *Contributions to Indian Sociology,* 11 (2), pp. 295-327.

Madan, T.N. 1965. *Family and Kinship*. Bombay: Asia Publishing House.

Mahalingam, S. 1990. *Role of Co-operative Organisation in Developing Tribal Economy* (A Study of LAMP Tribal Co-operative), New Delhi: Mittal Publications.

Maharatna, Arup. 2011. 'How Can 'Beautiful' Be 'Backward'? Tribes of India in a Long-term Demographic Perspective', *Economic and Political Weekly*, 46 (4), pp. 42-52.

Maharatna, Arup and Rasika Chikte. 2004. 'Demography of Tribal Population in Jharkhand 1951-1991', *Economic and Political Weekly*, 39 (46), pp. 5053-5062.

Mahapatra, Sitakant. 1992. 'Development and Culture: A View from India's Tribal World', in R. Malhotra (ed.) *Anthropology of Development:*

Commemoration Volume in Honour of Professor I.P. Singh, New Delhi: Mittal Publications.

Mahapatra, S. 1986. *Modernization and Ritual: Identity and Change in Santal Society*: Calcutta: Oxford University Press.

Majumdar, D.N. 1955. *The Santal, Study in Culture Change*. New Delhi: Department of Anthropology, Government of India.

Majumdar, D.N. 1965. *Races and Cultures of India*. Bombay: Asia Publishing House.

Makwana, M.H. and Richard Pais. (eds). 2011. Backward Classes and Social Justice, Jaipur and New Delhi: Rawat Publications.

Malinowski, B. 1906. *Ancient Law*. London: J. Murray.

Malinowski, Bronislaw. 1930. 'The Rationalization of Anthropology and Administration', *Africa: Journal of the International African Institute*, 3 (4), pp. 405-430.

Malhotra, Rikshesh. 1992. 'Tribals: Which Way Justice', in R. Malhotra (ed.) *Anthropology of Development: Commemoration Volume in Honour of Professor I.P. Singh*, New Delhi: Mittal Publications.

Malhotra, Rikshesh. (ed.) 1992. *Anthropology of Development: Commemoration Volume in Honour of Professor I.P. Singh*, New Delhi: Mittal Publications.

Man, E.G. 1983. *Sonthalia and the Santals*. Delhi: Mittal Publications.

Mane, Rahul Prahlad. 2006. 'Targeting the Poor or Poor Targeting: A Case for Strengthening the Public Distribution System of India', *Journal of Asian and African Studies*, 41 (4), pp. 299-317.

Mann, R.S. 1992. 'Creation of Change in Anthropological Parlance', in R. Malhotra (ed.) *Anthropology of Development: Commemoration Volume in Honour of Professor I.P. Singh*, New Delhi: Mittal Publications.

McAlpin, M.C. 1981. *Report on the Condition of the Sonthals in the Districts of Birbhum, Bankura, Midnapore and North Balasore*. Calcutta: Firma Mukhopadhyay.

Meenakshi, Ranjan Ray , Souvik Gupta. 2000. 'Estimates of Poverty for SC, ST and Female-Headed Households', *Economic and Political Weekly*, 35 (31), pp. 2748-2754.

Meher, Rajkishor. 2003. 'The social and ecological effects of industrialisation in a tribal region: The case of the Rourkela Steel Plant', *Contributions to Indian Sociology*, 37 (3), pp. 429-457.

Meher, Rajkishor. 2009. 'Globalization, Displacement and the Livelihood Issues of Tribal and Agriculture Dependent Poor People: The Case of Mineral-based Industries in India', *Journal of Developing Societies*, 25 (4), pp. 457-480.

Mehrotra, Nilika and S.M. Patnaik. 2008. 'Culture *versus* Coercion: Other Side of Nirmal Gram Yojana', *Economic and Political Weekly*, 43 (43), pp. 25-27.

Menon, Ajit. 2007. 'Engaging with the Law on Adivasi Rights', *Economic and Political Weekly*, 42 (24), pp. 2239-2242.

Menz, Diwakar and Delo Mai Hansda. 2010. *Encyclopedia of Scheduled Tribes of Jharkhand*, Delhi: Kalpaz Publications.

Mishra, AK. 1999. 'Orissa : Tribal Women against Liquor', *Economic and Political Weekly*, 34 (19), pp. 1089-1091.

Mishra, Banikanta. 2006. 'People's Movement at Kalinga Nagar: An Epitaph or an Epitome?', *Economic and Political Weekly*, 41 (7), pp. 551-554.

Misra, Kamal K. 1986. 'From Millenarianism to Jharkhand: The Changing Nature of Social Movements in Tribal Chotanagpur', *Journal of Asian and African Studies*, 21 (3-4), pp. 226-236.

Mohanty, Biswaranjan. 2005. 'Displacement and Rehabilitation of Tribals', *Economic and Political Weekly*, 40 (13), pp. 1318-1320.

Mohanty, Purna C. and Wilfrid C. Bailey. 2004. 'Development Programmes and the Koya of Orissa, India: A Test of Nehru's Philosophy' *Journal of Asian and African Studies,* 19 (1-2), pp. 49-63.

Mohanty, P.K. 2002. *Development of Primitive Tribal Groups in India*, Delhi: Kalpaz Publications.

Mondal, Sekh Rahim. 1999. 'Tribal Situation in West Bengal: Some Observations', in H.C. Upadhyay (Ed.), *Status of Scheduled Tribes in India*, pp. 39-52; New Delhi: Anmol Publications.

Mosse, David; Gupta, Sanjeev; Mehta, Mona; Shah, Vidya; Rees, Julia; and Team, KRIBP Project. 2002. 'Brokered livelihoods: Debt, Labour Migration and Development in Tribal Western India', *Journal of Development Studies*, 38 (5), pp. 59-88.

Mukherjea, Charulal. 1939. *The Santals*, Calcutta: A. Mukherjee & Co. Pvt. Ltd.

Mukhopadhyay, D.; H.R. Tewari, and S.B. Roy. 2007. 'Role of Community Institutions in Joint Forest Management', *Journal of Human Ecology,* 21 (1), pp. 37-42.

Nadkarni, 2003. 'Ethics and Relevance of Conversions', *Economic and Political Weekly*, 38 (3), pp. 227-235.

Nanda, Bikram Narayan. 1992. 'Vernacular Work, Wage Labour and Tribal Development: A Case Study of Highland Orissa', *Contributions to Indian Sociology*, 26 (1), pp. 115-132.

Narayana, M.R. 2006. 'Awareness of Policies and Programmes among Small-scale Industries in India: Evidence and Implications of a Case Study', *Journal of Asian and African Studies*, 41 (4), pp. 319-339.

Nongkynrih. 2010. 'Scheduled Tribes and the Census: A Sociological Inquiry', *Economic and Political Weekly*, 45 (19), pp. 43-47

Okongwu, A.F. and J.P. Mencher. 2000. 'The Anthropology of Public Policy: Shifting Terrains', *Annual Review of Anthropology*, 29, pp. 107-124.

Olsen, Wendy and Jamie Morgan. 2010. 'Aspiration Problems in Indian Microfinance: A Case Study Exploration', *Journal of Developing Societies*, 26 (4), pp. 415-454.

O'Malley, L.S.S. 1941. *Modern India and the West*. London: Oxford University Press.

Orans, Martin. 1965. *The Santal: A Tribe in Search of Great Traditions*, Detroit: Wayne State University Press.

Padh and Adve. 2006. 'Endemic to Development', *Economic and Political Weekly*, 41 (3), pp. 186-187.

Padhi, Ranjana; Pramodini Pradhan; D. Manjit. 2010. 'How Many More Arrests will Orissa See?', *Economic and Political Weekly*, 45 (10), pp.

Pai, et al. 2005. 'Uttar Pradesh in the 1990s', *Economic and Political Weekly*, 40 (21), pp. 2144-2146.

Pal, M. 2002. 'Haryana : Self-Employment Programme: A Stocktaking', *Economic and Political Weekly*, 37 (52), pp. 2157-2158

Parkin, Robert. 1990. 'Terminology and Alliance in India: Tribal Systems and the North-South Problem', *Contributions to Indian Sociology*, 24 (1), pp. 61-76.

Parry, Jonathan P. 2003. 'Nehru's dream and the village 'waiting room': Long-distance labour migrants to a Central Indian steel town', *Contributions to Indian Sociology*, 37 (1-2), pp. 217-249.

Patel, M.K. 1998. *Agrarian Transformation in Tribal India*, New Delhi: MD Publications.

Patel, Rajeev. 2006. 'International Agrarian Restructuring and the Practical Ethics of Peasant Movement Solidarity', *Journal of Asian and African Studies*, 41 (1-2), pp. 71-93.

Pathy, Suguna. 2003. 'Destitution, Deprivation and Tribal Development', *Economic and Political Weekly*, 38 (27), pp. 2832-2836.

Pati, B. 2010. 'Religion and Social 'Subversion': Re-examining Colonial Orissa', *Economic and Political Weekly*, 45 (25), pp. 43-52.

Pati, Biswamoy. 2001. 'Identity, Hegemony, Resistance: Conversions in Orissa, 1800-2000', *Economic and Political Weekly*, 36 (44), pp. 4204-4212.

Pati, R.N. and Jagannath Dash. 2002. *Tribal and Indigenous People of India: Problems and Prospects*, New Delhi: S.B. Nangia and A.P.H. Publishing House.

Patnaik, S.M. 2009. 'Situating NGOs in Tribal Development of Orissa', in Sachchidananda and V.K. Srivastava (eds). *Social Anthropology in Eastern India*, New Delhi: Serial Publications.

Patnaik, S.M. and Nilika Mehrotra. 2010. 'Micro-level Development Practices among Tribals: An Exploration in Bastar', *Social Action*, 60 (4), pp. 385-399.

Pattnaik, B.K. and S. Dutta. 1997. 'JFM in Southwest Bengal—A Study in Participatory Development', *Economic and Political Weekly*, 32 (50), pp. 3225-3232.

Patra, N. 2008. 'Exploring the Determinants of Childhood Immunisation', *Economic and Political Weekly*, 43 (12), pp. 97-104.

Paty, Saurab, A. 2005. 'Changing Ecology and its Impact on Lodha Tribe of West Bengal', in Chittaranjan Kumar Paty (ed.), *Forest, Government and Tribe*, pp. 60-70; New Delhi: Concept Publishing Company.

Pfeffer, Georg. 2002. 'The Structure of Middle Indian Tribal Society Compared', in Georg Pfeffer and D.K. Behera, (eds.), *Contemporary Society: Tribal Studies*, Vol. 5., The Concept of Tribal Society, pp. 208-229; New Delhi, Concept Publishing Company.

Pfeffer, Georg. 1983. 'Generation and Marriage in Middle India: The Evolutionary Potential of `Restricted Exchange', *Contributions to Indian Sociology*, 17 (1), pp. 87-121.

Pfeffer, G. and D.K. Behera. 2002. *Contemporary Society: Tribal Studies Vol. V (The Concept of Tribal Society)*, New Delhi: Concept Publishing Company.

Phansalkar and Verma. 2004. 'Improved Water Control as Strategy for Enhancing Tribal Livelihoods', *Economic and Political Weekly*, 39 (31), pp. 3469-3476.

Planning Commission. 2001. *Approach Paper to the Tenth Five-Year Plan.*

Planning Commission, Government of India, New Delhi.

Prakash, Padma. 2005. 'Where is the Woman in Preventive and Social Medicine?', *Economic and Political Weekly*, 40 (18), pp. 1828-1834.

Prasad, N. P. 2000. 'Health Care Access and Marginalised Social Spaces', *Economic and Political Weekly*, 35 (41), pp. 3688-3694.

Prasad, Onkar. *Santal Music: A Study in Pattern and Processes of Cultural Persistence*, New Delhi: Inter-India Publications.

Prasad, R.N. and S. Sengupta. 1973. *Santal Rural Economy: A Study Based on Village Survey in Santal Parganas*, Santiniketan: Agro-Economic Research Centre.

Prasad, R. Siva and Kasi. E. 2007. 'Tribal Livelihoods in a Limbo: Changing Tribe-Nature Relationship in South Asia' in *At the Crossroads: South*

Asian Research, Policy and Development in a Globalized World, Karachi, SDPI and SAMA Editorial and Publication.

Purohit and Purohit. 'Mobilising Non-Tax Revenue: An Empirical Analysis of Trends in States', *Economic and Political Weekly*, 44 (5), pp. 54-62.

Purushothaman. 2006. 'Land-Use Strategies for Tribals: A Socio-Economic Analysis', *Economic and Political Weekly*, 40 (53), pp. 5611-5619.

Radcliffe-Brown, A.R. 1922. *The Andaman Islanders*. Cambridge: Cambridge University Press.

Radcliffe-Brown, A.R. 1977. *The Social Anthropology*. London: Routledge and Kegan Paul.

Radhakrishna, Meena. 2009. 'Starvation among Primitive Tribal Groups', *Economic and Political Weekly*, 44 (18), pp. 13-16.

Radhakrishna et al. 2004. 'Chronic Poverty and Malnutrition in 1990s', *Economic and Political Weekly*, 39 (28), pp. 3121-3130.

Ramanna, M. 2004. 'Local Initiatives in Health Care', *Economic and Political Weekly*, 39 (9), pp. 4560-4567.

Ramaswamy, Gita and Bhangya Bhukya. 2002. Lambadas: Changing Cultural Patterns, *Economic and Political Weekly*, 37 (16), p. 1497-1499.

Ramdas, Sagari; R. Yakshi, and Girijana Deepika. 2001. 'Changing Livelihoods, Livestock and Local Knowledge Systems: Women Stake their Claim in Andhra Pradesh and Maharashtra', *Indian Journal of Gender Studies*, 8 (2), pp. 175-194.

Ramesh, Jairam. 2007. 'Self-Help Groups Revolution: What Next?', *Economic and Political Weekly*, 42 (36), pp. 3621-3624.

Rana, Kumar and Liby T. Johnson. 2002. 'Hot-Tempered Cold 'Fever', *Economic and Political Weekly*, 38 915), pp.

Rani, Sandhya, Saswata Ghosh, Mona Sharan. 'Maternal Healthcare Seeking among Tribal Adolescent Girls in Jharkhand', 42 (48), pp. 56-61.

Rao, K.M.; A. Laxmaiah; K. Venkaiah; and G.N. Brahmam. 2006. 'Diet and nutritional status of adolescent tribal population in nine States of India', *Asia Pacific Journal of Clinical Nutrition*, 15 (1), pp. 64-71.

Rao, M.V. 2003. *Community Health in Community Hands*, Midnapore, Mithun Enterprises.

Rao, M.V. 2002. *Development for the People: Innovations in Administration*, Kolkata: Subarnarekha.

Rao, Nitya. 2003. 'Jharkhand: Life and Livelihood in Santal Parganas: Does the Right to a Livelihood Really Exist?', *Economic and Political Weekly*, 38 (39), pp. 4081- 4084.

Rao, Nitya. 2001. 'Enhancing Women's Mobility in a Forest Economy: Transport and Gender Relations in the Santal Parganas, Jharkhand', *Indian Journal of Gender Studies*, 8 (2), pp. 271-290.

Rao, S. Laxman; Priya Deshingkar; John Farrington. 2006. 'Tribal Land Alienation in Andhra Pradesh: Processes, Impacts and Policy Concerns', *Economic and Political Weekly*, 41 (52), pp. 5401-5407.

Rao V.G.; R. Yadav; C.K. Dolla; S. Kumar; M.K. Bhondeley; and M. Ukey. 2005. 'Undernutrition and childhood morbidities among tribal preschool children', *Indian Journal of Medical Research*, 122, pp. 43-47.

Rao, V.M. 2007. 'A Self-Help Group Model for Farmer Insurance', *Economic and Political Weekly*, 42 (10), pp. 820-822.

Rao, Venkata, P., 2004. *Dimensions of Transformations in Tribal Societies with Reference to Andhra Pradesh*, New Delhi: Sarup & Sons.

Rapport, Nigel and Joanna Overing. 2007. *Social and Cultural Anthropology: Key Concepts*, London and New York: Routledge.

Rath, Chandra, Govinda. (ed.) 2006. *Tribal Development in India: Contemporary Debate*, New Delhi: Sage Publications.

Rath, Chandra, Govinda. 2006. 'Nehru and Elwin on Tribal Development: Contrasting Perspectives', in Rath, Chandra, Govinda. (ed.) *Tribal Development in India: Contemporary Debate*, New Delhi: Sage Publications.

Ravinder, D. 1999. "Adarana Programme and Vote Bank Politics in Andhra Pradesh', *Economic and Political Weekly*, 34 (30), pp. 2061-2062.

Ray, Lokenath. 2008. "Reflections on Mobilisation of Rural Peasant Women: Learning to Unlearn and Relearn in West Medinipur", *Indian Journal of Gender Studies*, 15 (1), pp. 149-157.

Ray, Niharranjan. 1972. 'Introductory Address' in K.S. Singh, *Tribal Situation in India*, Shimla: Indian Institute of Advanced Studies.

Ray, P.C. 1975. *Socio-Cultural Process and Psychological Adaptation of the Santal*, Calcutta: Anthropological Survey of India.

Ray, Subrata K. and Amitabha Basu. 1996. 'A Framework for Studying the Health Problems of the Tribes: The Oraon Case', in R.S. Mann (ed.), *Tribes of India: Ongoing Challenges*, New Delhi: M.D. Publications, 193-206.

Ray, T. 1983. *Santal Rebellion: Documents*, Calcutta, Sabarnarekha.

Raychaudhuri, Indu. 1973. *Folk Tales of the Santals*, New Delhi: Sterling.

Redfield, Robert. 1960. *The Little Community and Peasant Society and Culture*, Chicago: University of Chicago Press.

Reddy, M. Gopinath; K. Jayalakshmi; Anne-Marie Goetz. 2006. 'Politics of Pro-poor Reform in the Health Sector: Primary Healthcare in Tribal Areas of Visakhapatnam', *Economic and Political Weekly*, 41 (5), pp. 419-426.

Reddy, V. Ratna and B. Suresh Reddy. 2007. 'Land Alienation and Local

Communities: Case Studies in Hyderabad-Secunderabad', *Economic and Political Weekly*, 42 (31), pp. 3233-3240.

Risley, H.H. 1891. *The Tribes and Castes of Bengal*. Calcutta: The Bengal Secretariat Press.

Rizvi, B.R. 1996. 'A Vision in Disarray: The Nehruvian Model of Development', in R.S. Mann (ed.), *Tribes of India: Ongoing Challenges*, New Delhi: MD Publications, pp. 39-48.

Rodrigues, Valerian. 2011. 'Reading Texts and Traditions: The Ambedkar-Gandhi Debate', *Economic and Political Weekly*, 46 (2), pp. 56-66.

Rogaly, Ben, D. Coppard, K. Rana, A. Rafique, A. Sengupta and J. Biswas. 2003. 'Seasonal migration, employer-worker interactions, and shifting ethnic identities in contemporary West Bengal', *Contributions to Indian Sociology*, 37 (1-2), pp. 281-310.

Rottger-Hogen, Elizabeth.1982. 'Insurrection . . . Or Ostracism: A study of the Santal rebellion of 1855', *Contributions to Indian Sociology*, 16 (1), p. 79-96.

Roy Burman, B.K. 2002. 'Indigenous and Tribal Peoples: Global Hegemonies and Government of India', in RN Pati and Jagannath Dash (eds.). *Tribal and Indigenous People of India: Problems and Prospects*, pp. 15-28; New Delhi: S.B. Nangia and APH Publishing House.

Roy Burman, B.K. 2000. *Frozen Ice and a Silent Spring*. Accessed from internet: Source: http://www.india-seminar.com/2000

Roy, Dayabati. 2007. 'Politics at the Margin: A Tale of Two Villages', *Economic and Political Weekly*, 42 (32), pp. 3323-3329.

Roy, Mallarika Sinha. 2009. 'Magic Moments of Struggle: Women's Memory of the Naxalbari Movement in West Bengal, India (1967-75)', *Indian Journal of Gender Studies*, 16 (2), pp. 205-232.

Säävälä, Minna. 2001. 'Low caste but middle-class: Some religious strategies for middle- class identification in Hyderabad', *Contributions to Indian Sociology*, 35 (3), pp. 293-318.

Sabar, Bhubaneswar. 2010. 'Tribal Agriculture: The Chuktia Bhunjias in Central India', *Economic and Political Weekly*, 45 (12), pp. 77-79.

Sachchidananda and Vinay Kumar Srivastava. (eds.) 2009. *Social Anthropology in Eastern India*, New Delhi: Serials Publication.

Sah, D.C. and Y.S. Sisodia. 2004. *Tribal Issues in India*, Jaipur and New Delhi: Rawat Publications.

Sahu, Geetanjoy. 2008. 'Mining in the Niyamgiri Hills and Tribal Rights', *Economic and Political Weekly*, 43 (15), pp. 19-21.

Sankaran, S.R. 2000. 'Welfare of Scheduled Castes and Scheduled Tribes in Independent India: An Overview of State Policies and Programmes', *Journal of Rural Development*, 19 (4), 504-537.

Sarangi, D. 2003. 'State, NGOs and Tribals', *Economic and Political Weekly*, 38 (1), pp. 84.

Sarker, Debnarayan and Nimai Das. 2006. 'Towards a Sustainable Joint Forest Management Programme: Evidence from Western Midnapore Division in West Bengal', *South Asia Research*, 26 (3): 269-289.

Sarker, Debnarayan and Nimai Das. 2002. 'Women's Participation in Forestry: Some Theoretical Issues', *Economic and Political Weekly*, 37 (43), pp. 4407-4412.

Sarkar, R.M. 2009. *Primitive Tribal Groups in India*, New Delhi: Serial Publications.

Sarkar, R. and V. Sarkar. 1996. 'An Appraisal of the Economic Role of Women in the Central and Western Himalayas: Some Privileges and Constraints', in R.S. Mann (ed.), *Tribes of India: Ongoing Challenges*, New Delhi: MD Publications, pp. 279-286.

Sarkar, S.K. 2006. 'Present Status and Future Prospects of Joint Forest Management in West Bengal', *Indian Forester*, 132 (1), pp. 11-18.

Saumya. 2008. 'Communalism: Narratives in Chhattisgarh', *Economic and Political Weekly*, 43 (2), pp. 38-44.

Sen, Arnab and Esther Lalhrietpui. 2006. 'Scheduled Tribes (Recognition of Forest Rights) Bill: A View from Anthropology and Call for Dialogue', *Economic and Political Weekly*, 41 (39), pp. 4205-4210.

Sengupta, Arjun; K.P. Kannan; G. Raveendran. 2008. 'India's Common People: Who Are They, How Many Are They and How Do They Live?', *Economic and Political Weekly*, 43 (11), pp. 49-63.

Seth, D.L. 2009. 'Political Communalisation of Religions and the Crisis of Secularism', *Economic and Political Weekly*, 44 (39), pp. 71-79.

Sethuraman, Kavita and Nata Duvvury. 2007. 'The Nexus of Gender Discrimination with Malnutrition: An Introduction', *Economic and Political Weekly*, 42 (44), pp. 49-53.

Shah, Alpa. 2006. 'The labour of love: Seasonal migration from Jharkhand to the brick kilns of other States in India', *Contributions to Indian Sociology*, 40 (1), pp. 91-118.

Shah, Alpa. 2006. 'Markets of Protection: The 'Terrorist' Maoist Movement and the State in Jharkhand, India', *Critique of Anthropology*, 26 (3), pp. 297-314.

Shah, Mihir. 2005. 'First You Push Them In, Then You Throw Them Out', *Economic and Political Weekly*, 40 (47), pp. 4895-4899.

Shariff, Abusaleh. 2009. 'Rural Income and Employment Diversity in India during 1994 and 2005', *Journal of Developing Societies*, 25 (2), pp. 165-208.

Sharma, Chandan Kumar. 2001. 'Tribal Land Alienation:Government's Role', *Economic and Political Weekly*, 36 (52), pp. 4791-4795.

Sharma, M. Ursula. 1970. 'The Problem of Village Hinduism: "Fragmentation" and Integration', *Contributions to Indian Sociology*, 4 (1), pp. 1-21.

Sharma, P. Dash. (ed.). 2006. *Anthropology of Primitive Tribes in India*, New Delhi, Serials Publications.

Sharma, Pragya. 2005. *Tribal Society in a Flux: An Anthropo-Sociological Study of Raika*, Jaipur: Panchsheel Prakashan.

Sharan, Ramesh. 2005. 'Alienation and Restoration of Tribal Land in Jharkhand: Current Issues and Possible Strategies', *Economic and Political Weekly*, 40 (41), pp. 4443-4446.

Sharma, S.L. 2008. *Emerging Tribal Identity: A Study of Minas of Rajasthan*, Jaipur and New Delhi: Rawat Publications.

Singh, Bhupinder. 1992. 'Struggle to Survive: Isolated Tribal Communities', in R. Malhotra (ed.) *Anthropology of Development: Commemoration Volume in Honour of Professor I.P. Singh*, New Delhi: Mittal Publications.

Singh, J.P. 2010. 'Socio-cultural Aspects of the High Masculinity Ratio in India', *Journal of Asian and African Studies*, December 2010; Vol. 45, 6, pp. 628-644.

Singh, Kumar. A. 2003. *Dynamics of Tribal Economy*, New Delhi: Serial Publications.

Singh, K.S. 1985. *Tribal Society in India: An Anthropo-Historical Perspective*, Delhi: Manohar Publications.

Singh, K.S. 1982. 'Transformation of Tribal Society: Integration and Assimilation', *Economic and Political Weekly*, 17 (34), pp. 1376-1384.

Singh, Neera M. 2001. 'Women and Community Forests in Orissa: Rights and Management', *Indian Journal of Gender Studies*, 8 (2), pp. 257-270.

Singh, Netrapal. 2009. 'Rethinking the Concept of Tribe: Construction and Re-construction of Adivasi Identity', in Kasi Eswarappa and Ramesh C. Malik (eds.) *Theory and Practice of Ethnography: Readings from the Periphery*, pp. 220-250; Jaipur and New Delhi: Rawat Publications.

Singh, R.V. 2001. 'Contribution of Participatory Forest Management in the Livelihoods of Rural Communities in India', *Forests, Trees and Livelihoods*, 11 (2), pp. 159-166.

Singh, Shekhar. Mani and Aditya Bharadwaj. 2000. 'Communicating Immunisation: The Mass Media Strategies', *Economic and Political Weekly*, 35 (8), pp. 667-675.

Sinha, Saurabh; Michael Lipton; and Shahin Yaqub. 2002. 'Poverty and "Damaging Fluctuations": How do they Relate?', *Journal of Asian and African Studies,* 37 (2), pp. 186-243.

Skaria, Ajay. 1999. 'Some Aporias of History: Time, Truth and Play in Dangs, Gujarat', *Economic and Political Weekly*, 34 (15), pp. 897-904.

Skaria, Ajay. 1997. 'Shades of Wilderness: Tribe, Caste and Gender in Western India' *Journal of Asian Studies*, 56 (3), 726-745.

Southall, Aidan W. 1970. 'The Illusion of Tribes', *Journal of Asian and African Studies*, 5 (1-2), pp. 28-50.

Srinivas, M.N. 1962. "Changing Institutions and Values in Modern India" in *Collected Essays of M.N. Srinivas*, 2002. New Delhi: Oxford University Press.

Srinivas, M.N. 1966. *Social Change in Modern India.* Berkeley, C.A.: University of California

Srinivas, M.N. 1976. *The Remembered Village.* Delhi: Oxford University Press.

Srinivasan, K. and Sanjay Kumar. 1999. 'Economic and Caste Criteria in Definition of Backwardness', *Economic and Political Weekly*, 34 (40), pp. 3052-3057.

Srivastava, Vinay Kumar. 2008. 'Concept of 'Tribe" in the Draft National Tribal Policy', *Economic and Political Weekly*, 43 (50), pp. 29-35.

Srivastava, Vinay Kumar. 1997. Religious Renunciation of a Pastoral People, New Delhi: Oxford University Press.

Srivastava, Vinay Kumar. 1990. *Essays in Social Anthropology.* Kolkata: Institute of Social Research and Applied Anthropology.

Stavenhagen, Rodolfo. 2004. 'Indigenous People in Comparative Perspective: Problems and Policies', Human Development Report Office, Occasional Paper, Background Paper for HDR 2004, UNDP. http://hdr.undp.org/fr/rapports/mondial/rdh2004/documents/HDR2004_Rodolfo_Stavenhagen.pdf

Steward, Julian. H. 1986. 'Levels of Socio-cultural Integration: An Operational Concept', *Journal of Anthropological Research*, 42 (3), pp. 337-353.

Stewart, Frances. 2005. 'Groups and Capabilities', *Journal of Human Development*, 6 (2), pp. 185-204.

Strümpell, Christian. 2008. 'We work together, we eat together': Conviviality and modernity in a company settlement in south Orissa', *Contributions to Indian Sociology*, 42 (3), pp. 351-381.

Subba, T.B.; J. Puthenpurakal; and S.J. Puykunnel. (eds.). 2009. Christianity and Change in Northeast India, New Delhi: Concept Publishing Company.

Sundaram, K. 2006. 'On Backwardness and Fair Access to Higher Education: Results from NSS 55th Round Surveys, 1999-2000', *Economic and Political Weekly*, 41 (50), pp. 5173-5182.

Sundaram, K. and Suresh D. Tendulkar, 2003. 'Poverty among Social and Economic Groups in India in 1990s', *Economic and Political Weekly*, 38 (50), pp. 5263-5276.

Sudarshan, Ratna M. 2001. 'Managing Ecosystems for Women's Health and Sustainable Development: An Illustration from the Kumaon, Uttaranchal', *Indian Journal of Gender Studies*, 8 (2), pp. 207-222.

Sunder, Nandini. 2006. 'Bastar, Maoism and Salwa Judum', *Economic and Political Weekly*, 41 (29), pp. 3187-3192.

Suykens, Bert. 2011. 'The Gotte Koya IDP Mystery: Tribal Identity and the IDP—Migrant Continuum in the Chhattisgarh—Andhra Pradesh Borderland (India)', *Journal of Refugee Studies*, 24 (1), pp. 110-131.

Tagoe, Michael. 2011. 'Followership or Followersheep? Searching for Transformational Leaders for Accelerated National Development in Ghana', *Journal of Asian and African Studies*, 46 (1), pp. 87-103.

Thapar, Romesh (ed.). 1977. *Tribe, Caste and Religion in India*, New Delhi: Macmillan.

Thamizoli, P. 2001. 'Integrating Gender Concerns into Natural Resource Management: The Case of the Pichavaram Mangroves, Tamil Nadu', *Indian Journal of Gender Studies*, 8 (2), pp. 195-206.

Tharamangalam, Joseph. 1989. 'Religious Pluralism and the Theory and Practice of Secularism: Reflections on the Indian Experience', *Journal of Asian and African Studies*, 24 (3-4), pp. 199-212.

Thomas, Bejoy K.; Roldan Muradian; Gerard de Groot; and Arie de Ruijter. 2010. 'Resilient and Resourceful?: A Case Study on How the Poor Cope in Kerala, India', *Journal of Asian and African Studies*, 45 (1), pp. 29-45.

Thong, Tezenlo. 2010. 'Thy Kingdom Come': The Impact of Colonization and Proselytization on Religion among the Nagas', *Journal of Asian and African Studies*, 45 (6), pp. 595-609.

Tiwari, D.K., K.K.N. Sharma, and V.S. Dubey. 2001. 'Health Profile among Lodha and Munda Tribal Children of Midnapur District, West Bengal', *Anthropologist*, 3 (3), pp. 189-190.

Tiwari, Manish. 2004. 'NGOs in Joint Forest Management and Rural Development: Case Study in Jharkhand and West Bengal', *Economic and Political Weekly*, 38 (51), pp. 5382- 5390.

Troisi, J. (ed). 1979. *The Santals: Readings in Tribal Life*, New Delhi: Indian Social Institute.

Turner, Victor. 1967. *The Forest of Symbols: Aspects of Ndembu Ritual*, Cornell University Press.

Turner, Victor. 1969. *The Ritual Process: Structure and Anti-Structure*: Aldine Transaction.

Turner, Victor. 1974. *Dramas, Fields, and Metaphors: Symbolic Action in Human Society*: Cornell University Press.

Uberoi, Patricia; Nandini Sundar; Satish Deshpande, (eds). 2007. Anthropology in the East: Founders of Indian Sociology and Anthropology, Delhi: Permanent Black.

UNESCO. 1982. *Final Report of the World Conference on Cultural Policies*. Cited in World Decade Secretariat, *Culture and Development: A Study*. Paris: UNESCO.

Vajpeyi, Ananya. 2009. 'Old Words, New Worlds: Revisiting the Modernity of Tradition', *Economic and Political Weekly*, 44 (38), pp. 33-36.

Van Gennep, Arnold. 1909. Les *rites de passage*. Paris: Emile. Nourry, I909.

Varma, Mohan. M. 1996. *Tribal Development in India: Programmes and Perspectives*, New Delhi: Mittal Publications.

Varma, Mohan. M. 1996. 'Welfare Programmes for Primitive and Dispersed Tribal Groups in Uttar Pradesh', in Varma, Mohan, Mahendra. 1996. *Tribal Development in India: Programmes and Perspectives*, pp. 386-453, New Delhi: Mittal Publications.

Varman, P. Mahendra. 2005. 'Impact of Self-Help Groups on Formal Banking Habits', *Economic and Political Weekly*, 40 (17), pp. 1705-1713.

Vasimalai, M.P. and K. Narender. 2007. 'Microfinance for Poverty Reduction: The Kalanjiam Way', *Economic and Political Weekly*, 42 (13), pp. 1190-1195.

Vatta, Kamal. 2003. 'Microfinance and Poverty Alleviation', *Economic and Political Weekly*, 38 (5), pp. 432-433.

Vidyarthi, L.P. 1964. *Cultural Contours of Tribal Bihar*. Calcutta: Punthi Pustak.

Vira, Bhaskar. 2005. 'Deconstructing the Harda Experience: Limits of Bureaucratic Participation', *Economic and Political Weekly*, 40 (48), pp. 5068-5075.

Von Furer-Haimendorf, Christoph. 1982. *Tribes of India: Struggle for Survival*, Berkeley: University of California Press.

_____. 2005. *The Apa Tanis and their Neighbours:A Primitive Civilization of the Eastern Himalayas*. London: Routledge & Kegan Paul.

Wiebe, Paul. 1970. 'Protestant Missions in India: A Sociological Review', *Journal of Asian and African Studies*, October 1970; Vol. 5, 4: pp. 293-301.

World Bank 2005, *Drought in Andhra Pradesh: Long-term Impacts and Adaptation Strategies*, Draft Final Report, Volume 2: Technical

Annexes, South Asia Environment and Social Development Department, Washington: World Bank (www.worldbank.org).

Xaxa, Virginius. 2004. 'Women and Gender in the Study of Tribes in India', *Indian Journal of Gender Studies*, 11 (3), pp. 345-367.

Xaxa, Virginius. 2008. *State, Society and Tribes: Issues in Post-Colonial India*, New Delhi: Pearson Education.

Xaxa, Virginius. 2005. 'Politics of Language, Religion and Identity: Tribes in India', *Economic and Political Weekly*, 40 (13), pp. 1363-1370.

Xaxa, Virginius. 1999. 'Tribes as Indigenous People of India', *Economic and Political Weekly*, 34 (51), pp. 3589-3595.

Xaxa, Virginius. 1999. 'Transformation of Tribes in India: Terms of Discourse', *Economic and Political Weekly*, 34 (24), pp. 1519-1524.

Yorke, Michael. 1979. 'Kinship, marriage and ideology among the Raj Gonds: A tribal system in the context of South India', *Contributions to Indian Sociology*, 13 (1), pp. 85-116.

Zimmerman, Francis. 1999. *The Jungle and the Aroma of Meats: An Ecological Theme in Hindu Medicine*, Berkeley: University of California Press.

Index